100 Hikes in™

NORTHERN CALIFORNIA

100 Hikes in™

NORTHERN CALIFORNIA

John R. Soares and Marc J. Soares

THE
MOUNTAINEERS

Published by
The Mountaineers
1011 SW Klickitat Way
Seattle, Washington 98134

Published simultaneously in Canada by Douglas & McIntyre, Ltd., 1615 Venables Street, Vancouver, B.C. V5L 2H1

Published simultaneously in Great Britain by Cordee, 3a DeMontfort Street, Leicester, England, LE1 7HD

8 7 6 5 4
5 4 3 2 1

Manufactured in the United States of America

Edited by Dana Fos
Maps by Jody MacDonald
All photographs by John R. Soares and Marc J. Soares except as noted
Design, layout and typography by The Mountaineers

Cover photograph: Dick's Lake and Dick's Pass in the Desolation Wilderness of Northern California's Sierra Nevada
Frontispiece: Silver Falls

Library of Congress Cataloging in Publication Data
Soares, John R.
100 hikes in northern California / John R. Soares and Marc J. Soares.
          p.   cm.
  Includes index.
  ISBN 0-89886-385-6 (acid-free paper)
  1. Hiking--California, Northern--Guidebooks. 2. Backpacking--California, Northern--Guidebooks. 3. California, Northern--Guidebooks. I. Soares, Marc J. II. Title. III. Title: One hundred hikes in northern California.
  GV199.42.C2S63   1993
  796.5'1'09794--dc20   93-44838
                                   CIP

CONTENTS

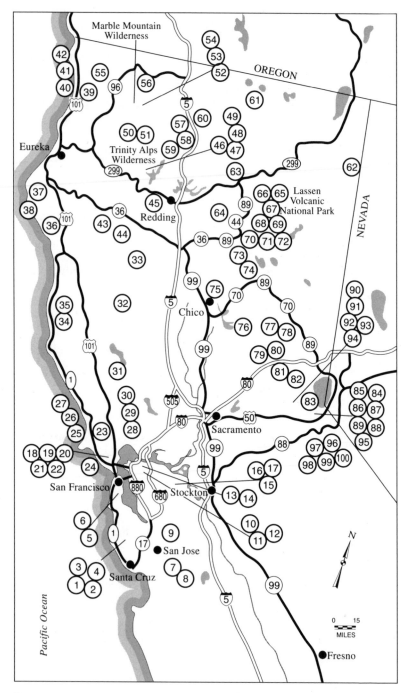

Marble Mountain
Wilderness

OREGON

Trinity Alps
Wilderness

Eureka

Redding

Lassen
Volcanic
National Park

NEVADA

Chico

Sacramento

Stockton

San Francisco

San Jose

Santa Cruz

Pacific Ocean

N

0   15
MILES

Fresno

ACKNOWLEDGMENTS

We give special thanks to our brother Eric Soares, commander of the Tsunami Rangers and sea kayaker extraordinaire, for hiking companionship, sage advice, and outdoors enthusiasm; and also to our mother, Mozelle Fitzhugh Berta, who gave us her total support and love throughout this project and was wise enough to know that children need freedom to explore and discover. The following wonderful people hiked the trails with us, making our trips even more enjoyable: Marc's wife Patricia Soares, daughter Dionne Soares, and son Jake Soares; our sister Camille Soares; and good friends Rick Ramos, Noelle Corder, Jim Kakuk, and Sue Loring. Other family members provided both good hospitality and plenty of encouragement. For this we gratefully thank Les Berta, Bob Soares, Phyllis Soares, and Lisa Soares. Yet other people provided us with valuable information and advice, including dozens of park and national forest employees. Special thanks in this category goes to Lee Dittmann and Barry Breckling of Henry W. Coe State Park. Finally, we offer the highest praise to Redding Arboretum horticulturist Gary Matson, our plant guru.

To our father, John Severin Soares,
who introduced to us the beauty and oneness of nature
and shared with us his love of outdoor adventure

Dick's Peak looms over Alta Morris Lake in the Sierra Nevada's
Desolation Wilderness (see hike 88).

INTRODUCTION

Secluded ocean beaches where powerful waves pulse against rock, sand, and cliff. Steep Sierra peaks stretching high above rock-ringed alpine lakes. The still, silent shade of ancient redwood forests. Hillsides carpeted with an explosion of spring wildflowers. *100 Hikes in Northern California* offers you this and much more as it takes you along trails that allow you to experience the infinite variety of nature.

The first region covers the San Francisco Bay Area, where a surprising number of trails allow both relative solitude and beautiful scenery. The second region describes hikes on and near the Pacific Coast and in the bordering Coast Range. The next region details hikes high in the remote Klamath Mountains of far Northern California, where you'll find the most solitude. The Cascade Mountains region stretches over the southern section of this vast range, with most trails traveling on or near volcanos and areas of past volcanic activity. The final region takes you to the foothills, lakes, and summits of the Sierra Nevada from Mokelumne Wilderness north. Whether you want to hike in spring, summer, fall, or winter, whether you want a strenuous seven-day backpacking trip or an easy day hike, you'll find just what you desire in the following pages.

How To Use This Book

The beginning of each hike description lists information in summary form that gives you a basic feel for the hike. Within the main body of the text you'll find directions to the trailhead; specific data regarding distances, trail junctions, and major sights; and a discussion of trailside natural history.

The following allows you to make the most use of the information preceding each hike description.

Length. This gives the total round-trip distance for the hike, unless otherwise specified. Note that if you are short on time or energy, you needn't do the entire hike in order to enjoy beautiful surroundings. Read the main body of the text for distances to good intermediate turn-around points such as lakes, meadows, and areas with scenic views.

Hiking time. This is a subjective indicator that allows the average hiker ample time for rest breaks, viewing scenery, and meals.

High point. This gives the elevation in feet of the highest point encountered on the hike.

Total elevation gain. This is the total number of feet you'll climb in getting to the main destination high point for hikes where you return the way you came. For loop hikes it gives the total number of feet climbed during the entire hike.

Difficulty. Total elevation gain, length, necessary physical exertion, and required agility determine whether a hike is rated easy, moderate, or strenuous; however, this can vary due to local or seasonal changes. A big storm can make a steep trail very slippery and turn an easy boulder-hop across a small stream into a tricky, waist-high wade through a swift-moving torrent. Most people, including younger children, can do hikes with an easy rating. Moderate and strenuous hikes require careful assessment of your abilities and preparedness. Keep in mind that some hikes rated moderate or strenuous may be easy for the first 2 or more miles to a good turnaround point; read the hike description to find out.

Season. This gives the approximate time period during the year that the trail is easily hikable. All trails below 2,000 feet elevation, including all of those on or near the coast and in mountain foothills, offer year-round hiking, although they may be hot and dry during the summer. Others in the 2,000- to 4,000-foot range will be snow-free for most of the winter, but before leaving, call the relevant government agency (see "Information," described below, and Appendix 1) to be sure of current conditions. For high-elevation hikes, season covers the estimated period between the time most of the trailside snow melts and the time that the first major fall snowstorm hits. These times can vary, depending on the amount of precipitation that falls in a given winter and

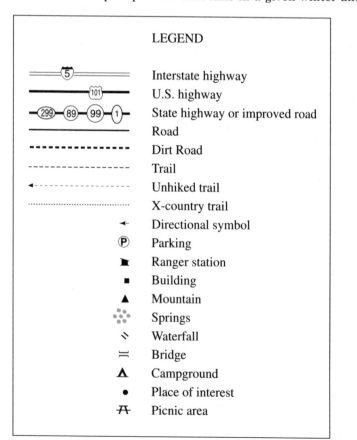

LEGEND	
	Interstate highway
	U.S. highway
	State highway or improved road
	Road
	Dirt Road
	Trail
	Unhiked trail
	X-country trail
	Directional symbol
℗	Parking
	Ranger station
■	Building
▲	Mountain
	Springs
	Waterfall
=	Bridge
⛰	Campground
•	Place of interest
	Picnic area

when that first fall storm actually arrives, so call the agency listed after "Information" first. If you desire solitude, hike on weekdays or off-season. Also, note that most state, county, and regional parks close from roughly dusk to dawn; prominently displayed signs at the park entrance and at trailheads usually give the exact times. In some cases, the access roads are locked during closed hours, which means your short moonlight stroll may turn into an overnight stay.

Water. This indicates the trailside availability of water, usually from lakes and streams, though some sources can dry up in late summer and early fall, especially in drought years. Also, be sure you understand how to properly purify water so you don't get giardiasis or other water-born diseases (see "Water," under "Safety"). However, for all but overnight backpacking trips, you should bring all the water you need from home. Of course, always stash some iodine tablets or other means of purification in your pack, just in case.

Maps. The maps in this book are for reference purposes only. Although they will be adequate for many hikes, you shouldn't rely solely on them. Get the listed United States Geological Survey (USGS) and United States Forest Service (USFS) topographical maps for more details on terrain, creeks, and so forth. These are usually sold at engineering supply stores and outdoor supply stores. Note that many USGS maps were made forty years ago and may not have some of the trails described in this book; they may also show trails that no longer exist. The USFS maps are much more up-to-date. The USFS also sells general maps for each national forest that show all the roads and many of the trails. These help you navigate when driving to trailheads but are usually inadequate for trail guidance. Most state, county, and regional parks offer brochures with trail maps at the park itself, often for a small fee.

Information. This lists the name of the government agency with jurisdiction over the trail. Look in Appendix 1 for the address and phone number. Call or visit these people to find out about trail access and conditions and to obtain maps and wilderness permits. Wilderness permits are required for most hikes in USFS wilderness areas and for overnight trips in Lassen Volcanic National Park. Some popular areas may impose a limit on the number of permits issued; it's always wise to call ahead before going. Note that some of the information in this book may have changed since the book went to press, such as trail access and the need for a wilderness permit; phone ahead to be sure that you can still do the hike.

Regarding driving directions. You'll find these in the second paragraph of each hike's text. They take you from the nearest highway or town to the trailhead. All trailheads in this book are generally accessible by all types of vehicles, including two-wheel-drive passenger cars, unless you go out of season when the road is very wet or covered with snow. Also, keep in mind that odometer accuracy varies, so look for described turnoffs and the like before you reach the mileage listed in the hike description. And be aware that you will be sharing some of those narrow national forest roads with behemoth logging trucks: Look out for them, and go slow around blind corners.

Regarding trailhead theft. Don't leave valuables in your car for potential thieves, and always lock the doors and close the windows tightly. Human rip-off artists aren't your only concern, however. Bears often visit trailhead parking areas and will "rip off" a door or window in search of a tasty snack. Because bears follow their noses, don't leave any food or garbage in your car for them to smell.

Regarding fees. Expect to pay entrance fees at Lassen Volcanic National Park and all state parks. Other agencies may charge fees in the future.

What To Take

The Ten Essentials. On all hikes, always take extra clothing, extra food, sunglasses, a knife (for first aid or emergency kindling), firestarter (for wet wood), a first-aid kit, matches (in a waterproof container), flashlight (with an extra bulb and batteries), maps, and a compass. In addition, take water, a water purifier, toilet paper, and a watch. Also include an emergency signaling device, such as a whistle, mirror, or piece of brightly colored plastic or cloth. (See Appendix 3 for a complete list of supplies for both day hikes and backpacking trips.)

Clothing. Include extra layers of clothes in your daypack: temperatures can drop suddenly, winds can kick up, or an unexpected storm could suddenly move in over a ridgetop. At a minimum, bring pants, a sweatshirt, a watchman's cap, and a poncho. For many hikes you'll find that a good pair of running shoes will do just fine; however, lightweight hiking boots can be just as comfortable while providing greater ankle support, more foot protection, and better traction. For protection from the sun, wear a wide-brimmed hat, good sunglasses, and a strong sunblock.

Safety

Most of this book's journeys travel through areas where the hiker faces potential dangers. The following information helps you to minimize the possibility of potential danger becoming reality, but it is no substitute for reading books and taking classes devoted solely to the subjects of wilderness safety, travel, and first aid. (See Appendix 2 for books on these subjects.)

Know your limitations. Don't exceed your or your group's physical conditioning, agility, and preparedness. Better prudent than dead.

Traveling alone. If you decide to hike alone, inform a responsible person of your route and the time you expect to return. Once home, call and confirm your safe arrival. Remember, when going alone, there is no room for error: Always be alert!

Weather. Check the weather forecast before you hike. In many areas you can call the National Weather Service, or check to see if your cable TV includes a weather channel, which often broadcasts up-to-the-minute forecasts several times an hour. Always bring a poncho or a space blanket. Both are lightweight and will keep you relatively dry and out of the wind if you're caught in a storm or have to spend an unexpected night in the wilderness. Backpackers should have a good tent, a sleeping pad, and a sleeping bag that's rated for temperatures below what you expect. Also, although thunderstorms and lightning can occur anytime of the year, they are most prevalent in summer and at higher elevations. If you see tall thunderheads gathering in the vicinity, stay away from exposed ridges and peaks, and wait out the show among the shorter trees in the nearest forest.

Hypothermia. This sometimes fatal physical condition occurs when body temperature drops drastically, usually due to some combination of wind, wetness, cold, and fatigue. Persons suffering from hypothermia usually exhibit coordination loss, shivering, and inarticulate speech. Forethought offers the best way to avoid hypothermia: bring warm clothes, including a windbreaker; stay dry; and avoid hikes that stretch your physical limits and those of your party. If you or an accompanying hiker shows signs of hypothermia, immediately seek shelter away from rain and wind, change into dry clothes, build a fire, and eat food (preferably grains, breads, or candy) that contains carbohydrates, which are quickly converted to heat energy.

Water. The days of drinking directly from lakes and streams are over, primarily due to *Giardia,* a microorganism that can cause intense intestinal distress and has spread to much of Northern California's waters. The best way to ensure you don't get infected by *Giardia* (or anything else) is to boil all water for at least twenty minutes. Chemical purifiers, usually iodine compounds, offer the second best option, but treated water tastes terrible. Finally, you can use a water-filtering device, hoping that it's not defective and that it actually meets the manufacturer's claims. Outdoor stores sell both chemical compounds and filtering devices. You'll find information about water availability at the beginning of each hike description. Keep in mind that you should always purify outdoor water. For those doing day hikes, pack your own water from the faucet at home.

Ticks. These occasionally carry Lyme disease, which they can pass to you when they drill a hole through your skin and drink your blood. Ticks inhabit brushy areas and tall grasses, where they hope to come in contact with unsuspecting animals—like you. To decrease the probability of a tick encounter, wear pants and a long-sleeve shirt and thoroughly check your skin and scalp after hiking through tick territory. If a tick does attach, you can attempt a careful removal with a tick removal kit or visit a doctor. Always visit a doctor if you feel any symptoms after a tick bite.

Rattlesnakes. This dangerous reptile's trademark is a jointed rattle at the tail end, but it will usually only bite if cornered or touched. Found below 6,000 feet elevation and active in warmer months, it frequents dry, rocky areas, brushy spots, and occasionally the sides of trails. Check both sides of the trail when you hike, and be especially careful of where you put your hands and feet when hiking off-trail. If you are bitten by a rattlesnake, stay calm and relaxed. Get to a hospital as soon as possible (preferably within twelve hours) for an antivenin shot.

Black bears. These creatures generally avoid humans and will usually turn tail and run away at high speed when they see you. To lessen the chance of an unhappy encounter with a bear around the campsite, use a rope to suspend all food, garbage, and scented products (like deodorant and toothpaste) from a tree at night (at least 10 feet from the ground, 10 feet from the trunk, and 5 feet from the branch). The tree should be both downwind and as far from camp as practical. Also, don't leave food scraps lying around the campsite, and be sure that no food or smell of food is on your body or clothes. Of course, never feed bears (or any other wild animals). The greatest danger occurs when you get between a mother bear and her cub. If this happens, slowly back away and speak to the mother in a nonthreatening voice. If a confrontation seems imminent, roll into the fetal position and play dead. Often a bear will leave once it asserts its dominance.

Horses. If you encounter these creatures and their riders on the trail, you must give them the right-of-way. Step to the side of the path, and talk in a calm voice to the riders. This lets the horses know that you are a human being, not some strange beast that may harm them.

Poison oak. This deciduous plant, quite common below 5,000 feet, takes the form of either a vine or a shrub. Its leaves, green in spring and summer and red in fall, usually form clusters of three, although size and shape vary. When in doubt, assume a plant is poison oak. You may develop a red itchy rash after coming into contact with poison oak. If you think you've touched it, wash immediately with soap and cool water, and also wash the clothes you were wearing. Pharmacies stock ointments that help relieve the symptoms.

Ocean. When near this vast and powerful body of water, always watch for rogue waves, especially in winter. These waves, much larger than other waves, can sweep you or members of your party into the cold, turbulent waters. Also, be careful when hiking near ocean cliffs, which are often unstable and have a habit of breaking off and falling to the rocks, sand, and surf below.

A Note About Safety

Safety is an important concern in all outdoor activities. No guidebook can alert you to every hazard or anticipate the limitations of every reader. Therefore, the descriptions of roads, trails, routes, and natural features in this book are not representations that a particular place or excursion will be safe for your party. When you follow any of the routes described in this book, you assume responsibility for your own safety. Under normal conditions, such excursions require the usual attention to traffic, road and trail conditions, weather, terrain, the capabilities of your party, and other factors. Keeping informed on current conditions and exercising common sense are the keys to a safe, enjoyable outing.

The Mountaineers

Wilderness Ethics

Walking in the wilderness. Resist the temptation to shortcut up and down switchbacks.This destroys trailside plant life and accelerates trail erosion. And always try to minimize the impact of your feet on the land by stepping on rock or firm, dry ground when possible. Be especially careful in meadows, which contain a variety of sensitive plants.

Indeed, your philosophy should be that of minimum impact, which means you strive to leave no trace of your visit.

Camping. Minimum-impact philosophy also applies to campsites. Select a site at least 100 feet away from streams and rivers so that you won't disturb waterside plants or pollute the water. However, if the only site you find is an *established* site less than 100 feet from the water, then use it carefully. Whenever possible, use an existing site in the forest or on bare rock that's far from the water. Finally, put a plastic tarp under your tent to protect yourself from rain water. Never dig ditches.

Fires. The minimum-impact hiker doesn't need a fire. Burning wood removes organic material from the ecosystem, contributes to air pollution, and scares away animal life. Bring enough clothes to ensure night warmth. Those addicted to caffeine can bring caffeine pills as a substitute for morning coffee. If you must have a hot meal, bring a gas stove; however, you can enjoy a wide variety of foods that don't require cooking. If you insist on having a fire, do so only in or near heavily wooded areas, and use only down deadwood in an established campfire ring. When finished, douse the fire thoroughly with water until you're sure it's completely out.

Washing. Detergents and food particles harm water life and can alter water chemistry, so wash yourself and your dishes far from lakes and streams. Carry water off to the woods or bare rock for washing, and use biodegradable soaps available at outdoor stores.

Sanitation. Defecate in a shallow hole 6 to 10 inches deep, preferably in forest duff where the covered feces will quickly decompose. Be sure your spot is at least 200 feet from water and well away from trails and campsites. You needn't be so careful with urine because it's sterile. But do stay away from water sources, and don't pee all over any single plant. Spread it around and let it provide the soil with valuable nitrogen.

Garbage. Pack it all out, including any you find that's not yours.

Hiker courtesy. Your goal is to be as unnoticeable and unobtrusive as possible. Choose subdued colors such as gray, green, and brown for your clothing and equipment. Travel only in small groups. Set up an inconspicuous camp. Talk in quiet tones. And leave the dog at home. Dogs pollute the water, scare away wildlife, and sometimes threaten other hikers.

BERRY CREEK FALLS AND SKYLINE TO THE SEA TRAIL

Length: 16.3 miles round trip
Hiking time: 10 hours or over-
night
High point: 1,500 feet
Total elevation gain: 1,700 feet
Difficulty: strenuous up McCrary
Ridge, otherwise easy
Season: year-round

Water: bring your own
Maps: USGS 7.5' Big Basin, USGS
7.5' Davenport, USGS 7.5' Ano
Nuevo, USGS 7.5' Franklin
Point
Information: Big Basin Red-
woods State Park

Hike through redwood forest and native chaparral and along quiet creeks, and enjoy views of Waddell Beach, the Pacific Ocean, the Santa Cruz Mountains, and graceful Berry Creek Falls. For a complete Skyline to the Sea journey, combine the last part of this trip with the first 4 miles of hike 2 (Silver Falls and Skyline to the Sea Trail). Backpackers must make advance reservations for trailside camping (call [408] 338-6132).

The trailhead, signed for Waddell Beach, is on the west side of Highway 1, 18 miles north of Santa Cruz and 26 miles south of Half Moon Bay.

Skyline to the Sea Trail begins across Highway 1. Pass Waddell Creek's marsh, followed by Horse Trail Camp, and then bear left at 0.3 mile. Climb through a knobcone pine and coast live oak forest, then gain a view of Waddell Beach, its marsh, and the Pacific Ocean as the trail levels at 0.6 mile. Hike past Douglas fir, alder, and redwood, then cross Waddell Creek at 1.4 miles. Reach a signed trail junction 0.1 mile farther, where you bear left. Backpackers can stay the night here at Alder Trail Camp or at Twin Redwoods Trail Camp another 0.2 mile farther.

Over the next 1.5 miles, the riparian habitat along Waddell Creek

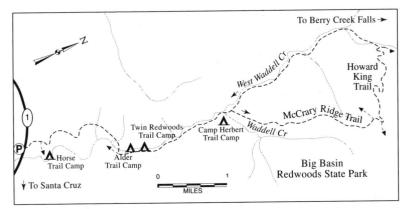

Opposite: *Berry Creek Falls*

consists of an impressive array of native trees that grow taller than usual while competing for sunlight: look for alder, bigleaf maple, buckeye, Douglas fir, redwood, and California laurel. Below the trees you'll see redwood sorrel, thimbleberry, fern, horsetail, and periwinkle.

Camp Herbert Trail Camp, another backpack camp, comes up at 3.1 miles. Cross a tributary of Waddell Creek 100 yards farther, then, after another 100 yards, leave Skyline to the Sea Trail and bear right onto the signed McCrary Ridge Trail. This 2.9-mile footpath initially climbs under welcome shade before entering an open area where manzanita and knobcone pine dominate.

At 6 miles the trail ends at a signed trail junction, where you bear right onto a fire road. Watch closely for a signed trail junction partially concealed by shrubs 0.2 mile farther, where you go left onto Howard King Trail for a shaded 2.5-mile descent through a forest of madrone, California laurel, and Douglas fir.

Reach West Waddell Creek at 8.7 miles and bear right onto Skyline to the Sea Trail. At 9 miles turn left onto Berry Creek Falls Trail. Magnificent Berry Creek Falls, which plunges 70 vertical feet to a small, clear pool, awaits 0.1 mile farther. Allow time to explore the cascades and pools found all along enchanting Berry Creek. Also, consider a visit to Silver Falls, only 0.4 mile farther up the trail, and to the nearby Sunset Trail Camp (see hike 2, Silver Falls and Skyline to the Sea Trail).

To return to Waddell Beach, backtrack to Skyline to the Sea Trail for the final 6 miles downhill, accompanied the whole time by peacefully meandering Waddell Creek. The same flora encountered on the second and third miles of the hike decorate this scenic section of the wide dirt road. Stay on the road past three junctions.

2 SILVER FALLS AND SKYLINE TO THE SEA TRAIL

Length: 10.2 miles round trip
Hiking time: 6 hours or overnight
High point: 1,300 feet
Total elevation gain: 1,900 feet
Difficulty: moderate

Season: year-round
Water: bring your own
Maps: USGS 7.5' Big Basin, USGS 7.5' Franklin Point
Information: Big Basin Redwoods State Park

Walk past tall redwoods to three splendid sets of waterfalls along enchanting Berry Creek. To hike the complete Skyline to the Sea Trail to Waddell Beach, combine the first 4 miles of this hike with the last 6.3 miles of hike 1 (Berry Creek Falls and Skyline to the Sea Trail). Backpackers must make advance reservations for trailside camping (call [408] 338-6132).

Ferns, horsetails, and a fallen redwood tree grace Kelly Creek.

From the interchange of Highways 9 and 236 (6 miles west of Highway 35), drive west on Highway 236 a steep 8.4 miles to the Big Basin Redwoods State Park headquarters. Or, from Highway 9 at the town of Boulder Creek (13 miles northeast of Santa Cruz), travel 9 miles on Highway 236.

To start, head west from just behind the fee kiosk, follow signs for Skyline to the Sea Trail, then turn left at the huge signpost just after

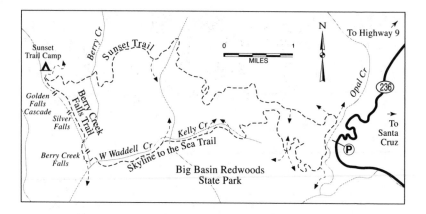

crossing a wooden bridge. Bear right at a signed trail junction at 0.2 mile, then cross a fire road at 1 mile and continue on Skyline to the Sea Trail toward Berry Creek Falls.

Tall redwoods reach skyward along a moderate descent past a signed trail junction at 1.6 miles, where you continue left. Cross Kelly Creek 0.5 mile farther, and stay left at three signed trail junctions. Reach a series of small pools at around 3 miles, near where Kelly Creek merges with West Waddell Creek.

See magnificent Berry Creek Falls from a wooden bench at 4.1 miles. The trail drops another 0.1 mile to where Berry Creek pours into West Waddell Creek. Backpackers and car-shuttle day hikers can reach Waddell Beach by turning left here (for a description of the rest of Skyline to the Sea Trail, see hike 1, Berry Creek Falls and Skyline to the Sea Trail). Bear right for a 0.1-mile climb to Berry Creek Falls, which plunges 70 feet into a sand-bottomed pool. Berry Creek Falls Trail then escorts you upward for a closer view of the top of the waterfall.

At 4.6 miles reach Silver Falls, which drops 60 feet into a small, oblong pool dammed by a toppled redwood trunk. The trail climbs to a dramatic vista of Silver Falls and then gives strikingly gorgeous views of Golden Falls Cascade, a peanut-butter-and-orange-colored series of pools and cascades that decorate the trailside for 200 yards.

After a 0.1-mile climb away from West Berry Creek, reach a signed trail junction at 5 miles, where you bear right onto Sunset Trail (backpackers can go left 100 yards to Sunset Trail Camp). Break out of the redwood forest shade into a brief section of chaparral consisting of knobcone pine, manzanita, and chamise. You now canyon-hop twice to a signed trail marker at 7.7 miles and turn left.

Smaller redwoods appear over the final 2.5-mile leg. Bear left at the signed trail junction at 9.2 miles. The final mile travels past three signed trail junctions (take a left and two rights), then alongside attractive Opal Creek under massive redwoods, and finally to park headquarters.

3 BUTANO STATE PARK TRAILS

Length: 6.2 miles round trip
Hiking time: 4 hours
High point: 1,100 feet
Total elevation gain: 1,300 feet
**Difficulty: strenuous up the Ano
  Nuevo Trail, otherwise easy**

Season: year-round
Water: none, bring your own
Map: USGS 7.5' Franklin Point
Information: Butano State Park

This mostly shaded excursion into whisper-quiet, old-growth redwood forests travels four different trails past a variety of plant habitats.

From Highway 1 near Pescadero Beach (15 miles south of Half Moon Bay), head east for 2 miles on Pescadero Road. Turn right onto Cloverdale Road, then park 2.3 miles farther near the kiosk.

After visiting the nature center and garden next to the kiosk, begin climbing steeply on Ano Nuevo Trail past lush fern gardens and Douglas fir, the latter covered with staghorn lichen. Tree shade coupled with constant moisture from the nearby Pacific Ocean nourishes this rich, green jungle.

The path climbs relentlessly until you reach a crest at 0.8 mile, where a bench offers great views on clear days of Ano Nuevo Island

Coast live oak leaves frame a sunny Butano State Park meadow with Douglas firs and redwoods in the distance.

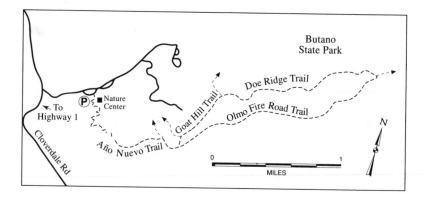

and the Pacific Ocean. The rare Douglas iris flower grows here beneath a canopy of madrone and Douglas fir.

At 1.1 miles turn right onto Olmo Fire Road Trail, and then go left 0.2 mile farther onto the Goat Hill Trail connector. Bear right 0.1 mile farther on the actual Goat Hill Trail. Travel past level, lush, and shaded scenery for 0.5 mile to the Doe Ridge Trail marker, where you bear right.

For the next 1.4 miles, travel through a huge redwood forest on the serene Doe Ridge Trail. These huge redwoods survived two fires long ago, which explains the charred trunks. Twin redwood stalks sharing a 10-foot-wide trunk catch your attention at 2.9 miles.

Bear right onto Olmo Fire Road Trail at 3.2 miles. The next 1.8 miles stays level past coast live oak, a few redwoods, and Douglas fir. Enjoy occasional views of the Pacific Ocean by leaving the trail when you see parting branches. Reach a crest at 5 miles, then walk downhill for 0.1 mile, where you turn left onto the previously encountered Ano Nuevo Trail.

4 CASTLE ROCK AND GOAT ROCK

Length: 5.8 miles round trip
Hiking time: 3 hours
High point: 3,214 feet
Total elevation gain: 800 feet
Difficulty: moderate
Season: year-round

Water: bring your own
Map: USGS 7.5' Castle Rock Ridge
Information: Castle Rock State Park

This journey in Castle Rock State Park has many features: sweeping vistas of Monterey Bay, odd-looking sandstone slabs, and groves of black oak and coast live oak.

Young hikers play in Castle Rock's sandstone caves.

From the Saratoga Gap vista point, at the junction of Highways 9 and 35 (Skyline Boulevard), drive south on Highway 35 for 2.6 miles to the Castle Rock State Park dirt parking lot on the right.

Begin your hike by taking the 0.6-mile-long Castle Rock Trail. (Watch for poison oak growing abundantly on this trail and sporadically on the others.) Douglas fir, madrone, black oak, and coast live oak furnish ample shade as you climb the initial 0.2 mile and then bear right onto an old dirt road. At 0.3 mile a cluster of giant coast live oak surround 40-foot Castle Rock, where you can explore sandstone caves.

From Castle Rock descend the obvious trail to join Saratoga Gap Trail at 0.6 mile. Serene black oak forest accompanies you down to a creek at 0.8 mile. Hug its bank for 0.1 mile, then bear left at a signed junction, staying on Saratoga Gap Trail.

At 1.1 miles an attractive madrone canopies an observation deck ideal for viewing Castle Rock Falls. You'll also see a vertical sandstone slab, the Santa Cruz Mountains, Monterey Bay, and the distant Pacific Ocean.

The path now departs the creek and travels along a steep hillside and through chaparral. Peer past eastwood manzanita and Scotch

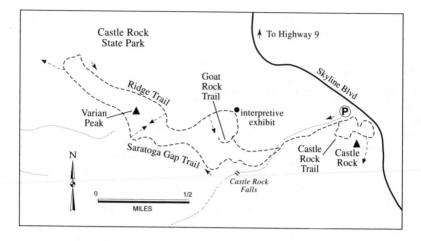

broom for more distant ocean and bay views at 1.5 miles. The trail continues its gradual ascent past a few steep, rocky spots. Cross a shaded wooden bridge at 1.8 miles, and stay left 0.2 mile farther at a signed trail junction. The next 0.8 mile stays mostly level along the slope of 2,865-foot Varian Peak. Head right at the signed junction at 2.8 miles into a community of tall madrone. Reach a trail fork at 3.1 miles. Left leads 0.2 mile to Castle Rock Trail Camp—first come, first served. Bear right on Ridge Trail, and climb to a scenic vista point at 3.6 miles. The path levels to a junction at 4.4 miles—stay left.

At 4.7 miles go left at the signed trail fork, and 0.2 mile farther arrive at the interpretive exhibit. Find the signed Goat Rock Trail, then reach the scenic overlook. From here, explore Goat Rock's numerous formations: some feature interesting crevices, and others give good views of the Santa Cruz Mountains.

Return to Ridge Trail and go right. Bear left at 5.4 miles onto the signed Saratoga Gap Trail for the final 0.4 mile back to the trailhead.

5 PURISIMA CREEK AND HARKINS RIDGE

Length: 7.5 miles round trip
Hiking time: 4 hours
High point: 1,600 feet
Total elevation gain: 1,200 feet
Difficulty: moderate

Season: year-round
Water: bring your own
Map: USGS 7.5' Woodside
Information: Midpeninsula Regional Open Space District

This redwood tree journey parallels cool and peaceful Purisima Creek, passes tranquil, natural herb gardens on the secluded Soda

Blue blossom ceanothus and dense redwood forest on Harkins Ridge Trail

Gulch Trail, and finally travels a view-filled, slender finger of Harkins Ridge.

Turn east on Higgins-Purisima Road 1.3 miles south of the intersection of Highways 1 and 92 at Half Moon Bay. Park 4.5 miles farther near Purisima Creek.

The first mile along Purisima Creek Trail, a dirt road, stays level and shaded, with an equal mix of tall redwood, alder, and bigleaf maple. Come to a large clearing at 1.1 miles, which supports thistle, thimbleberry, poison hemlock, and a few rushes.

The trail noticeably ascends after crossing a bridge roofed by a drooping maple at 1.3 miles. Reach the Grabtown trailhead junction 0.1 mile farther and continue straight. You soon cross another bridge that overlooks a tributary originating from Soda Gulch, higher up to the left. Note the tall redwoods and towering maples that provide shelter for a lady fern community at creekside, then climb gently to the Soda Gulch Trail junction at 2.4 miles and go left.

The climb moderates as you leave the creek and enter a jungle of redwood and various herbs, including mint, mugwort, and nettle. At 3.5 miles observe two redwoods joined at the trunk, then continue to a sweeping view of the Santa Cruz Mountains at 3.7 miles. The narrow

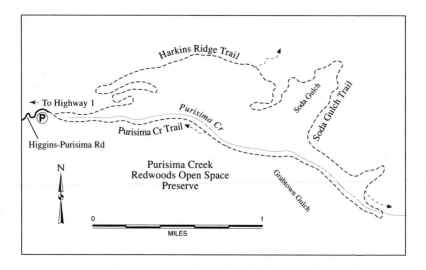

path arcs toward the distant Pacific Ocean at 4 miles and then enters dense chaparral.

As you approach the top of a knoll, you'll have another view of the Santa Cruz Mountains rolling into Half Moon Bay. California poppy, cow parsnip, and yerba santa then decorate the landscape leading up to the Harkins Ridge Trail junction at 4.8 miles, where you bear left.

Harkins Ridge Trail, another dirt road, takes you past blue blossom ceanothus and madrone with a back-setting of Purisima Creek's redwood groves as you gradually descend over the next 1.4 miles. Views disappear at 6.2 miles, where the trail bends toward Purisima Creek and descends more rapidly through shaded forest to the trailhead.

6 NORTH PEAK MONTARA MOUNTAIN

Length: 6 miles round trip
Hiking time: 4 hours
High point: 1,898 feet
Total elevation gain: 2,200 feet
Difficulty: strenuous
Season: year-round

Water: none, bring your own
Map: USGS 7.5' Montara Mountain
Information: Half Moon Bay State Beaches

This hike offers an impressive array of wildflowers and chaparral plants as well as a superb top-of-the-world panorama of the San Francisco Bay area and Pacific Ocean.

Watch for an unsigned entrance gate on the east side of Highway 1 several yards north of the access road to Montara State Beach (10 miles north of Half Moon Bay). If this small lot is packed, you may have to park farther south at Gray Whale Cove parking area on the east side of the highway or at the Montara State Beach parking lot.

The path initially travels east and parallels a grove of tall cypress trees. Bear sharply left onto unsigned Old San Pedro Road at 0.2 mile, just in front of the ranger's residence. Thankfully, this dirt path is wide, because poison oak, identifiable by its three-leaved branchlets, dominates trailside to 0.4 mile.

At 0.5 mile walk past a shady grove of Scotch broom and pampas grass, both hardy, exotic plants. The path now climbs relentlessly, with improving views of the towns of Half Moon Bay behind you and Pacifica northward.

Bear right at 1.4 miles onto Montara Mountain Trail, a fire road. The steepest climbing occurs from 1.6 to 1.9 miles, accompanied by California poppy and lupine. Blue-blossom California lilac dominates trailside from 2 to 2.5 miles as monumental rock outcrops attract attention in the distance.

You may be tempted to stray off the beaten path to climb a number

A northward view of the Pacific Coast from the chaparral-lined Montara Mountain Trail

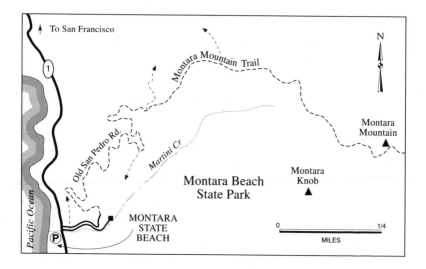

of small peaks from 2.7 to 2.9 miles, but remain on the main dirt road and reward yourself with a 360-degree view from the microwave/weather station atop 1,898-foot North Peak Montara Mountain at 3 miles. Look for Mount Diablo to the east and Scarper's Peak and the Santa Cruz Mountains to the southeast. Half Moon Bay and its neighboring beaches stretch below to the southwest, and mighty Mount Tamalpais hovers to the north above San Francisco's skyscrapers.

7 HENRY W. COE STATE PARK: CHINA HOLE

Length: 13.4 miles round trip
Hiking time: 8 hours or overnight
High point: 3,041 feet
Total elevation gain: 3,200 feet
Difficulty: moderate
Season: year-round

Water: available only from Frog Lake and China Hole; bring your own
Maps: USGS 7.5' Mt. Sizer, USGS 7.5' Mississippi Creek, Henry W. Coe State Park
Information: Henry W. Coe State Park

Admire ongoing views of rolling foothills as you hike atop ridges, along steep canyon sides, and beside creeks, each supporting a diverse array of plants. Register at the visitor center if you plan an overnight trip.

From Highway 101 in Morgan Hill (south of San Jose), take the East

Dunne Avenue Exit, then drive 12.5 miles to the Henry W. Coe State Park visitor center.

To start, get on the Pacheco Route dirt fire road in front of the red house (by the visitor center), climb 75 yards, and then bear left onto Monument Trail. The slender footpath bisects a sloping field to a stand of ponderosa pine at a three-way trail fork. Take the 0.2-mile spur trail on the left for an impressive view of the Santa Clara Valley.

Return to the three-way trail fork, and go left for 0.1 mile through valley oak savanna to the Northern Heights Route, where you turn left. Continue down this wide dirt road past a trail junction, some huge big berry manzanita specimens, and then another junction signed for Frog Lake. Cross attractive Little Fork Coyote Creek, then climb briefly in a blue oak forest to overlook a murky former cattle pond (Frog Lake) at 1.9 miles, where backpackers can camp by the cattails and rushes.

Climb as juvenile gray pine and larger blue oak gradually yield to graceful ponderosa pine, big black oak, and huge manzanita. Reach a trail junction at 2.6 miles and bear right onto Middle Ridge Trail. Stay left at the signed trail junction 0.2 mile farther. (For an abbreviated hike, consider bearing right onto the signed Fish Trail at 4.2 miles. This footpath connects with the Pacheco Route for a 6.7-mile total round trip.)

As you continue on Middle Ridge Trail, occasionally leave the path for westward views of Pine Ridge and eastward views of Blue Ridge

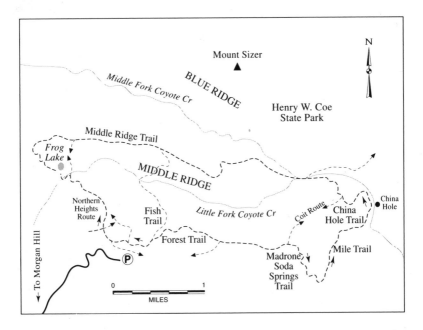

Mature blue oaks and young gray pines seen from the Middle Ridge Trail

and the Middle Fork Coyote Creek drainage. The final leg of Middle Ridge Trail plunges through black oak– and madrone-shaded woodland to the Y of Middle and Little Fork Coyote creeks and then travels along Coyote Creek to the Poverty Flat campsite at 6.5 miles.

The up-and-down climb to China Hole begins with a right turn on the unsigned Cougar Trail, which climbs 0.7 mile to the signed junction with China Hole Trail, where you bear left. At 8.8 miles reach this year-round pond, which is suitable for swimming in the warmer months and doubles as a good campsite. Note that here you can connect with the trails of hike 8 (Henry W. Coe State Park: Coit Lake).

Retrace your steps, then turn left on the signed Mile Trail, which stays mostly shaded until its junction with the unsigned Madrone Soda Springs Trail, where you turn right at 10.1 miles. Climb for 0.8 mile, turn left onto the signed Coit Route for another 0.8 mile, then go right at 11.7 miles onto the signed Forest Trail near a valley oak.

At 12.8 miles, go right onto Corral Trail. Travel a steep, grassy slope, which features a bench for admiring the rolling hills westward, then continue past canyon live oak, valley oak, and open chamise chaparral areas to the parking lot at 13.4 miles.

8 HENRY W. COE STATE PARK: COIT LAKE

Length: 26 miles round trip
Hiking time: 3 to 5 days
High point: 2,640 feet
Total elevation gain: 4,800 feet
Difficulty: moderate to strenuous
Season: year-round

Water: available at China Hole,
Coit Lake, and Los Cruzeros;
always have plenty
Maps: USGS 7.5' Mississippi
Creek, USGS 7.5' Mount Sizer,
Henry W. Coe State Park
Information: Henry W. Coe State
Park

Take a secluded backpack trip in gently sculpted hills past oak savanna to Coit Lake. Along the way you'll have grand views of foothill slopes and canyons. Note that spring and fall are the best times to hike. Backpackers must register at the visitor center.

From Highway 101 in Morgan Hill (south of San Jose), take the East Dunne Avenue Exit, then climb 12.5 miles to the Henry W. Coe State Park visitor center.

To start, take the signed Corral Trail in front of the visitor center. When you reach an open area covered with oat grass, look for a magnificent valley oak decorated with profuse mistletoe growth. Bear right 50 yards farther onto the signed Springs Trail next to another valley oak.

The 1.4-mile-long Springs Trail begins in shade, passes two springs which shrivel up by midsummer, and continues along an open hilltop featuring sweeping vistas of the steep-sided, rolling hills that epitomize this large park. As a bonus, this level stretch supports a four-oak-species savanna: valley oak, coast live oak, black oak, and blue oak.

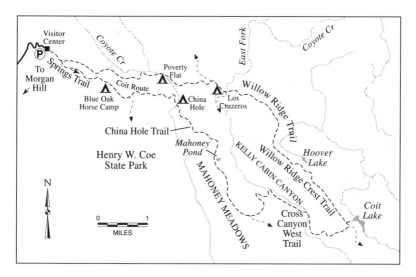

A flower-bordered spring and a vista of distant hills near tne Pacheco Route

At 1.7 miles pass an attractive third spring lined with native rushes. The trail then leads to a multisigned trail intersection at 1.9 miles, where you go right onto the Coit Route dirt road. Several picnic tables and two outhouses mark Blue Oak Horse Camp 0.2 mile farther. You'll find water at a nearby bass pond, where a spur loop trail leads to one of the Manzanita Point Group camps, which are available to backpackers.

At 2.5 miles stay straight at the signed trail junction with Madrone Soda Springs Trail (see hike 7, Henry W. Coe State Park: China Hole). The path becomes the China Hole Trail 0.2 mile farther and descends past a variety of native flora, including big berry manzanita, ponderosa pine, black oak, chamise chaparral, and eventually blue oak woodland, to popular China Hole, which doubles as a swimming spot and a camp for backpackers.

Continue on to Mahoney Meadows and Mahoney Ridge by crossing Coyote Creek, which can be impassable in winter months (check with the visitor center ahead of time). The 1.5-mile section from Mahoney Pond to the signed junction of Cross Canyon Trail West (where you turn left) consists of an oak savanna ridge walk that curves past tall gray pine. Admire views to the right of Coyote Creek Canyon, and turn around to view Blue Ridge, Middle Ridge, and Pine Ridge to the northwest. Your mile-long journey down Cross Canyon Trail West encompasses a mix of shady and open vegetation. The primary shrub species include ceanothus, ocean spray, and big berry manzanita. Watch for sporadic madrone and black oak closer to the canyon's bottom.

When you get down to Kelly Cabin Canyon, the trail veers abruptly southeast and follows the seasonal creek upstream past laurel, bigleaf maple, sycamore, and coast live oak. After 1 mile the trail departs the creek and then ascends in and out of side canyons to the signed junction with Willow Ridge Crest Trail (a dirt road), where you turn left.

After 0.1 mile pick up the 0.2-mile-long trail on your right that leads to Coit Lake, which offers good swimming and camping for backpackers.

Return to Willow Ridge Crest Trail and pass shallow Hoover Lake and several sections of chamise chaparral as you appreciate ongoing views of the Pacheco drainage to the east and previously mentioned vistas to the north and west. Turn left onto the signed Willow Ridge Trail (a section of the Pacheco Route) 3.5 miles past Coit Lake. You'll spot an unsigned side trail 0.2 mile farther that leads to a spring that usually shrivels up by early summer.

Back on Willow Ridge Trail, descend 1,000 feet of elevation over 1.3 miles to the East Fork Coyote Creek. Los Cruzeros, another backpack camp, is a short side trip downstream. Cross the creek, then continue on the Pacheco Route, now a dirt road. Climb 0.4 mile to a signed trail junction, bear left, and then continue left at another signed junction 0.3 mile farther.

Gradually descend for 1 mile to Poverty Flat, another favorite creekside camping spot. From here, briefly follow Coyote Creek to two signed trail junctions, then cross the creek (which may be impassable in winter). Stay straight on the Pacheco Route for a 1.6-mile climb past a variety of oaks, plus gray pine and laurel, to a previously encountered trail junction (hike 7, Henry W. Coe State Park: China Hole, describes Forest Trail), where you stay straight on the Pacheco Route. The trail now climbs to a plateau, with splendid views of canyons and rolling hills, and then descends to the trailhead.

9 GRANT PARK'S PEAK 2987

Length: 9 miles round trip
Hiking time: 5 hours
High point: 2,987 feet
Total elevation gain: 1,900 feet
Difficulty: moderate

Season: year-round
Water: none, bring your own
Map: USGS 7.5' Lick Observatory
Information: Joseph D. Grant
    County Park

Oak trees dotting an open landscape can take on unique, sculpted shapes. Such is the case on this hike as you climb through oak woodlands to an oak-ringed meadow and then to Peak 2987 for a 360-degree view of the South Bay, Mount Hamilton, and rolling hills.

From the east side of San Jose on I-680, take the Alum Rock Avenue Exit (2 miles north of the interchange with Highway 101), then drive east 2.2 miles. Turn right onto Mount Hamilton Road and climb 7.7 twisting miles to the Joseph D. Grant County Park kiosk. Go 150 yards, then park in the dirt lot on the left.

Get on the dirt road that skirts the northeastern shoreline of scenic, coyote brush–lined Grant Lake. After 0.2 mile bear right onto the signed Halls Valley Trail. Then cross a willow-lined seasonal stream,

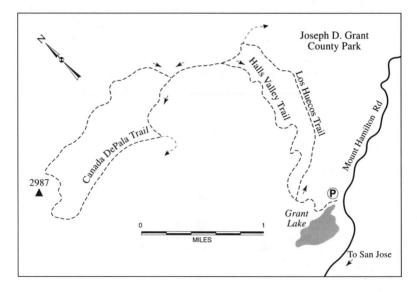

A mistletoe-infested valley oak grows high above Grant Lake on Grant Park's Los Huecos Trail.

climb past a stand of eucalyptus, and bear right 0.2 mile farther onto the signed Los Huecos Trail.

This wide dirt road immediately climbs, rewarding you with views of Grant Lake beyond scattered valley oak and Lick Observatory atop 4,209-foot Mount Hamilton ahead. When these views vanish, look southward into the broad valley housing San Felipe Creek.

Just prior to reaching the ridgetop, look west at San Jose and the South Bay. Reach the crest at 2.1 miles, and bear left onto Cañada De Pala Trail, noting the nearby twin patriarch valley oaks. A grove of hardy buckeye trees appears 0.2 mile farther at a signed trail junction. Stay straight, but remember that Halls Valley Trail on the left is the return route. Admire a rare, high ridge wetland patch on the left when you reach a signed trail junction at 2.8 miles. Bear left here, and then, at 3.1 miles, come to a large meadow. Bear right 0.2 mile farther at the signed trail junction, then skirt the meadow for the next 0.4 mile along a rush-lined seasonal stream. Climb another 0.8 mile to regain the ridgetop, then gain this journey's best panorama by taking the spur trail left to Peak 2987, highest in the park, which combines all of the previously encountered views.

Back on the main trail, a long ridgetop stroll reveals Mount Hamilton and the steep foothills and nearby canyon eastward. At 6.1 miles go left at a previously encountered junction, descend past an old corral, and then bear right onto Halls Valley Trail at 6.4 miles. After 0.1 mile note the huge buckeye on the left and two sycamore trees growing by a seasonal stream on the right. Enjoy the only semishaded trail on this hike as you make a long descent under black oak, blue oak, California laurel, and buckeye. At 8.8 miles turn left at the signed trail junction and stroll past Grant Lake to the parking area.

10   REDWOOD REGIONAL PARK TRAILS

Length: 8.4 miles round trip
Hiking time: 5 hours
High point: 1,619 feet
Total elevation gain: 1,300 feet
Difficulty: easy to moderate

Season: year-round
Water: bring your own
Map: USGS 7.5' Oakland East
Information: East Bay Regional
 Park District

This ridgetop journey travels the outer edges of Redwood Regional Park past huge redwood and offers numerous views of San Francisco Bay and its surrounding cities and mountains.

From Highway 13 in Oakland, take the 35th Street/Redwood Road Exit, travel northeast 1.1 miles, then turn left on Skyline Boulevard. Drive 3.7 miles to the parking area at the corner of Skyline Boulevard and Pine Hills Road.

Begin on West Ridge Trail, a mostly level dirt road that travels past coast live oak, eucalyptus, coyote brush, and California laurel. Mature

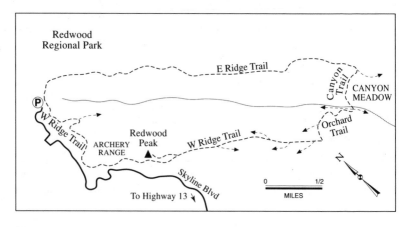

Monterey pine and a handful of redwood trees show up at a signed trail junction at 0.4 mile, where you keep right. Obtain views of Mount Diablo and San Francisco Bay as the trail climbs to a tall grove of slender eucalyptus trees at 1.3 miles. Look near an archery range at 1.5 miles for a redwood stump that's 33 feet in diameter. Botanists theorize that the magnificent specimen that once stood here was perhaps the biggest redwood ever known.

Climb 0.2 mile up 1,619-foot Redwood Peak by bearing left at the signed trail junction at 1.8 miles. You'll pass coast live oaks and redwoods before reaching a cluster of closet-sized boulders at the top.

At 2.5 miles bear left at a trail fork. Descend with views of Mount Diablo and numerous other Bay Area landmarks, then continue on West Ridge Trail at a trail junction at 3.1 miles. Trek into a gigantic eucalyptus forest, then continue straight past two signed trails on the right. Bear left down the signed Orchard Trail at 3.7 miles, then go right 0.2 mile farther at a group of madrone. At the first of two consecutive trail intersections, make a right at 3.7 miles, then bear left 20 yards farther to Canyon Meadow. Cross the streambed and head straight to pick up Canyon Trail. This dirt fire road promptly ascends past dense chaparral and hugs a seasonal stream for awhile. Bear left onto East Ridge Trail at 4.5 miles, and climb to a crest at 5.7 miles, where you capture the hike's best southward views from a bench. Enjoy expansive vistas as you remain on East Ridge Trail past stands of Monterey pine to the trailhead at 8.4 miles.

The East Ridge Trail offers views of forested hills and distant Mount Diablo.

⏸ ROCKY RIDGE

Length: 6.3-mile loop
Hiking time: 4 hours
High point: 2,000 feet
Total elevation gain: 1,150 feet
Difficulty: moderate
Season: year-round

Water: bring your own
Map: USGS 7.5' Las Trampas
  Ridge
Information: East Bay Regional
  Park District

This hike takes you through several of the East Bay's plant communities: flower-filled meadows, vast thickets of multiscented chaparral, and lush streamside habitat. As an added bonus, you'll also get expansive ridgetop views.

First, get to the intersection of Crow Canyon Road and Bollinger Canyon Road by traveling 7.3 miles on Crow Canyon Road from I-580 in Castro Valley or by traveling 1.6 miles on Crow Canyon Road from I-680 in San Ramon. Then, reach the trailhead parking lot by taking Bollinger Canyon Road 4.4 miles northwest to its end.

Hikers crest Rocky Ridge.

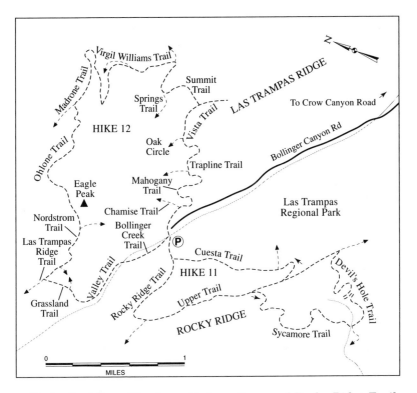

Begin the hike with a long climb on the paved Rocky Ridge Trail. Groves of live oak and California laurel dot the open hillside, interrupting extensive meadows that burst forth in spring with orange fiddlenecks, California poppies, yellow buttercups, blue lupines, and purple vetch. At 0.4 mile Cuesta Trail comes in on the left. You'll use this path to complete the loop journey but, for now, continue up to a road gate at 0.7 mile and turn left onto Upper Trail.

You now travel just below Rocky Ridge. A look eastward shows Bollinger Canyon below, with chaparral-cloaked Las Trampas Ridge just above and Mount Diablo looming in the distance beyond. As you continue, look for fossil clam shells embedded in the sandstone rock.

Turn right onto Sycamore Trail at 1.5 miles and immediately have fantastic views of the East Bay hills rolling to the bay, the entire peninsula, including San Francisco, and the Santa Cruz Mountains and Coast Range stretching to the south. Reach a shoulder at 1.7 miles, a good spot to explore the wind-swept sandstone rock that punctuates Rocky Ridge. The trail then drops past chaparral, grassy hillsides, and occasional coast live oak groves to a seasonal creek at 2.7 miles, which is amply shaded by California laurel, canyon live oak, and a few California sycamores. Go briefly downstream and cross the creek. Stay on the main trail at a fork just beyond the creek, then turn left onto the signed Devil's Hole Trail at 2.8 miles.

The way now climbs steeply, alternating between chaparral and open hillside. You eventually regain the spine of Rocky Ridge and its encompassing vistas and then turn left back onto Upper Trail at 4.1 miles.

Take a right onto Cuesta Trail at 4.5 miles, and stay on it when you reach a trail junction at 4.7 miles. You now hike downhill past a feast of wildflowers and several groves of California laurel, coast live oak, canyon live oak, and bigleaf maple. Connect with Rocky Ridge Trail at 5.9 miles and go right for the final 0.4 mile. If you want to hike more, do all or part of hike 12 (Las Trampas Ridge Trails).

12 LAS TRAMPAS RIDGE TRAILS

Length: 9.2 miles round trip
Hiking time: 6 hours
High point: 1,720 feet
Total elevation gain: 2,100 feet
Difficulty: moderate
Season: year-round

Water: bring your own
USGS map: 7.5' Las Trampas
   Ridge
Information: East Bay Regional
   Park District

Expect a change in scenery on all the numerous trails encountered while climbing up and down Las Trampas Ridge and gaining views of Mount Diablo and other Bay Area landmarks. Get the brochure at the parking area, which shows all of Las Trampas' paths and allows you to choose alternative trails.

From I-580 in Castro Valley, take the Crow Canyon Road Exit and then turn left. Drive 7.4 miles on Crow Canyon Road, turn left on Bollinger Canyon Road, and drive 4.4 miles to the trailhead. From I-680, take the Crow Canyon Road Exit, drive 1.6 miles west, and turn right onto Bollinger Canyon Road.

Pick up Creek Trail on the west side of Bollinger Creek next to a huge coast live oak, cross the creek at 0.6 mile underneath some California laurel trees, and bear left 25 yards farther onto the unsigned Valley Trail. Go right onto Grassland Trail 0.3 mile farther at a saddle and begin climbing.

At 1.7 miles bear right onto the unsigned Las Trampas Ridge Trail. It levels in a chaparral thicket and then meets a three-way signed trail junction, where you go left onto Nordstrom Trail. Hike 0.3 mile past madrone, then bear left onto the unsigned Ohlone Trail. After 150 yards the trail becomes a sandstone gulch that climbs straight toward Eagle Peak. Scamper up to its knoll for excellent views. Eastward, Mount Diablo guards the San Ramon Valley. San Pablo Bay lies northward while Rocky Ridge (hike 11) dominates the western skyline.

Continue down Ohlone Trail past lupine and blue oak to a saddle at 4.3 miles, where you bear right onto the signed Madrone Trail. This

Las Trampas Ridge's Virgil Williams Trail allows good views of Mount Diablo.

new trail drops past oak woodlands, arcs sharply right, and gradually climbs to the signed Virgil Williams Trail at 5.2 miles, where you bear right. Admire Mount Diablo on the left, then go right at 6.2 miles onto the unsigned Springs Trail, where the steepest climb of the journey promptly ensues to the crest. Head left here at 7 miles onto the signed Summit Trail, and enjoy views similar to those previously encountered.

Go right at 7.5 miles on the mostly level Vista Trail, and stroll past chamise, salvia sage, artemisia sage, and ceanothus scrub. Turn left onto the unsigned Trapline Trail at 8 miles next to Oak Circle and then left again 0.1 mile farther. At 8.6 miles bear left onto the signed Mahogany Trail. Hug a rapidly descending seasonal stream, then, at 8.8 miles, go left onto the signed Chamise Trail. Reach Bollinger Canyon Road 0.2 mile farther, and turn right for the brief walk to the trailhead.

13 WILDCAT CANYON REGIONAL PARK TRAILS

Length: 11.5 miles round trip
Hiking time: 6 hours
High point: 1,250 feet
Total elevation gain: 1,400 feet
Difficulty: moderate

Season: year-round
Water: bring your own
Map: USGS 7.5' Richmond
Information: East Bay Regional
**   Park District**

Stroll alongside scenic Wildcat Creek, then climb Wildcat Peak to enjoy spectacular views of the Bay Area.

From I-80 northbound in Richmond, take the Amador/Solano Exit,

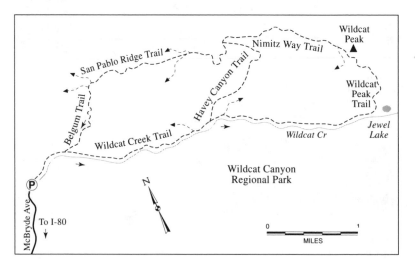

San Pablo Reservoir from the summit of Wildcat Peak

then go east on Amador Street. Drive three blocks, then turn right on McBryde Avenue and go 0.5 mile to the trailhead at Alvarado Park. From I-80 southbound, take the McBryde Avenue Exit and go east on McBryde Avenue until it dead-ends at the trailhead.

Wildcat Creek Trail promptly climbs on an old paved road. Continue straight at a signed trail junction at 0.5 mile. At 0.9 mile sprawling Wildcat Creek canyon appears on the right. Large coast live oak and mature California laurel coat the canyon sides, and alder and willow cover Wildcat Creek.

The first union with Wildcat Creek occurs near a wooden bridge amid eucalyptus trees at 2.1 miles. Continue straight, then begin a brief climb at a signed three-way intersection a few yards farther. Note that you can substantially shorten your trip here by going left onto Havey Canyon Trail for 1.2 miles to Nimitz Way Trail.

The main path remains mostly flat over the next 2 miles past a sequence of gullies choked with willow and blackberry bushes; all empty into Wildcat Creek during winter and spring's wet months.

At 4.1 miles, and a few yards before reaching a duck pond called Jewel Lake, bear left onto the unsigned Wildcat Peak Trail next to two signposts (one is labeled "9"). Your climb commences through a eucalyptus forest and then open chaparral. Be sure to follow sign arrows with drawn pictures of the peak at the numerous intersections.

Reach the peace grove platform atop 1,250-foot Wildcat Peak at 5.6 miles, and admire extensive views: Mount Diablo towers to the east beyond San Pablo Reservoir, and to the west you'll see Mount Tamalpais, Angel Island, the Golden Gate, the San Francisco skyline, and San Francisco Bay. Choose one of the numerous footpaths and head north down to the obvious asphalt intersection of Conlon and Nimitz Way trails, where you go north on Nimitz Way Trail.

Scattered Monterey pine and coyote brush adorn the open grasslands along this ridgetop path. At 8.2 miles, stay on Nimitz Way Trail as it goes left and becomes a dirt road. When you pass a corral at 8.5 miles, bear left, then right 100 yards farther onto the signed San Pablo Ridge Trail. This secluded dirt road climbs a few knolls, which provide pleasing panoramas of rolling hills and the Bay Area.

Bear left onto Belgum Trail at 10 miles. The path gives great vistas of San Pablo Ridge behind you and San Francisco Bay ahead. Cactus, eucalyptus, and palm trees precede a right turn onto the signed Wildcat Creek Trail at 10.9 miles, which returns you to the trailhead.

14 BRIONES REGIONAL PARK TRAILS

Length: 8.4 miles round trip
Hiking time: 5 hours
High point: 1,483 feet
Total elevation gain: 1,300 feet
Difficulty: easy to moderate
Season: year-round

Water: bring your own
Maps: USGS 7.5' Briones Valley,
USGS 7.5' Walnut Creek
Information: East Bay Regional
Park District

Explore a creek and a pond, then climb Briones Peak for views of rolling hillsides, Mounts Diablo and Tamalpais, and San Pablo and Suisun bays.

From Highway 24 in Lafayette, take the Pleasant Hill Boulevard Exit, go north for 0.6 mile, then turn left on Reliez Valley Road. Drive 4.8 miles, turn left onto the road signed for Alhambra Creek Staging Area, then go 0.8 mile to the parking lot. From Highway 4 take the Alhambra Avenue Exit south, then go right onto Alhambra Valley Road. Drive 1.7 miles, turn left on Reliez Valley Road for 0.5 mile to the staging area, then go right for 0.8 mile.

Take Alhambra Creek Trail past riparian habitat, buckeye, live oak, and blue oak to a signed trail junction at 0.9 mile, where you bear right onto Spengler Trail. Climb away from the creek past coast live oak, poison oak, coyote brush, and California laurel to two ponds called Maricich Lagoons at 1.6 miles, where you turn left onto Old Briones Road Trail. Climb gradually along gently rolling grassy hillsides that

Maricich Lagoons and Carquinez Straits from the Briones Crest Trail

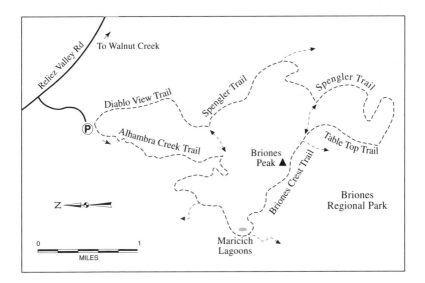

typify the Briones region to a signed trail junction at 1.9 miles, where you bear left on Briones Crest Trail.

Take the spur trail on the left at 2.5 miles to a bench marking the top of 1,483-foot Briones Peak, the highest spot in Briones Regional Park. To the north you can see the San Joaquin and Sacramento rivers converge into Suisun Bay; San Pablo Bay sprawls northwesterly, Mount Tamalpais looms westward beyond the Berkeley hills, and Mount Diablo juts to the east.

Bear left at the next signed trail junction, then climb briefly and go right onto the signed Table Top Trail. Walk past chaparral and scattered coast live oak to a signed trail junction at 3.3 miles, where you turn left back onto Spengler Trail. This wide road plunges steeply at times through a canyon shaded by coast live oak, huge toyon, buckeye, California laurel, and the occasional bigleaf maple.

Ignore an unsigned trail junction near a water tank, and continue left to a signed trail junction at 5.7 miles, where you turn right. Bear right at an unsigned trail junction and then left at a signed trail junction at 6.3 miles. Continue left on Spengler Trail at a three-way, unsigned trail junction 25 yards farther. The trail stays shaded while dropping 0.4 mile to an unsigned fork, where you bear left for a brief climb. Go right onto Diablo View Trail at 7.3 miles. Turn left at a signed trail junction 0.5 mile farther. After 100 yards the trail drops to the Alhambra Creek canyon and to the trailhead at 8.4 miles.

15 MOUNT DIABLO LOOP

Length: 7.1 miles round trip
Hiking time: 4 hours
High point: 3,849 feet
Total elevation gain: 2,050 feet
Difficulty: moderate
Season: year-round

Water: bring your own
Maps: USGS 7.5' Clayton, Mount Diablo State Park
Information: Mount Diablo State Park

This hike begins at Mount Diablo's summit, which offers a far-reaching panorama encompassing more square miles than any other view in the United States. You'll then take a loop trip along the flanks of this famous mountain, encountering a vast array of different plant species along the way.

If driving south on I-680 toward Walnut Creek, take the Treat Road Exit and go east. In 1.2 miles turn right onto Bancroft Road, which crosses Ygnacio Valley Road after another 0.6 mile and then turns into Walnut Avenue. You can also reach the intersection of Ygnacio Valley Road and Walnut Avenue by driving north on I-680 from the Highway 24 interchange, taking the Ygnacio Valley Road Exit, and driving 2.6

miles east on Ygnacio Valley Road to Walnut Avenue. Drive Walnut Avenue for 1.6 miles, then go right onto Oak Grove Road and take an immediate left onto North Gate Road. From here, it's 12.4 curvy miles to the trailhead at the summit of Mount Diablo. Alternatively, you can reach the summit by taking the Diablo Road Exit off I-680 in Danville, traveling Diablo Road for 3.4 miles, and turning left onto South Gate Road. From here, it's 6.6 curvy miles to the junction with North Gate Road. Go right, and proceed another 4.5 miles to the summit.

Before starting the hike, absorb the fantastic view from the 3,849-foot summit of Mount Diablo. On an exceptionally clear day, you can see the Delta, the Sacramento Valley, the Sutter Buttes, and Lassen Peak to the north; the San Joaquin Valley and the Sierra Nevada (including half-dome in Yosemite) to the east; Mount Hamilton and its surrounding

Eagle Peak from Murchio Gap

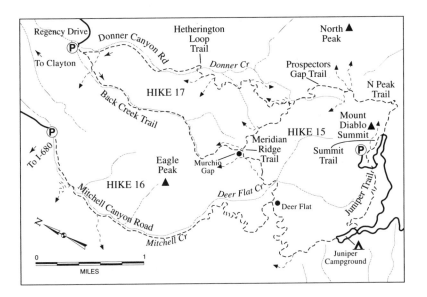

hills and valleys to the south; and the East Bay Hills, San Francisco Bay, the Santa Cruz mountains, and Mount Tamalpais to the west.

Take Summit Trail downhill from the southeast side of the lower parking area, and turn left at the unsigned North Peak Trail at 0.3 mile, which is also close by the main road and offers an alternative starting point. Descend past California laurel, interior live oak, scrub oak, orange California poppy, blue lupine, and purple brodiaea. At 1.4 miles you reach a four-way junction at Prospectors Gap, an excellent spot to picnic under the shade of blue oak and gray pine as you enjoy open views to the east and west.

Take the dirt road heading downhill that's signed "Prospector's Gap Trail" and heads toward Deer Flat, one of your intermediate destinations. You'll pass several side trails along the way; always stay on the main dirt road. At 2.2 miles you'll reach seasonal Donner Creek and then stroll level past chaparral to Murchio Gap at 3.3 miles, where you can connect with hike 17 (Mount Diablo's Back and Donner canyons) trails. Near the road look for a low knob, which offers good westward views.

Cross seasonal Deer Flat Creek, then reach Deer Flat at 4.1 miles, where you can rest under the shade of large blue oak. Go left at a road fork, and start the occasionally steep ascent (hike 16, Mount Diablo Summit via Mitchell Canyon, describes the right fork). Stay left at a road fork at 4.9 miles, and continue to climb as you enjoy the open views and wildflowers.

Juniper Campground awaits at 5.9 miles. Head left on the paved road past the restrooms and drinking fountain, then turn left on the signed Juniper Trail. It initially passes through a large grove of tall California laurel trees and then climbs to a ridge, which hosts chaparral shrubs, gray pine, and interior live oak. You'll pass a radio tower and then reach the main road to the summit at 6.9 miles. Go right for 100 feet, then turn left and take the unsigned trail uphill 0.1 mile to the lower parking lot. From here, you can proceed across the parking lot to your car.

16 MOUNT DIABLO SUMMIT VIA MITCHELL CANYON

Length: 14.2 miles round trip
Hiking time: 9 hours
High point: 3,849 feet
Total elevation gain: 3,300 feet
Difficulty: moderate
Season: year-round

Water: bring your own
Maps: USGS 7.5' Clayton, Mount Diablo State Park
Information: Mount Diablo State Park

This hike to the top of Mount Diablo hosts the greatest variety of flora of all the hikes in this book. It begins along shady Mitchell Creek,

View from Mount Diablo's Moses Rock during a spring storm

climbs open hillsides covered with flowers, and culminates with far-reaching views atop Diablo's summit.

On I-680 from Walnut Creek (1.8 miles north of the interchange with Highway 24), take the Treat Boulevard Exit. Drive east 2.6 miles, then turn right onto Oak Grove Road. After 1 mile, turn left on Ygnacio Valley Road, drive 4.4 miles, and turn right onto Clayton Road. After 0.8 mile turn right, and drive 1.7 miles on Mitchell Canyon Road to the trailhead.

The gentle currents of swirling Mitchell Creek take center stage for the first part of this journey. European grasses, poison hemlock, blackberry bushes, mustards, thistles, filaree, cow parsnips, white-flowered and tall mugwort, and other introduced flora accompany native plants such as poppy, yerba santa, alder, and maple. Stay left at two trail junctions, then reach a grassy flat at 2.5 miles, where canyon oak and coast live oak grow tall near the creekside.

Leave Mitchell Canyon at 2.7 miles, and climb steeply. Mature coast live oak and gray pine soon yield to younger members, and toyon, poison oak, and ceanothus crowd the landscape. Pause often during this steady climb to admire views of Eagle Peak to the north, Mount Diablo's flanks straight ahead, and the entire East Bay to the west.

Two picnic tables mark Deer Flat at 3.8 miles. Turn right at the signed intersection at 4 miles (for trails to the left, see hike 15, Mount Diablo Loop). The 1.7-mile climb from Deer Flat to Juniper Campground passes impressively diverse native vegetation. Blue oak and gray pine canopy the landscape, with a chaparral understory of chamise, ceanothus, poison oak, and occasional elderberry. Also, the spring wildflower show is among the most profuse anywhere in Northern California. Poppies, blue lupines, orange fiddlenecks, brodiaea, white yarrow, and numerous others adorn the sunny hillsides.

Reach Juniper Campground at 5.7 miles, go left on the paved road, pass through the campground, and bear left on the signed Juniper Trail. The final 1.0-mile-long climb begins in California laurel and then climbs past gray pine and interior live oak to the main road. Head right for 30 yards, then go left onto the unsigned trail that heads uphill 0.2 mile to the summit.

Mount Diablo's summit allows extensive views of the entire Bay Area and much of Northern California. Bring your binoculars, and enjoy a view that encompasses more area than any other in the nation. If you want to be picked up here, see the trailhead directions for hike 15 (Mount Diablo Loop).

17 MOUNT DIABLO'S BACK AND DONNER CANYONS

Length: 7.3 miles round trip
Hiking time: 4 hours
High point: 2,350 feet
Total elevation gain: 1,800 feet
Difficulty: strenuous on Back Creek Trail, otherwise easy

Season: year-round
Water: bring your own
Maps: USGS 7.5' Clayton, Mount Diablo State Park
Information: Mount Diablo State Park

Contrasting, colorful native plants escort you up secluded Back Canyon to Murchio Gap, where views of Eagle Peak, North Peak, and surrounding foothills await.

From Highway 24, take I-680 north, then take the Ygnacio Valley Road Exit after 0.3 mile and drive east for 7.8 miles to Clayton Road. To get to Clayton Road from I-680 south, go east on Treat Boulevard in Walnut Creek and then right on Bancroft Road at 1.2 miles. This connects with Ygnacio Valley Road after 1 mile, where you turn left, drive 5.3 miles to Clayton Road, and bear right. After 2.8 miles on Clayton Road, turn right onto Regency Drive, and follow it 0.5 mile to its dead end.

Opposite: *Blooming yarrow, rock outcrop, and the Clayton Valley from upper Donner Canyon*

To gain Back Creek Trail, descend the 20-foot embankment, cross through the park gate, then take the right road at the fork, which departs from Donner Creek. For 0.1 mile walk past oat grass and a few valley oak, then bear right at an unsigned road fork and quickly left at another unsigned trail junction.

Slender Back Creek runs below as you walk past buckeye, interior live oak, blue oak, and gray pine. The canyon narrows at 0.5 mile, where you cross a gate and continue past fragrant sage, orange sticky monkey flower, yarrow, toyon, and mugwort. Farther on, various unsigned paths break to the left amid yerba santa, chamise, wild grape, and poison oak; always stay right and continue up Back Canyon.

The climb steepens at 1.3 miles, but you're rewarded with better views of the surrounding countryside. From 2.1 miles to the saddle at 3 miles, chamise dominates, interspersed with yerba santa, chaparral pea, and finally profuse white-leaf manzanita just prior to reaching Murchio Gap, where you can connect with the trails of hike 15 (Mount Diablo Loop).

The route bears left onto Meridian Ridge Road. As you climb, collect bountiful views in all directions except south: Eagle Peak beckons from the northwest, rolling hills stretch to the San Joaquin Delta and Suisun marshes to the north, and the steep cliffs of North Peak hover to the east.

Continue straight at the signed trail junction at 3.4 miles, then bear left onto the signed Middle Trail, a level 0.4 mile farther. Go down the dry chaparral hillside, then bear left at an unsigned trail junction at 4.6 miles. At 5.5 miles bear right onto the unsigned Meridian Ridge Road. Go left 100 yards farther down the signed Donner Canyon Trail. Make a right onto the signed Hetherington Loop Trail 0.2 mile farther, which descends to Donner Creek. Live oak joins the massive toyon specimens along this creekside stretch until you rejoin the Donner Creek fire road at 6.4 miles. Buckeye and oak border the final 0.9 mile to the trailhead.

18   TENNESSEE VALLEY BEACH

Length: 6.5 miles round trip
Hiking time: 3 hours
High point: 500 feet
Total elevation gain: 550 feet
Difficulty: easy

Season: year-round
Water: bring your own
Map: USGS 7.5' Point Bonita
Information: Golden Gate
    National Recreation Area

The Tennessee Valley gradually unfolds into the Pacific Ocean on this family journey as you trek past wildflowers and grasslands to a lagoon and scenic Tennessee Valley Beach.

On Highway 101 about 5 miles north of the Golden Gate Bridge, take the Highway 1 exit marked Mount Tamalpais/Muir Woods. Follow

View from coastal cliffs above Tennessee Valley Beach

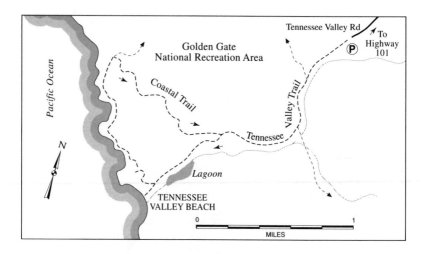

the highway 0.5 mile, then turn left onto Tennessee Valley Road, which takes you to the large parking lot 2.2 miles farther.

The trail (an old road) begins paved and level as it travels past numerous flowers, including wild radish, mustard, fennel, dock, and California poppy. A large grove of tall eucalyptus decorates a creek at 0.2 mile. Wild oat grass mingles with cow parsnips at 0.3 mile, where you bear left at the marker indicating Tennessee Valley Beach.

For the next 1.7 miles, head directly west in the bottom of the U-shaped canyon down to the beach. Ignore the two trails on the right along the way, staying instead on the wide gravel path that hugs the creek.

At 1.8 miles you reach a waterbird-frequented freshwater lagoon that's surrounded by bush lupine and cow parsnip. Continue 0.1 mile farther to popular Tennessee Valley Beach for picnicking, wave watching, beachcombing, and castle building.

After your break at the beach, take the narrow, unsigned trail between the lagoon and the beach, then climb north, refraining from brushing against the poison oak that can dominate trailside. At 2.4 miles, after an exhilarating 500-foot climb, reward yourself with refreshing southward views of Tennessee Valley Beach and the mouth of San Francisco Bay. The Tennessee Valley and surrounding foothills spread eastward, and massive rock outcrops block the ocean surf to the west.

These splendid views continue as you stroll amid level, sea-misted grasslands until reaching a signed trail junction, where you bear sharply right onto Coastal Trail at 3.1 miles. Head inland, gradually descending through rolling hills over the next 1.8 miles to the junction with Tennessee Valley Trail. Go left for the final 1.6 miles to the parking area.

19 COYOTE RIDGE AND GREEN GULCH TRAILS FROM MUIR BEACH

Length: 4.6 miles round trip
Hiking time: 3 hours
High point: 700 feet
Total elevation gain: 1,100 feet
Difficulty: easy to moderate

Season: year-round
Water: bring your own
Map: USGS 7.5' Point Bonita
Information: Golden Gate
    National Recreation Area

Enjoy great views of Muir Beach, the Pacific Ocean, and rolling coastal hills, then finish your journey with a visit to Zen gardens and fertile farmlands.

Five miles north of the Golden Gate Bridge on Highway 101, take the Mount Tamalpais/Muir Woods Exit. Follow the signs and stay on Highway 1 for 9 winding miles to the Muir Beach parking area.

Face the beach, then stroll left until you cross a wooden bridge over a bog. You'll then spot the signed Coastal Trail on the left. At 0.1 mile stay right on Coastal Trail at the signed Green Gulch Trail junction, where poison hemlock towers to 9 feet.

The path winds gently upward past a bird's-eye view of an affluent neighborhood above Muir Beach. At 0.6 mile take the short spur trail to the overlook of the Pacific Ocean, where pelicans and other waterbirds frequently fly above a designated wildlife study area. Regain the main trail, then look southeast at 0.7 mile to admire the wide expanse of rugged coastline.

Reach a saddle 0.1 mile farther, then go left on the unsigned Coyote Ridge Trail. A summit featuring commanding views of the ocean awaits at 1.7 miles, where you bear left at a sign. Spot Richardson Bay 0.1 mile farther on the right, then turn left onto the signed Green Gulch Trail. Continue on the wide trail and reach Hope Castle, a Zen meditation center, at 2.7 miles.

From the cluster of Monterey pine near Hope Castle's backdoor, bear

Blooming poison hemlock near the Coastal Trail

Muir Beach from wildlife study area

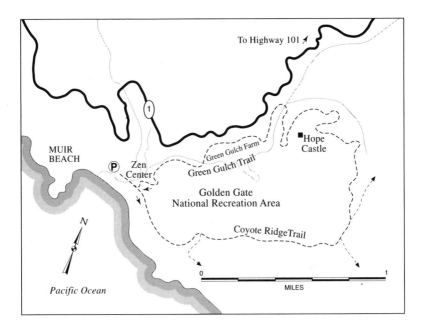

right on an unsigned footpath. At 3 miles you'll reach a small spring enclosed by a fern garden and then a cattail swamp. Spot a huge eucalyptus tree at 3.4 miles next to a large water storage tank, after which you'll pass several Zen retreat cabins amid a grove of eucalyptus.

At 3.7 miles you'll come to a green gate next to a signed trailhead. Go right and stroll through the productive Zen nursery and then past a small farm. Close the gate behind you at 4.1 miles, go left for 50 yards, and bear right when you spot the inconspicuous trail. Reach a pasture at 4.4 miles, then continue back to Muir Beach at 4.6 miles.

20 MUIR WOODS

Length: 6 miles round trip
Hiking time: 3 hours
High point: 950 feet
Total elevation gain: 1,050 feet
Difficulty: easy to moderate
Season: year-round

Water: available first half of trip
   from Redwood Creek
Map: USGS 7.5' San Rafael
Information: Golden Gate
   National Recreation Area

This hike in Muir Woods begins with an informative self-guided, interpretive nature trail displaying spectacular redwood trees, followed by quiet creekside walking, and then climaxed by bird's-eye views down upon some of the tallest redwoods in California.

Five miles north of the Golden Gate Bridge on Highway 101, go west on Highway 1 at the Stinson Beach Exit. After 3.3 miles turn left on Muir Woods Road, and go 1.5 miles to the visitor center parking lot.

The paved, populated path (starting as the self-guided interpretive nature trail) begins through a level old-growth redwood forest. In this high-usage first half-mile, posted signs provide interesting information about redwoods. Cross any of the four wooden bridges over Redwood Creek that lead to several redwood groves (all paths shortly rejoin the main trail). Wander into Cathedral Grove, highlighted by tall redwoods, then visit the William Kent Memorial, where you'll spot a 273-foot-tall Douglas fir, the tallest tree in the entire monument area.

Refreshing seclusion awaits at 0.9 mile as you take your first steps onto Bootjack Trail and leave the crowds behind. The quiet solitude is comforting: the steady splash of tumbling Redwood Creek is virtually the only sound you hear.

The path climbs past bigleaf maple and bracken, sword, and lady fern to reach a large wooden bridge across Redwood Creek, which originates near the top of Mount Tamalpais's west peak. The trail cuts a steep course up the hillside, reuniting with a bouldery section of Redwood Creek at 1.9 miles.

The climb persists 0.4 mile to small Van Wyck Meadow and its surrounding Douglas fir, coast live oak, and California laurel. From the meadow bear left onto TCC Trail. It provides a 1.4-mile level excursion across a series of canyon sides in tranquil, shady woods. Teasing glimpses of Mount Tamalpais intermittently appear beyond the low-hanging limbs of majestic Douglas fir.

At 3.6 miles reach a wooden bridge and bench, where you make two

The Muir Woods Nature Trail travels through an old-growth redwood forest.

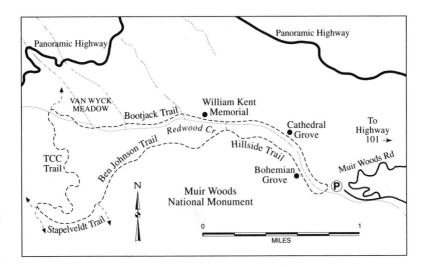

successive left turns on Stapelveldt Trail. This trail descends past two huge redwoods that form an archway at 4.1 miles. Reach a signed trail intersection 0.1 mile farther, and bear left onto Ben Johnson Trail.

Depart this gradually descending trail at 5.2 miles with a right turn onto the signed Hillside Trail. This scenic, level trail offers several vistas of Redwood Creek and its surrounding massive redwoods before reaching the parking lot.

21 MOUNT TAMALPAIS: THE SUMMIT TO PANTOLL RANGER STATION

Length: 8.2 miles round trip
Hiking time: 5 hours
High point: 2,571 feet
Total elevation gain: 1,400 feet
Difficulty: moderate

Season: year-round
Water: bring your own
Map: USGS 7.5' San Rafael
Information: Mount Tamalpais
State Park

This hike features commanding vistas of the entire San Francisco Bay area from the summit of Mount Tamalpais and then alternates shaded forest with open views of city, hills, and ocean. Note that you can eliminate the climbing by arranging to be picked up at Pantoll Ranger Station.

Five miles north of the Golden Gate Bridge on Highway 101, take the Muir Woods/Mount Tamalpais Exit. Continue west on Highway 1 for 3 miles, then turn right onto Panoramic Highway. Follow all obvi-

San Francisco Bay from Mount Tamalpais's east summit

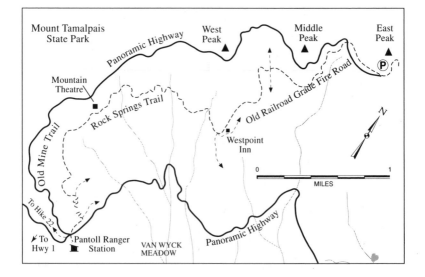

ous signs labeled "Mount Tamalpais" from here for 10.2 miles to the parking lot at East Peak. From Highway 1 in Stinson Beach, turn east onto Panoramic Highway, then drive 3.8 miles to Pantoll Ranger Station. Turn left onto Ridgecrest Road, and climb 5.7 miles to the summit of Mount Tamalpais.

From the parking lot, first take the 0.4-mile path to Mount Tamalpais's east summit. From this well-known landmark, you'll have far-reaching views of Marin County, San Francisco, Mount Diablo, and the entire Bay Area.

Return to the parking lot and follow the paved loop road 0.1 mile west to a rusty gate, where you head left on Old Railroad Grade Fire Road. Douglas firs, numerous oaks, and yerba santa combine with sweeping scenes of the Pacific Ocean at the onset, then the path travels past chaparral, highlighted by orange sticky monkey flower. At 0.5 mile you'll come to a sign noting Westpoint Inn near where a graceful Douglas fir highlights a view of the Bay Bridge, San Francisco skyscrapers, and Alcatraz Island. Then, next to a wooden water storage tank at 1.2 miles, you'll get views of San Pablo Bay and Mount Diablo.

At 1.8 miles turn right onto the signed Rock Springs Trail next to the deserted Westpoint Inn. At 2 miles the path ascends gently, with views of Westpoint Inn framed by the Golden Gate Bridge and Angel Island. Cross the first of three wooden bridges at 2.8 miles on Rock Springs Trail, where you'll find fern and California laurel along a tiny brook. At 3.3 miles reach Mountain Theatre, featuring seat rows built from rocks.

Climb the stone stairs and find the large sign that directs you to Old Mine Trail. This path travels along a vast hillside of pure oat grass and coast live oak with sweeping views of the sea and bay for another 0.8 mile to Pantoll Ranger Station. From here, you can continue all the way to Stinson Beach (see hike 22, Mount Tamalpais: Pantoll Ranger Station to Stinson Beach).

22 MOUNT TAMALPAIS: PANTOLL RANGER STATION TO STINSON BEACH

Length: 6.8-mile loop
Hiking time: 4 hours
High point: 1,500 feet
Total elevation gain: 1,500 feet
Difficulty: moderate
Season: year-round

Water: bring your own
Maps: USGS 7.5' San Rafael,
   USGS 7.5' Bolinas
Information: Mount Tamalpais
   State Park

This hike takes you from open views on the slopes of Mount Tamalpais to Stinson Beach and the Pacific Ocean and, finally, under the shade of tall redwoods.

From Stinson Beach on Highway 1, turn east on Panoramic Highway, drive 3.8 miles, then park at Pantoll Ranger Station. Or, 5 miles north of the Golden Gate Bridge on Highway 101, take the Muir Woods/Mount Tamalpais Exit, go west for 3 miles on Highway 1, then turn right onto Panoramic Highway and go 6 miles to Pantoll Ranger Station.

To begin the hike, cross Panoramic Highway and turn left onto the signed Matt Davis Trail. After 0.1 mile stroll under the shade of Douglas fir, California laurel, and alder. After you cross a seasonal creek at 1.2 miles, look south for a view of San Francisco Bay joining the Pacific Ocean. Go straight at a signed trail intersection 0.1 mile farther, then

Orange sticky monkey flowers adorn a hillside above Stinson Beach on the Dipsea Trail.

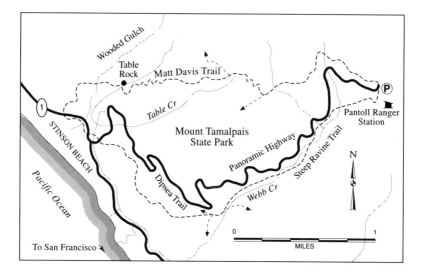

climb the bare knoll for an impressive panorama that includes San Francisco Bay and the Pacific Ocean.

At the far end of a California laurel grove at 1.6 miles, bear left at a signed trail junction. Reenter forest at 2.1 miles, then descend past sword ferns, coast live oak, Douglas fir, and California laurel. At 2.7 miles the continuous roar of the Pacific Ocean ahead accompanies the steady rumble of Table Creek on the right. Depart Table Creek's riparian habitat at 3.4 miles, then continue downhill past chaparral to forested Wooded Gulch just before reaching a signed trail fork at 3.7 miles, where you go right.

The trail ends at a paved street at 3.9 miles. At all street junctions, take the road that heads downhill to popular Stinson Beach, which offers excellent swimming, beachcombing, and picnicking. After enjoying the beach, pick up the signed Dipsea Trail at the intersection of Shoreline and Panoramic Highways just south of town (0.1 mile south of Arenal Avenue).

After a short climbing burst in shaded woods, enter open chaparral country, which allows continuous views of the sprawling sea behind you. Ignore the first unsigned dirt road 1.3 miles from Stinson Beach, then continue straight 0.1 mile farther at a trail junction.

Go left onto the signed Steep Ravine Trail when you get down to Webb Creek. This shaded footpath crosses the stream five times via wooden bridges as it travels past bouldery cascades that slide gracefully into small pools. You'll duck under toppled redwood archways several times, pass through profuse communities of thimbleberry and sword fern, and climb a fifteen-rung ladder during the 1.6-mile climb back to Pantoll Ranger Station. If you want to hike more, see hike 21, Mount Tamalpais: The Summit to Pantoll Ranger Station.

23 BOLINAS RIDGE

Length: 10.2 miles round trip
Hiking time: 5 hours
High point: 1,800 feet
Total elevation gain: 700 feet
Difficulty: easy to moderate
Season: year-round

Water: bring your own
Maps: USGS 7.5' San Geronimo,
**   USGS 7.5' Inverness**
Information: Golden Gate
**   National Recreation Area**

Bolinas Ridge Trail provides commanding views of bald hills, wooded ridges, and expansive Tomales Bay as it escorts you past large coast live oak and eventually through Douglas fir.

From Olema on Highway 1, turn east on Sir Francis Drake Boulevard, go 0.8 mile, then park off the road at the signed trailhead.

At the outset pick up the dirt road, which promptly ascends to an old corral next to a patch of cypress trees at 0.1 mile. Then travel past treeless rolling hills covered with pasture grasses, yellow-flowered mustard, plantain, and low-growing filaree.

Reach the first crest at 0.6 mile. A lone boulder outcrop and a single coast live oak impressively frame a northwesterly view of Tomales Bay and Point Reyes Peninsula. Turn right and head up the bare hillside at a signed trail junction at 1.3 miles.

A ridgetop field rewards you 0.2 mile farther with a splendid westward view of lush, dark-forested Inverness Ridge, which hides the Pacific Ocean. The dirt road now hugs a double–barbed wire fence, affording intermittent glimpses of the slender Olema Valley below Inverness Ridge. At 2.4 miles you walk past a long stretch of Douglas fir on the

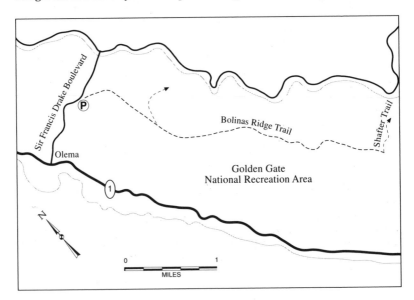

Exploring Bolinas Ridge

left, fronted by coyote brush. Pass a rush-lined pond on the right at 3.6 miles, then climb gently past another pond 0.2 mile farther. Reach the open ridgetop at 4.1 miles, where you'll enjoy great northward views of rolling hillsides and Tomales Bay. The trail gains its highest point when you pass a row of five huge eucalyptus trees at 4.8 miles and capture another view of Tomales Bay.

An excellent vista point awaits at 5.1 miles. At the Shafter Trail junction, climb any knoll on the right for the spectacular views of Inverness Ridge and the Pacific Ocean.

24 PELICAN LAKE AND WILDCAT BEACH

Length: 11.4 miles round trip
Hiking time: 6 hours
High point: 700 feet
Total elevation gain: 1,100 feet
Difficulty: moderate

Season: year-round
Water: bring your own
Map: USGS 7.5' Double Point
Information: Point Reyes
    National Seashore

This varied journey leads past three ponds and four freshwater lakes to attractive, secluded Wildcat Beach. On the way you'll admire continuous vistas of the Pacific Ocean and its rugged shoreline. If you prefer a backpack trip, register for Wildcat Camp at Bear Valley Visitor Center (for directions, see hike 25, Bear Valley, Arch Rock, and Kelham Beach).

From Highway 1 about 4.1 miles north of Stinson Beach and 8.6 miles south of Olema, turn west on an unsigned road (signed "Olema/ Bolinas Road" farther on) that's just north of Bolinas Lagoon, where a Golden Gate National Recreation Area sign stands next to a big white house, both on the east side of the highway. After 1.8 miles on Olema/ Bolinas Road, turn right on Mesa Road. Travel 3.5 miles, turn right where the pavement ends, then go 1.3 miles to the Palomarin trailhead.

The trail quickly reaches a tall eucalyptus forest and then stays mostly level for the first 1.1 miles as it offers views of the Pacific Ocean. Climb to a signed trail fork at 2.2 miles, then continue left on Coastal Trail. Spur trails lead to three freshwater ponds on the left.

A quarter mile past the third small pond, you'll spot swimmable Bass Lake. A westward view down on Pelican Lake arrives at 3.2 miles, enhanced by the Pacific Ocean appearing through a rock hillside archway just beyond. For the next 0.5 mile, you're treated to view after view of the lake's dark gray waters, inaccessible due to dense chaparral.

At 4.2 miles you'll reach a signed trail junction next to profuse coyote brush and orange sticky monkey flower. Make a mental note of the left-hand trail (the return loop), then continue straight on Coast Trail for the 1.3-mile stroll past Wildcat Lake to Wildcat Camp and Wildcat Beach.

Wildcat Camp, a huge field, serves as an excellent backpacking camp facility. There are several picnic tables and benches and a spring-fed water spigot plus easy access to pristine Wildcat Beach. (To gather more views of the ocean and beaches, continue along Coast Trail past Wildcat Camp to Arch Rock [see hike 25, Bear Valley, Arch Rock, and Kelham Beach] for 3.5 miles along chaparral-covered bluffs.)

To return, double back to the north side of Wildcat Lake and take the lower loop trail past Ocean Lake. This slender footpath (0.2 mile from Wildcat Beach) quickly climbs to a series of perches offering inspiring oceanic vistas. Poppy and yarrow decorate the area, but

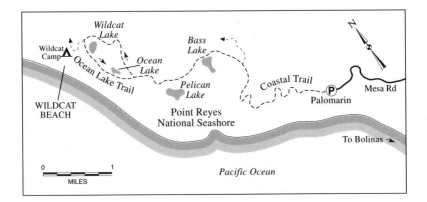

The Coastal Trail winds past Ocean Lake to Wildcat Beach.

thistles and poison oak occasionally intrude on the trail, so proceed cautiously. Gain an eastward view of Wildcat Lake, followed by a brief drop that takes you next to rush-lined Ocean Lake, then rejoin previously encountered trails for the final 4.2 miles to the trailhead.

25 BEAR VALLEY, ARCH ROCK, AND KELHAM BEACH

Length: 8.2 miles round trip
Hiking time: 4 hours
High point: 400 feet
Total elevation gain: 500 feet
Difficulty: easy
Season: year-round

Water: seasonally available from Bear Valley and Coast Creeks; bring your own
Maps: USGS 7.5' Inverness, USGS 7.5' Double Point
Information: Point Reyes National Seashore

This journey, suitable for the whole family, stays shaded along Bear Valley and Coast creeks most of the way and then leads to Arch Rock on a coastal bluff, where you'll admire views of the Pacific Ocean before strolling on a gorgeous beach.

Hikers are rewarded with commanding views of Kelham Beach from Climbing Arch Rock (right).

From Highway 1 in Olema (13 miles north of Stinson Beach), turn west onto Bear Valley Road, drive 0.5 mile, then turn left into the Bear Valley Visitor Center parking lot.

Pick up Bear Valley Trail, a dirt road, by walking south past the Morgan Horse Ranch. The 1.6-mile, 200-foot elevation climb to Divide Meadow travels under the shade of Douglas fir and alder and follows Bear Valley Creek. Divide Meadow supports an assortment of tall annual grasses that dry up by early summer.

Once past the meadow, the native tree habitat expands. Look for alder, California laurel, buckeye, coast live oak, willow, and Douglas fir. Now follow Coast Creek on its gradual descent to the Pacific Ocean. Continue on the wide Bear Valley Trail past all signed trail junctions, while watching for five-finger fern, chain fern, sword fern, thimble-

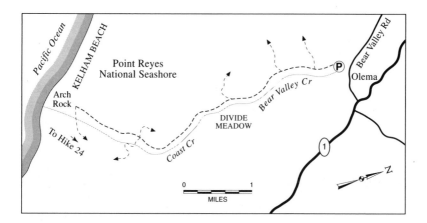

berry, stinging nettle, poison hemlock, cow parsnip, and thistle.

At 3.7 miles you break out of the shaded, riparian habitat and into an open chaparral section where coyote brush dominates along with young Douglas fir. Gather the first view of the sea 0.1 mile farther, quickly followed by a signed trail junction, where you go right for 0.3 mile to prominent Arch Rock.

Set aside a lot of time for Arch Rock, where you'll enjoy splendid views of beach and ocean, enhanced by rock outcrops that host a variety of seabirds. Take the spur trail from Arch Rock down to spectacular Kelham Beach, strollable as long as it's not high tide.

For an excellent backpacking trip, take Coastal Trail (retrace your steps 200 yards from Arch Rock and bear right at the signed trail junction) 3.5 miles southeast to Wildcat Beach (see hike 24, Pelican Lake and Wildcat Beach). This side trip allows continuous views of the ocean from high chaparral-clad bluffs.

26 HOME BAY, DRAKE'S ESTERO, AND SUNSET BEACH

Length: 7 miles round trip
Hiking time: 4 hours
High point: 400 feet
Total elevation gain: 800 feet
Difficulty: easy to moderate

Season: year-round
Water: bring your own
Map: USGS 7.5' Drake's Bay
Information: Point Reyes
National Seashore

Bring your binoculars for close-ups of shorebirds and packs of basking harbor seals on this journey along mudflats and *estero* (Spanish for "estuary"). The spectacular views include Inverness Ridge and numerous overlooks of Home Bay and Drake's Estero.

From Highway 1 in Olema (13 miles north of Stinson Beach), turn

Eroded cliffs and secluded Sunset Beach

west on Sir Francis Drake Boulevard. Drive 9.9 miles to a sign marked "Estero," then turn left and drive 0.9 mile to the trailhead.

The obvious trail starts level near cattle ranchlands where clover grows among pasture grasses, native bunchgrasses, and rushes. It twists sharply right at 0.5 mile near a small community of Scotch broom, offering good views of Inverness Ridge eastward beyond the fields.

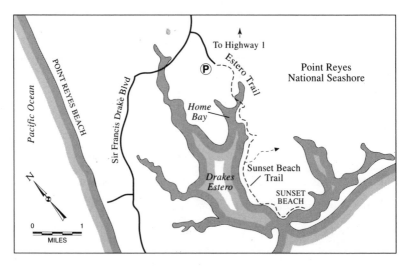

Proceed past a thick forest of Monterey pines, all the same height because they were planted simultaneously as a Christmas tree farm. At 0.6 mile stroll past a gateway and travel briefly alongside this small forest's outskirts.

Your first view of Home Bay arrives at 1 mile next to a boggy pond. At 1.1 miles cross the bridge dividing the pond and Home Bay. From here, the trail ascends past cow parsnip and bush lupine. As you continue climbing gradually to 1.9 miles, keep checking Home Bay's mudflats and water's edge for a variety of waterbirds, including widgeons, ducks, blue herons, godwits, and willets.

The trail levels to a pasture and then heads southeast to two ponds and your first sighting of Drake's Estero. At 2.2 miles go straight at a trail fork, pass several stands of rushes, which front premium views of the *estero* below, and skirt two dinky ponds at 2.5 miles.

The trail stays flat the rest of the way as it overlooks the *estero,* where freshwater runoff meets the ocean's saltwater, creating rich habitat for numerous shorebirds. A pond at 3.5 miles marks your arrival at Sunset Beach, which offers seclusion, rocky bluffs, beachcombing opportunities, and possible harbor seal sightings.

27 TOMALES POINT

Length: 9.4 miles round trip
Hiking time: 5 hours
High point: 400 feet
Total elevation gain: 800 feet
Difficulty: easy

Season: year-round
Water: bring your own
Map: USGS 7.5' Tomales
Information: Point Reyes
National Seashore

This excursion along gently rolling, slender Tomales Point offers premium views of the Pacific Ocean and Tomales and Bodega bays and the chance to observe tule elk and various seabirds.

From Olema on Highway 1, drive northwest on Sir Francis Drake Boulevard for 8.5 miles, then turn right on Pierce Point Road. Go 9.2 miles farther to the Tomales Point trailhead.

At 0.2 mile you'll see striking scenes of Tomales Bay to the right and the Pacific Ocean to the left as you walk past yellow bush lupine and purple-flowered Canada thistle. Stroll gently upward to 0.3 mile for your first view of McClure's Beach (a recommended 0.6-mile walk from the trailhead).

The path gradually climbs eastward, revealing White Gulch and Hog Island on Tomales Bay at 0.7 mile. Reach a crest at 1.4 miles, punctuated by a 7-foot-high boulder on the left. You'll see Bodega Bay at 2 miles where it joins Tomales Bay at Avalis Beach.

Study Bodega Bay through tall lupine from 2.6 miles and beyond. The trail snakes east at 2.8 miles near a small pond where tule elk come to drink. This herd was brought to this sanctuary a couple of decades ago, after nearly a century-long absence from the area.

Views of the tiny town of Dillon Beach come from just above the pond. The worn ranch road trail transforms into a scant footpath 0.3 mile farther as you begin another gentle climb. At 3.3 miles the trail reaches open ocean vistas at a crest.

The tread becomes sand at 3.7 miles where a sign indicates Tomales Point. Stay with the barely discernible path to the final crest at 4.2 miles. Wander west from here past bush lupine, and get out the binoculars for great views of birds perched atop aptly named Bird Rock, which rests just offshore.

A northward view of Tomales Point

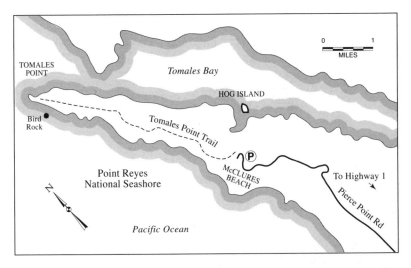

The final 0.5 mile gradually descends to the Tomales Point bluffs, which slid nearly 20 feet north during the 1906 earthquake. Spend time in solitude with ocean and cliff before returning to the trailhead.

28 BALD MOUNTAIN

Length: 6.4-mile loop
Hiking time: 4 hours
High point: 2,729 feet
Total elevation gain: 1,700 feet
Difficulty: moderate
Season: year-round

Water: bring your own
Maps: USGS 7.5' Kenwood, USGS 7.5' Rutherford
Information: Sugarloaf Ridge State Park

Before you tour Sonoma Valley's famous wineries, climb Bald Mountain for a panoramic view of the Sonoma Valley and many of Northern California's high mountains.

Reach Adobe Canyon Road, located on Highway 12 midway between Santa Rosa and Sonoma, then go 3.6 miles to Sugarloaf Ridge State Park and park on the left just past the kiosk.

Bald Mountain Trail begins by a large signboard containing a map of all the park's trails. As you begin the trek along the ever-climbing path, you'll pass briefly through an oak forest and then turn left at two trail forks to travel along an open hillside that hosts a multihued wildflower display in spring. At 0.6 mile the trail continues through a lush forest of coast live oak, madrone, and California laurel, which eventually gives way to dryer chaparral. This pattern of alternating between oak woodland forest and brushy areas repeats throughout the hike.

At 1 mile the dirt path meets a paved road. Turn right and head up-

The hike to Bald Mountain begins in open grassland.

hill. As you climb note the blue-green serpentine rock exposed by the road cuts. Stay on the pavement past Vista and Mountain trails.

At 2.3 miles turn right at the signed junction for Bald Mountain onto a wide dirt path. Follow this steep trail up grassy slopes for another 0.4 mile to a three-way trail junction just below Bald Mountain's summit. Follow Digger Pine Trail for 200 feet, then turn right for the last 150 feet to the summit.

Bald Mountain, part of the Mayacamas Mountains, offers broad vistas in all directions. To the north rises Mount Saint Helena, and even further beyond, to the northwest, is Snow Moun-

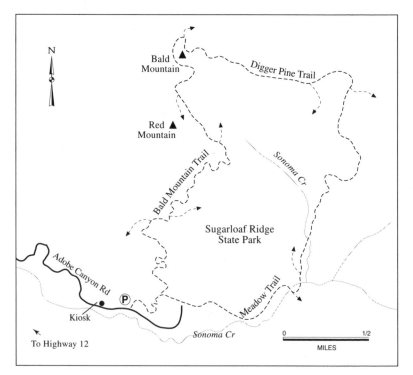

tain. The Napa Valley lies northeast, and on exceptionally clear days you can even see high peaks rising over 10,000 feet in the Sierra Nevada 125 miles away. Beyond nearby Red Mountain's microwave station, Mount Diablo looms. The San Francisco Bay area, including Mount Tamalpais, anchors the southeast horizon. Mount Hood, 1 foot higher than Bald Mountain, rises 3 miles due west, and just beyond is the Sonoma Valley.

To complete the loop trip, take Digger Pine Trail as it travels along the ridge past California laurel and large black oak. Follow this dirt road as it descends, staying on it when Red Mountain Trail comes in from the right 0.7 mile from Bald Mountain's summit.

You'll first encounter the crazily twisted trunks and branches of gray (digger) pine about 1 mile from the summit, just before Brushy Peaks Trail. Head right at this junction, and go downhill for another 1.4 miles, where you'll meet Sonoma Creek and the turnoff for Vista Trail (stay left). After crossing the creek and walking another 0.1 mile, turn right onto Meadow Trail (a gravel road) and follow it 0.8 mile through the broad, flower-filled Sonoma Creek valley to a parking lot by a campsite. Cross through the lot, bear left at two trail junctions within the next 0.1 mile, then hike the last 0.3 mile back to the trailhead.

29 RITCHEY CREEK TRAIL

Length: 5.4 miles round trip
Hiking time: 3 hours
High point: 1,850 feet
Total elevation gain: 1,400 feet
Difficulty: moderate
Season: year-round

Water: available from Ritchey Creek
Map: USGS 7.5' Calistoga
Information: Bothe–Napa Valley State Park

Take a break from wine tasting to walk beside the tumbling waters of Ritchey Creek. Tall Douglas fir and one of the easternmost stands of redwood provide cool shade for most of the hike, which ends at an old homestead site.

Drive to Bothe–Napa Valley State Park, located on the west side of Highway 128 about 5 miles northwest of Saint Helena and 3 miles southeast of Calistoga. After passing the entrance station, take the first right, drive to the far end of the campground, and park at a small lot on the left near restrooms and showers.

The trail begins next to a hiker symbol just up the road from the parking lot. After passing a few campsites, the paved trail ends at the intersection of two dirt roads. Take the one on the left. An old barn lies near the path at 0.2 mile—bear right at a trail fork just before the barn and go right again just past it.

The way now travels under the sheltering branches of tall Douglas fir and redwood trees as it parallels the course of Ritchey Creek. Shorter trees such as madrone and bigleaf maple are also numerous,

Douglas firs shade a barn near Ritchey Creek.

and just past the barn look for several large buckeye trees, which display large spikes of white flowers in spring.

Go right when you encounter a trail fork at 0.3 mile and then left at another fork at 0.6 mile. At 0.8 mile turn right again up a steep path that affords good views of the creek's canyon. At 1.1 miles the trail crosses Ritchey Creek. On the creek's other side, climb steeply and bear right at two trail forks over the next 0.2 mile. As the path continues its steady uphill climb, vegetation alternates between moister areas dominated by Douglas fir, redwood, and bigleaf maple and drier areas populated by California laurel, interior live oak, and toyon. About 0.5 mile past the creek crossing, the trail passes through an exposed area inhabited by chaparral plants such as chamise, manzanita, and buckbrush and also allows open views of the mountain ridge on the canyon's north side.

At 2.7 miles a faint trail on the right leads to an old homestead site. It crosses a seasonal creek near a small grove of 100-foot-high redwood trees—an excellent picnic site. Continue past the redwoods through a thick patch of purple-flowered vinca to the meadow. All traces of the cabin are gone, but several fig, apple, and other fruit trees remain. A

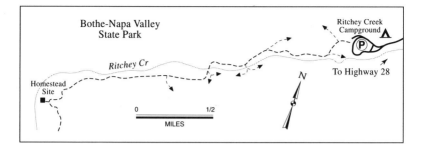

climb to the top of the meadow rewards you with open views of the Ritchey Creek canyon.

If you want more hiking, take the main trail another 0.5 mile uphill to the park's boundary.

30 MOUNT SAINT HELENA

Length: 10 miles round trip
Hiking time: 6 hours
High point: 4,343 feet
Total elevation gain: 2,300 feet
Difficulty: moderate
Season: year-round

Water: none, bring plenty
Maps: USGS 7.5' Detert Reservoir, USGS 7.5' Mount St. Helena
Information: Bothe–Napa Valley State Park

The journey to Mount Saint Helena's summit takes you high above the Napa Valley vineyards and through territory that inspired some of Robert Louis Stevenson's writing. Upon reaching your lofty goal, you'll see Northern California's hills, ridges, and mountains stretching in all directions. Bring binoculars.

To reach the trailhead, drive to Robert Louis Stevenson State Park, located on both sides of Highway 29 at a saddle 8 miles north of Calistoga and 31 miles south of Highway 20.

The trail begins on the west side of Highway 29 near some old building foundations, the last remains of the abandoned mining town of Silverado. Initially, you gently switchback uphill under the shade of Douglas fir, madrone, black oak, and California laurel, accompanied by an understory of tan oak, interior live oak, and the sharp-needled California nutmeg.

At 0.7 mile the trail enters a small, level clearing and then ascends steeply up a slippery slope 0.2 mile to meet the dirt road, which you follow uphill all the way to the summit. This is where you first encounter the large forests of knobcone pine stretching up the flank of Mount Saint Helena. Note the numerous cones tightly bound to the trunks and branches.

As you climb you'll see more and more of the surrounding country. Initially, the road travels past manzanita, chamise, and other chaparral plants and then by abundant outcroppings of volcanic rock. Mount

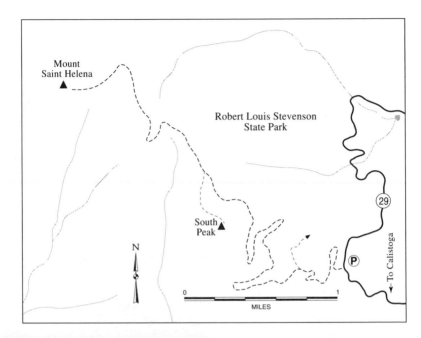

Trees line the lower part of Mount Saint Helena's summit trail.

Saint Helena, though composed primarily of volcanic rock, has never been an active volcano.

At 3 miles you reach the 0.5-mile spur trail to the top of the 4,003-foot South Peak. Continue up the main path another 2 miles to the summit.

The top of Mount Saint Helena, elevation 4,343 feet, offers exquisite views in all directions. To the north lies Snow Mountain, and on an exceptionally clear day you can even see Northern California's two most famous volcanos, Mount Shasta and Lassen Peak. To the east are the mountains leading to the Sacramento Valley and the Delta, with the Sierra Nevada in the far distance. The Napa Valley vineyards lie immediately south, with the Bay Area and Mount Diablo farther away. To the west, low mountain ranges stretch seaward.

31 ANDERSON MARSH

Length: 5 to 6.5 miles round trip
Hiking time: 3 hours
High point: 1,500 feet
Total elevation gain: 300 feet
Difficulty: easy
Season: year-round

Water: bring your own
Maps: USGS 7.5' Clear Lake,
   USGS 7.5' Lower Lake
Information: Anderson Marsh
State Historical Park

Visit an old Indian village and oak woodlands before exploring a marsh shoreline that hosts a variety of birds. Wear long pants and a long-sleeve shirt, and be prepared for some mud along Anderson Marsh.

From the junction of Highways 20 and 53 on Clear Lake's east side, drive south 7 miles on Highway 53, then turn into Anderson Marsh State Historical Park, which is 0.7 mile north of Highway 29.

Pick up the trail by heading west across the field next to a chain-link fence. Go left at an unsigned trail junction at 0.4 mile, then continue alongside another chain-link fence past the occasional valley oak. You'll reach a Pomo Indian village at 0.6 mile. Explore the teepees and other structures, and spend some time learning about the interesting Pomo ways of life and culture from signboards.

Regain the trail next to the circular wooden fence structure. It gradu-

Cottonwood and willow trees grow in and around Anderson Marsh.

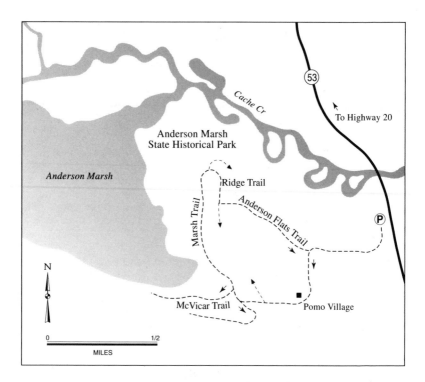

ally climbs a hill under the shade of blue oak and green leaf manzanita to a signed trail junction at 0.9 mile, where you bear left and promptly spy Anderson Marsh. As you bisect the grassy meadow next to the marsh, watch for a herd of deer. Gray pine hug the foothill on the left, while cottonwood and willow surround the marsh on the right.

Without warning the trail becomes mucky and jungled, with up to 2-yard-high grasses, teasel, and sporadic patches of poison oak. Quite soon the marsh extends next to your feet near wood rose bushes. Pause quietly for a few moments and observe an impressive variety of waterbirds including pelicans, green herons, and blue herons.

At 1.5 miles spot the sign indicating McVicar Audubon Sanctuary. Bear left, then climb 100 yards to a sloping walnut orchard. The trail now heads westerly between the orchard and a thicket of redbud, California elderberry, and buckeye, topped by an occasional black oak. Another brief climb rewards you with a view of the marsh at 1.8 miles. The trail peters out at this vista, so retrace your steps to the marsh and McVicar Trail. Although moist and clogged with weeds, it goes for 0.7 mile alongside the marsh, offering ample opportunity for further bird-watching.

When you've had enough of this path, retrace your steps to an unsigned trail fork atop the hill, and bear left at a rattlesnake sign onto

Marsh Trail, which allows you to explore the east side of Anderson Marsh.

Depart the blue oak belt after 0.4 mile, and move slightly closer to the marsh and a tall stand of valley oak on the right. After another 0.2 mile, the trail abruptly departs the marsh and climbs 20 yards to another unsigned trail junction, where you head straight on Ridge Trail toward a huge valley oak.

The trail soon heads south to a picnic bench under a massive valley oak. Pause here to admire the moist lowlands northeast that stretch to the riparian habitat bordering Cache Creek, then turn left and follow the unsigned Anderson Flats Trail east through the oak-studded meadow for another 1 mile to the trailhead.

32 SNOW MOUNTAIN

Length: 8 miles round trip
Hiking time: 6 hours or overnight
High point: 7,056 feet
Total elevation gain: 2,150 feet
Difficulty: moderate
Season: mid-June to early October
Water: none, bring your own

Maps: USGS 7.5' Potato Hill, USGS 7.5' Fouts Springs, USGS 7.5' St. John Mountain, USGS 7.5' Crockett Peak, USFS Snow Mountain Wilderness
Information: Stonyford Ranger District, Mendocino National Forest

The trip to the twin summits of Snow Mountain offers scenery that includes serene forests of pine and fir, a psychedelic assortment of multihued rocks, and sweeping vistas of mountains and valleys stretching to the far horizons.

The last stretch of trail climbs gently to the summit of Snow Mountain East.

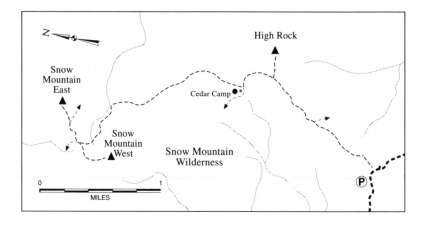

Reach the town of Stonyford by exiting I-5 at either Maxwell or Willows. Take Road M-10 (18N01), which is initially called Fouts Springs Road, and follow signs for Snow Mountain and Summit Springs. After 24 miles turn right at a "Trailhead 1" sign for the final, steep 1.4 miles to the Summit Springs trailhead parking area.

The path begins in a small forest of Jeffrey pine and white fir and then quickly enters open areas created by a huge 1987 fire. As you climb over the next mile, note the variety of shrubs and other plants that have begun a long process of succession, which should eventually restore much of this area to forest.

Go left at a trail fork at 0.7 mile, then cross two small, seasonal creeks at 1 mile. From here, switchback uphill to a ridge at 1.5 miles. Look to the right for High Rock, about 300 yards east of the trail; it offers expansive westward, southward, and eastward views similar to those of the Snow Mountain summits, lacking only a northward vista.

The path now climbs along the ridge, passing through a forest of Jeffrey pine and red and white fir. Ignore the faint trails that disappear into the trees, and continue to Cedar Camp at 2 miles, which has an excellent campsite beside a small pond and a green meadow but no cedars. Bear right here at a trail fork, taking the path signed for Snow Mountain.

After a steady ascent through the forest, enter the open, glaciated basin below Snow Mountain's summits. Climb steadily 0.7 mile to the saddle between the two summits, then turn left at a three-way trail junction.

After a brief climb, reach the 7,038-foot summit of Snow Mountain West. From here, you have northward views of Mount Linn, Mount Shasta, and the Klamath Mountains; eastward views of Stony Creek Gorge, the Sacramento Valley, Sutter Buttes, and the Cascade and Sierra Nevada mountains; and southward and westward views of endless chains of Coast Range ridges and peaks. Be sure to look at the odd assortment of green, gray, and purple rocks at your feet.

After you've rested and enjoyed the view, go back to the saddle and take the right-hand trail up to the 7,056-foot summit of Snow Mountain East, which offers views similar to those of its sibling.

If you have the ambition, consider camping on one of the summits. You'll have far-reaching, earthly views during the day and an open universe above at night. Bring all the water you'll need, be prepared for possible high winds, and make sure you don't get caught in a thunderstorm.

IDES COVE LOOP TRAIL

Length: 11.3-mile loop
Hiking time: 7 hours or overnight
High point: 7,500 feet
Total elevation gain: 1,200 feet
Difficulty: moderate
Season: early June through late September

Water: available from streams, springs, and lakes
Maps: USGS 7.5' South Yolla Bolly Mountain, USFS Yolla Bolly Middle Eel Wilderness
Information: Corning Ranger District, Mendocino National Forest

This hike takes you through lush meadows and dense pine/fir forest to two small lakes and then up to a ridge with excellent views. Solitude and gentle terrain combine to make this an easy overnight backpacking trip or a good day hike.

Take the Corning Exit off I-5, head west on Road A-9 for 20 miles to Paskenta, then bear right at the fork onto Road M2 (23N01). Road M2

The Ides Cove Loop Trail offers numerous vistas of the Coast Range.

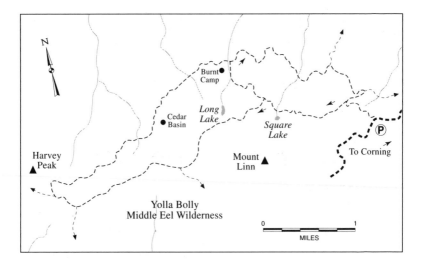

is paved for 20 miles; afterward you travel dirt roads. Follow Road M2 for 25 miles to Cold Springs Fire Station, then turn onto Road M22 (25NO1). Go 8 miles, then turn left at the sign for Ides Cove trailhead for the last 2 miles.

The trail starts out relatively level as it passes by several springs under the shade of red fir, Jeffrey pine, and western white pine. The lower portion of the loop trail appears on the right at 0.5 mile. Stay straight and enjoy open views of the Trinity Alps, Mount Shasta, and Lassen Peak as you continue to tiny Square Lake at 1.3 miles. The lake itself is too shallow for swimming, but it and the surrounding meadow provide a pleasant foreground for Mount Linn, the Coast Range's highest peak at 8,092 feet.

Continue another 0.3 mile to where Burnt Camp Cutoff Trail comes in on the right. Go straight and continue until you see a small rock cairn at 2.2 miles, which marks the faint path down to Long Lake. This body of water shares size and depth characteristics with Square Lake but offers a couple of campsites nestled among Jeffrey pine and red fir.

Back on the main trail, pass immediately through a green meadow housing the small stream feeding Long Lake, the last source of water for the next several miles. Climb moderately to reach the spine of a ridge dropping from Mount Linn at 3.2 miles. This open, windswept area, home to only a few stunted Jeffrey pine, offers good views of nearby Coast Range ridges, peaks, and valleys including the North Yolla Bollys (hike 44, North Yolla Bolly Trails). You'll also see the Trinity Alps and Klamath Mountains to the north, snow-clad Mount Shasta, Lassen Peak, and other Cascade volcanos to the northeast, and a portion of the Sacramento Valley.

Go right at a junction with South Yolla Bolly Trail, then walk along the open ridge. Stay right when you reach Thomes Pocket Ridge Trail at 4.7 miles, continue toward Harvey Peak, then turn right at another trail fork at 4.9 miles. The path loses some elevation and then begins a relatively level, eastward stretch past several springs and small creeks which water mountain alder and willow thickets. At 6.9 miles you'll enter aptly named Cedar Basin, which hosts numerous incense cedars, several small creeks, and a campsite.

Slides Creek slithers through a meadow at Burnt Camp at 8.4 miles. A campsite lies on the creek's west side, and a trail fork awaits on the east side. If you wish to take a half-mile off the distance back to the trailhead, go right on Burnt Camp Cutoff Trail, and climb a steep 0.8 mile to the top of the loop just west of Square Lake.

The main trail continues east, meeting Cottonwood Connector Trail at 9.9 miles. Bear right, begin a climb, and then bear right again at another trail fork at 10.6 miles. After another 0.2 mile, reach the top of the loop trail. Go left for the final 0.5 mile to the trailhead.

34   FERN CANYON TRAIL TO PYGMY FOREST

Length: 7.9 miles round trip
Hiking time: 4 hours
High point: 500 feet
Total elevation gain: 500 feet
Difficulty: easy
Season: year-round

Water: available from Little River
Map: USGS 7.5' Mendocino
Information: Van Damme State Park

This path travels through the lush environs of multiferned and redwood-shaded Little River canyon and then heads up to the ecologically intriguing Pygmy Forest.

Drive to Van Damme State Park, which is on Highway 1's east side 3.5 miles south of Mendocino. Follow the paved main road past the campground for 0.8 mile to the trailhead. As you begin the walk down

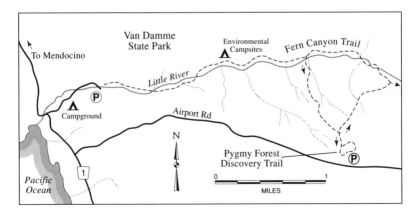

Studying ecology on the Pygmy Forest Discovery Trail

the signed Fern Canyon Trail, you'll surely agree that it's aptly named: sword, bracken, five-finger, and several other species of fern flourish in the moist soil of the Little River canyon. Numerous berry-producing shrubs compose the understory, and redwood and Douglas fir tower high above.

The mostly level trail makes the first of several crossings of Little River at 0.8 mile. If you hike here during periods of high water flow (winter and spring), you might have to get your feet wet. At 1.7 miles you'll pass ten environmental campsites designed for hikers and bikers (inquire at park headquarters if you wish to camp here) and then meet a trail fork at 2.3 miles. Go either way: The two halves rejoin 0.2 mile farther, where you'll find another fork. Go right where a sign directs you the final 1.3 miles up an old dirt logging road to the Pygmy Forest.

Cross Little River on a wooden bridge, then climb moderately under redwood and Douglas fir. As you approach the Pygmy Forest, bishop pine becomes the dominant tree species.

The 0.3-mile-long Pygmy Forest Discovery Trail, this hike's final destination, lies 3.8 miles from the trailhead. It begins from the paved parking lot just off Airport Road. (You can drive to this lot by going 3.5 miles down Airport Road, which leaves Highway 1 about 0.7 mile south of Van Damme State Park.) Grab the brochure available at the trail's beginning, which explains the interaction of geological and biological processes that lead to the formation of pygmy forests and also identifies Mendocino cypress, rhododendron, and five other plant species.

You can extend your walk back to the trailhead by taking the trail that leaves the logging road about 0.1 mile below the Pygmy Forest. This trail heads northeast to Fern Canyon and eventually leads you back to the trail fork encountered at 2.5 miles. It adds another 1.1 miles to the round-trip hiking distance.

35 ECOLOGICAL STAIRCASE NATURE TRAIL

Length: 5.4 miles round trip
Hiking time: 3 hours
High point: 450 feet
Total elevation gain: 500 feet
Difficulty: easy
Season: year-round

Water: bring your own
Maps: USGS 7.5' Fort Bragg,
 USGS 7.5' Mendocino
Information: Jughandle State
 Reserve

Enjoy spectacular views of seastacks attacked by the pulsing waves of the Pacific Ocean, then climb past a series of different ecological communities, each with a diverse array of plants. Be sure to invest in the immensely informative brochure for this self-guided nature trail. It explains the 500,000-year interaction of land, ocean, and biological processes that created the five different terraces and the plant communities that now grow upon them. It's available from a machine by the parking lot.

To reach the trailhead, turn into the signed Jughandle State Reserve, which is on Highway 1's west side 5 miles south of Fort Bragg.

The trail begins by an interpretive signboard near the parking lot. Follow it due west, where you'll find the first of thirty-two numbered posts corresponding to natural history descriptions in the nature trail brochure. Out near the cliff edge beyond post 2, you'll have an excellent view of beach, seastacks, Jug Handle Bay, and the coastline stretching to the north and south.

The trail then heads toward Highway 1, eventually passing under-

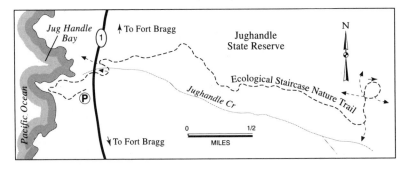

The Ecological Staircase hike begins with a view of Jug Handle Bay.

neath it. In this section you'll see first a small path heading downhill to the beach at Jug Handle Bay and then, just after crossing Jughandle Creek on a wooden bridge, another small path traveling along the creek to the same destination. Both paths make excellent side trips.

From here, the main trail begins a relatively gentle northward climb, initially passing under the native two-needled Bishop pine and then the introduced three-needled Monterey pine, which is native to the central California coast. Grand fir and Sitka spruce eventually join the forest.

About 2.4 miles from the trailhead, the trail meets a dirt road just before encountering post 23. Turn left on the dirt road, follow it for 200 yards, then look for the continuation of the actual trail on the right. You now enter the pygmy forest, which is an association of bolander pine, manzanita, and other plants that can tolerate the highly acidic hardpan soil, though just barely, as their small stature indicates.

From post 32, the nature trail's last post, go right and follow the ditch to a dirt road. Go west for about 200 feet on this road, then turn left onto another dirt road. Follow this previously encountered road for 200 yards south, then turn right onto the actual trail and return to the trailhead.

36 TAN OAK SPRINGS/ DURPHY CREEK LOOP

Length: 4.2-miles loop
Hiking time: 3 hours
High point: 1,450 feet
Total elevation gain: 1,100 feet
Difficulty: easy to moderate

Season: year-round
Water: bring your own
Map: USGS 7.5' Garberville
Information: Richardson Grove
State Park

This hike takes you far away from the noise and traffic of Highway 101's heavily traveled Avenue of the Giants. You'll climb past redwoods to a ridge, visit a small spring, and then walk near the banks of a year-round stream.

Enter Richardson Grove State Park, which is on Highway 101's west side 8 miles south of Garberville and 17 miles north of Leggett. Drive 0.3 mile along the main road, and park on the right just after the road crosses Durphy Creek. If there's no room here, continue into the campground and park near campsite 58.

From the parking site near Durphy Creek, walk 150 yards through the campground to campsite 58, where you'll find the trail, signed for Lookout Point. Go 100 feet, turn left, and begin a gentle climb, initially skirting behind campsites. You'll enter a fire-scarred area in the vicinity of a seasonal creek shaded by tall redwoods and then reach Lookout Point at 0.3 mile. From the wooden railing, you can look west and south over the South Fork of the Eel River and part of its mountainous, heavily forested watershed.

You'll encounter two trail forks over the next 0.2 mile; go left at the first and right at the second. The trail now begins a relatively steep climb over the next 0.5 mile and then undulates along a ridge shaded by Douglas fir, tan oak, and madrone. As you walk the leaf-littered path, you'll have occasional views of the forested slopes on the north side of Durphy Creek.

At 2 miles the trail begins a steep descent. Shortly thereafter an unsigned trail heads left for 100 yards to Tan Oak Springs, a small, lush area of ferns, cattails, and other water-loving plants.

Back on the main trail, continue downhill 0.9 mile to where

Numerous madrone trees line the trail to Tan Oak Springs.

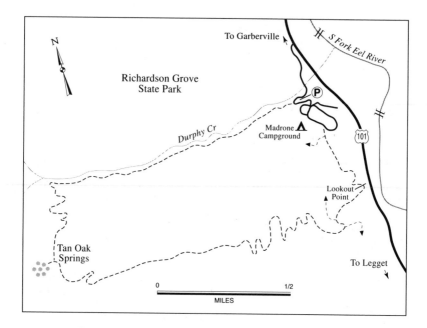

the trail approaches Durphy Creek just downstream of the confluence of its two forks. You now head east, following the white alder–lined creek downstream as bigleaf maple and California laurel join Douglas fir and tan oak as the primary tree species. The path passes ever-increasing numbers of massive redwood trees as it alternates between level creekside stretches and steep, but brief, climbs along the mountainside.

Cross nine small wooden bridges across seasonal streams as you continue. A redwood-ringed picnic spot lies just below the last one, and you'll find a similar picnic site 0.1 mile farther, at 3.9 miles. These picnic sites, located at 0.3 and 0.4 mile from the trailhead, make good destinations if you only want a short, level hike into tall redwood groves.

37   BULL CREEK FLATS

Length: 9.4 miles round trip
Hiking time: 5 hours
High point: 300 feet
Total elevation loss: 100 feet
Difficulty: easy

Season: year-round
Water: available from Bull Creek
Map: USGS 7.5' Weott
Information: Humboldt Redwoods State Park

Take a leisurely stroll through the heart of a virgin redwood forest, where the deep quiet complements the majesty of the massive trees soaring skyward.

Take the South Fork/Honeydew Exit off Highway 101, about 23 miles north of Garberville and 15 miles south of Scotia. Following signs for Honeydew, travel west on Bull Creek Flats Road. After 4.8 miles turn left at the sign for Giant Tree, and go 100 yards down the dirt road to the parking area.

From the picnic site near the parking area, cross the clear waters of Bull Creek on a wooden bridge. Be sure to pause at the bridge's midpoint to admire the bigleaf maple and white alder that grow in the moist soil near the stream's banks.

Immediately on the other side, turn left onto Bull Creek Flats Trail, which offers a nearly level downstream descent through a forest of redwood trees that measure over 10 feet in diameter and tower up to 200 feet. You'll soon reach the aptly named Giant Tree, cross Squaw Creek at 0.3 mile, and bear left at a trail fork at 0.5 mile.

Bull Creek Flats Trail continues east under the shade of redwoods. You'll see a variety of plants that have adapted to the paucity of sunlight on the forest floor. Look for trillium, redwood sorrel, and calypso, among others. As you cross Miller Creek at 1 mile, look for Douglas fir trees that have managed to make an inroad into the dense redwood forest.

The path eventually crosses Connick Creek at 1.6 miles and Tepee Creek at 2.9 miles. At 3.9 miles turn left onto a trail that leads down to a bridge across Bull Creek. (Note that this bridge is only in place during summer. In winter you'll have to wade.)

On the creek's far side, head right at a trail fork up to Bull Creek Flats and Rockefeller Loop Trail. This 0.5-mile loop passes through a dense redwood grove, and on the far side a trail goes 150 yards to a

South Fork Eel River near Bull Creek Flats

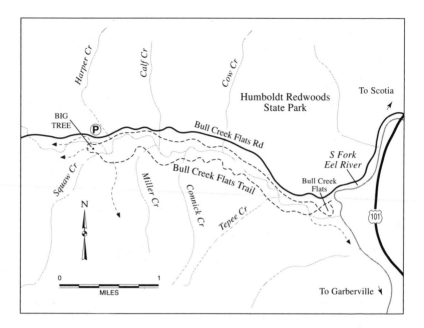

bridge across the South Fork of the Eel River. If you wish to arrange a car shuttle, the Rockefeller Forest parking area (from which Rockefeller Loop Trail begins) is 1.5 miles west of Highway 101 on Bull Creek Flats Road.

If you are returning to the trailhead, consider taking the first left after crossing the bridge across Bull Creek. This path travels between Bull Creek and Bull Creek Flats Road and leads back to the trailhead. Although not as pretty and private as Bull Creek Flats Trail, it does offer an alternative to retracing your footsteps.

38 PUNTA GORDA LIGHTHOUSE

Length: 6 miles round trip
Hiking time: 3 hours
High point: 25 feet
Total elevation gain: 100 feet
Difficulty: easy

Season: year-round
Water: bring your own
Map: USGS 7.5' Petrolia
Information: Bureau of Land
Management

Hike along one of California's wildest stretches of ocean shoreline, the Lost Coast, past the Punta Gorda promontory to an abandoned lighthouse. An abundance of wildflowers grows on the sea-hugging, steep hills, and numerous animals of the sea and coast inhabit the ocean waves, the rocky tidepools, and the beach.

To reach the trailhead, you must first get to Petrolia. Either take the Honeydew Exit off Highway 101 and drive 38 miles along Honeydew Road and Mattole Road to Petrolia, or drive 30 miles southwest from Ferndale on Mattole Road to Petrolia. Once in Petrolia, go 50 feet south of the bridge across the Mattole River, turn west on Lighthouse Road, and drive 4.9 miles to the parking area.

Before heading for the lighthouse, be sure to walk 0.25 mile north of the parking area to the Mattole River's mouth. Here you'll see a wide variety of waterbirds where the mountains' freshwater meets the ocean's saltwater.

To begin the main portion of the hike, let your ears lead you over low dunes to the ocean's roar. As you walk south along Mattole Beach's black sand, observe numerous pelicans, cormorants, sea gulls, and other birds skimming between the ocean's tall waves or perching on the seastacks that puncture the surf zone. Also, be prepared for otters to spy on you from just offshore during the entire journey.

After passing a sea lion rookery, you'll see at 2 miles a small cave in the cliff side near Punta Gorda (Spanish for "thick point"). Walk a 0.5-mile stretch of actual trail from here if you wish firmer tread.

Shortly after spying the lighthouse in the distance at 2.5 miles, you'll reach two old ranch cabins on private property beside a year-round stream. Walk along a dirt road past another cabin and a barn, to finally reach the lighthouse at 3 miles. The lighthouse, in operation from 1911 to 1951, was built after several ships wrecked on the rocks

Mattole Beach just north of Punta Gorda

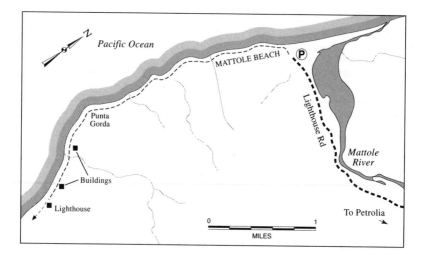

offshore. You can see a remnant of one unlucky vessel embedded in the beach below.

If you wish to extend your hike, walk farther down the beach. The Lost Coast extends another 21 miles to Shelter Cove and makes an excellent backpacking trip, especially if you can arrange a car shuttle. Contact the Bureau of Land Management for a detailed map and more information.

39 REDWOOD CREEK TO TALL TREES GROVE

Length: 18 miles round trip
Hiking time: 1 to 3 days
High point: 300 feet
Total elevation gain: 400 feet
Difficulty: easy to moderate
Season: May through October

Water: available from Redwood Creek the whole way
Maps: USGS 7.5' Orick, USGS 7.5' Rodgers Peak, USGS 7.5' Bald Hills
Information: Redwood National Park

Take a pleasant, shaded day hike or backpack trip near the banks of Redwood Creek on your way to visit the world's tallest tree. Be aware that Redwood Creek often swells to uncrossable depths from November into May. Movable bridges allow easy crossing in the busy warmer months, but you'll have to wade the rest of the time. You can camp on the creek's numerous gravel bars (register first). Wear long pants to avoid rubbing against trailside plants. Consider a one-way hike by arranging for a car shuttle at the south end of C-Line Road (9 miles farther on Bald Hills Road, then right) or meeting the shuttle bus. Call the Redwood Information Center at (707) 488-2171 for seasonal shuttle times or the combination to the locked gate.

Just north of Orick and 0.1 mile north of the Redwood Creek bridge, turn east off Highway 101 onto Bald Hills Road. Turn right after 0.25 mile, then drive 0.5 mile to the Redwood Creek Trail parking lot.

The flat trail takes you past red alder to cross a seasonal creek at 0.4 mile, where a towering bigleaf maple bears thickly covered Spanish moss. In late spring and early summer, you can pick salmonberries here or blackberries a little farther on.

Briefly depart the red alder forest at 1.6 miles to enter a gravel plain covered with wild mustard, then cross Redwood Creek via the bridge. If the bridge is gone, find the widest portion of the creek and wade across. Look for the red, diamond-shaped marker on the other side to reunite with the trail.

Attractive views down on Redwood Creek greet you at 2 miles, where the few redwood trees outgrow huge bigleaf maple that shade sorrel and fern communities. At 2.7 miles, two huge, lightning-charred redwoods grow together. The trail is briefly overgrown at 3 miles; look for the moss-covered maple next to a prime picnic spot at a scenic gravel bar in this vicinity. From 4.2 miles on, a series of seasonal streams drains into Redwood Creek until you cross Bond Creek at 5.6 miles. A mile farther, admire lush, shaded canyon walls as you cross Forty Four Creek.

From 6.4 to 7.5 miles, climb away from Redwood Creek and eventually obtain a view of the creek and the first sighting of the tallest redwoods in the world from Tall Trees Overlook. At 8.2 miles you reach the alluvial flat where Redwood Creek bends and the tallest trees tower.

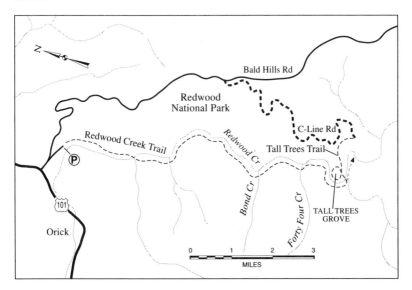

This redwood, found at Tall Trees Grove, is the tallest tree in the world, rising 387 feet above the forest floor.

Cross the creek and take the 0.7-mile Tall Trees Trail to spend some time underneath the 600-year-old tallest tree in the world. This redwood stands 387 feet high, with a 44-foot circumference and a 14-foot diameter. It thrives here because of moderate temperatures, plentiful rainfall, and rich soil.

Climb out of the grove and follow Tall Trees Trail up to the end of C-Line Road if you've arranged a car shuttle or are meeting the bus. Otherwise, retrace your steps to the trailhead.

40 FERN CANYON AND GOLD BLUFFS BEACH

Length: 6.3 miles round trip
Hiking time: 4 hours
High point: 500 feet
Total elevation gain: 500 feet
Difficulty: easy to moderate
Season: year-round

Water: available from Home and
**   Squashan creeks**
Map: USGS 7.5' Fern Canyon
Information: Prairie Creek
**   Redwoods State Park**

Walk through an extensive redwood forest featuring a floor blanketed with sea-misted ferns, then finish the peaceful journey along scenic Gold Bluffs Beach.

Travel 2 miles north of Orick on Highway 101, turn left onto

Davison Road, then drive 6.8 miles to the Fern Canyon trailhead parking lot.

Fern Canyon Loop Trail continually crosses Home Creek on planks as you walk through misty, dark Fern Canyon. Five-finger and sword fern, with a small mix of lady and bracken fern, coat 60-foot walls that shade thimbleberry and salmonberry. Near the end of 30-foot-wide Fern Canyon, a large red alder fronts a spiral staircase that leads to a smaller side canyon flourishing with five-finger ferns and highlighted by a 12-foot trickling waterfall. At 0.4 mile a walkway departs the canyon and ascends past groves of redwood trees. Bear right at the ridgetop onto the signed James Irvine Trail, named after a man who helped create Northern California's redwood parks.

Ferns and a fallen redwood

Five-foot-tall sword fern lead you to a footbridge at 0.8 mile, where a waterfall tumbles 20 feet into Home Creek, viewable from two thronelike redwood chairs. The tallest collection of redwood and Douglas fir on this hike await at 2.2 miles near the signed junction of the James Irvine and Clintonia trails, where you head right on the latter. The 1.0-mile jaunt on this snaking trail turns narrow, dark, and quiet

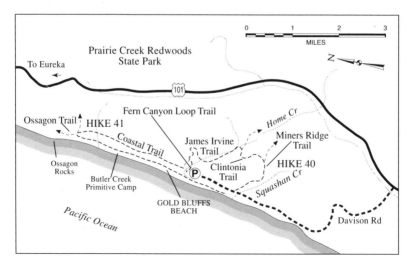

as it leaves Home Creek and links with Miners Ridge Trail, where you bear right at 3.1 miles.

The next 2.2 miles feature whisper-still solitude and wooden walkways as the path crosses babbling brooks that merge with nearby Squashan Creek. Observe the ground here for long, yellow banana slugs and orange, lizardlike Pacific salamanders.

At 5.3 miles cross Davison Road, and bear right when you reach Gold Bluffs Beach, named long ago when prospectors spotted a few gold flakes on the sand. Gold Bluffs Beach offers opportunities to beachcomb, wave watch, and observe wildlife, including Roosevelt elk. When you spot the red alder forest that surrounds Home Creek at 6.3 miles, turn right and walk 150 feet to the trailhead.

41 OSSAGON ROCKS AND GOLD BLUFFS BEACH

Length: 7 miles round trip
Hiking time: 4 hours
High point: 50 feet
Total elevation gain: 100 feet
Difficulty: easy

Season: year-round
Water: none, bring your own
Map: USGS 7.5' Fern Canyon
Information: Prairie Creek Redwoods State Park

Admire massive Roosevelt elk as you stroll through spruce and alder forests, then picnic amid Gold Bluffs Beach's rugged Ossagon Rocks and breathe the cool mist from the Pacific Ocean.

Turn west on Davison Road 2 miles north of Orick on Highway 101, then drive 6.8 miles to the Fern Canyon trailhead parking lot.

The slender, level Coastal Trail (also called Beach Trail here) starts by crossing Home Creek to travel through a red alder forest for 0.2 mile and then hugs the bottom of cliffs with constant views of the grass-covered sandy plain on the left and numerous strips of Sitka spruce. The grassy areas provide perfect habitat for the small herds of Roosevelt elk, named for President Theodore Roosevelt. These grazers, native to the north coast, are California's largest land animals—a stag can weigh a half ton. Stay your distance from the protective females during the calving season in May.

At 1.6 miles the trail skirts a marsh, then 0.2 mile farther you pass near Butler Creek Primitive Camp (for bicyclists). Native grasses reach 6 feet here, and Butler Creek swirls by to soon reach the sea.

At 2.1 miles a 50-yard cobblestone section of the trail leads into a dark and moist jungle that hosts banana slugs, California salamanders, frogs, and pigeons. Reenter the sandy plain 0.2 mile farther.

When you reach a small brook at 3 miles, Ossagon Trail heads inland and upward. You, however, stay left near Gold Bluffs Beach. Hike 0.5 mile along the open plain, staying near, but never in, the dense alder.

Sand verbena and fescue grasses flourish in the dunes along the short scamper to wild, wave-worn Ossagon Rocks, where the surf

The Coastal Trail passes through prime Roosevelt elk habitat on the way to Ossagon Rocks and Gold Bluffs Beach.

sprays white water onto the massive outcrops. You'll also find an ideal section of beach for watching California gray whales and seabirds while collecting sand dollars and seashells.

To complete this varied journey, leisurely beachcomb your way back to the Fern Canyon parking area via secluded Gold Bluffs Beach.

42 HIDDEN BEACH AND FALSE KLAMATH ROCK

Length: 8 miles round trip
Hiking time: 4 hours
High point: 300 feet
Total elevation gain: 600 feet
Difficulty: easy to moderate

Season: year-round
Water: none, bring your own
Map: USGS 7.5' Requa
Information: Redwood National Park

This excursion features vistas of notable highlights, including the mouth of the Klamath River, the Pacific Ocean, Hidden Beach, and False Klamath Rock.

Turn west on Requa Road 2 miles north of the town of Klamath on Highway 101. Go 2.3 miles on Requa Road to the trailhead next to a stop sign.

Coastal Trail drops at the onset as you view the wide mouth of the Klamath River. Look for both California gray whales and barking sea lions. Commanding, eagle's-eye views continue as the trail travels 0.7 mile past open grasslands, where a mix of bracken fern, horsetail, lupine, and berry bush grow.

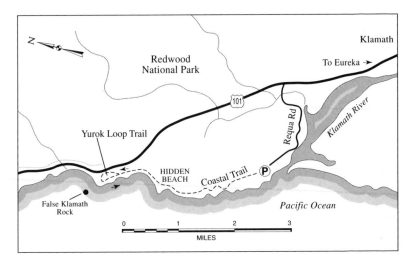

Pause at 0.7 mile by a trailside bench to admire the Klamath River valley to the south, where the river, loaded with sediment washed down from the coastal mountains, joins the sea. Proceed into a red alder forest highlighted by Sitka spruce.

The main attraction of the hike awaits at 2.7 miles, where a spur trail takes you to driftwood-covered Hidden Beach. Spend some time exploring this secluded area, featuring dark gray sand, wildflowers, and large waves exploding on jagged rocks.

Regain Coastal Trail, which at 2.8 miles descends near beachside and then enters grasslands as a steady surf chant accompanies continuous open views of the ocean. A spectacular view of Hidden Beach awaits at the end of a 50-yard loop spur trail to the left at 3.3 miles.

Go right onto the signed Yurok Loop Trail 0.1 mile farther, which

A hiker inspects a dead whale. (photo by Rick Ramos)

takes you under a dense canopy of willow, oak, and alder. The fresh-water pond on Lagoon Creek on the right provides a setting for yellow pond lilies and native and migrating birds. Spot massive False Klam-ath Rock offshore to the north at 3.8 miles. The trail winds westward at 4 miles to rejoin the main path back to the trailhead.

43 SOUTH FORK NATIONAL RECREATION TRAIL

Length: 5.6 miles round trip
Hiking time: 3 hours
High point: 2,250 feet
Total elevation gain: 450 feet
Difficulty: easy
Water: available from South Fork of the Trinity River

Season: year-round, occasional winter snow
Map: USGS 7.5' Forest Glen
Information: Hayfork Ranger District, Shasta-Trinity National Forest

This historic trail, hikable year-round, offers multihued foliage in autumn, quiet solitude in winter, a wildflower explosion in spring, and refreshing swimming in summer.

Drive Highway 36 to Forest Glen, which is 66 miles east of Highway 101 and 69 miles west of Red Bluff. Turn south at the sign for Hell Gate Campground onto Road 29N58. Avoid the right turn into the campground, cross a bridge, then stay on the main road, which changes to Road 1S25 at a fork 0.3 mile from Highway 36. Continue another 0.5 mile past a small right-hand spur road leading to some campsites, then turn right into the parking area, indicated by a South Fork River Trail sign.

The hike begins next to a signboard, which has a map and gives the history of the trail. Cross the river on a swinging steel and wood bridge,

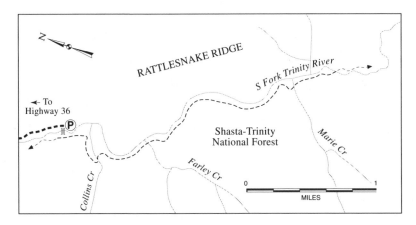

Several footbridges cross tributaries of the South Fork Trinity River.

then turn left on a dirt road. For the remainder of the hike, you'll walk an old wagon trail used to haul lumber in the early twentieth century.

A good swimming hole awaits on the left, just 100 yards past the bridge. After passing a cabin, cross Collins Creek at 0.3 mile, then continue through a forest of Douglas fir, black oak, madrone, and an occasional ponderosa pine. As the trail climbs high above the river, bigleaf maple and dogwood trees grow in abundance. Through gaps you'll have good views of the forested ridge to the east.

The trail eventually approaches the river. Cross Farley Creek at 0.9 mile, then spot a campsite and swimming hole at 1.1 miles. The path now again climbs up the ridge, passes briefly through a mining claim (stay on the trail), then enters a young second-growth forest at 2.2 miles.

Cross a wooden bridge over Marie Creek at 2.4 miles, the third year-round stream encountered so far, then approach the alder-lined banks of the river. A trail fork awaits at 2.6 miles. Bear left, and cross a seasonal stream just before reaching the final destination of this hike, a steel bridge across the river. From the center of the bridge, you have good views of the bordering, steep, forested mountain ridges (Rattle Snake Ridge on the west and South Fork Ridge on the east) and the slow-moving river water beneath you. If you wish to extend your hike, continue south on the far side of the bridge toward Smokey Creek, another 4.4 miles down the trail.

44　NORTH YOLLA BOLLY TRAILS

Length: 13.7 miles round trip
Hiking time: 9 hours or overnight
High point: 7,900 feet
Total elevation gain: 3,900 feet
Difficulty: moderate to strenuous
Season: mid-June through mid-October

Water: available from lakes and streams
Maps: USGS 7.5' Black Rock Mtn, USGS 7.5' North Yolla Bolly Mtn, USFS Yolla Bolly Middle Eel Wilderness
Information: Yolla Bolly Ranger District, Shasta-Trinity National Forest

This hike's trail system takes you into the heart of the North Yolla Bolly Mountains, the southernmost section of the vast Klamath mountain range. You can choose from four different trails that leave the central trail: the lower two visit secluded lakes; the upper two climb high summits with extensive views.

From Redding drive 40 miles on Clear Creek Road (off Highway 273) to Platina. From Red Bluff drive 47 miles on Highway 36 (off I-5) to Platina. From Platina drive west 11 miles on Highway 36, then turn south onto Wildwood–Mad River Road (Road 30) about 0.25 mile west of the Hayfork Creek bridge and about 81 miles east of Highway 101.

North Yolla Bolly Mountain summit

Go 9 miles to Pine Root Saddle, then turn left onto Road 35. Drive 10 miles to the intersection of several roads. Take the one signed for Stuart Gap trailhead for the last 1.8 miles to the parking area. All roads are paved except for the last 1.8 miles.

From the parking area, take Pettijohn Trail, the central path for this hike. It climbs gently for the first mile and then much steeper for the final 1.5 miles to a broad ridge. Several small streams cross it and usually provide water until late summer.

Black Rock Lake Trail. The right-hand trail leaves Pettijohn Trail 1 mile from the trailhead. It quickly descends to Pettijohn basin, an expansive meadow with a good view of North Yolla Bolly Mountain, one of this hike's destinations. The basin also holds several campsites and the fledgling South Fork of the Trinity River, a sure source of year-round water. Cross the river and continue on the gently rolling path through a forest of Jeffrey pine, incense cedar, and red fir. Shallow Black Rock Lake awaits 1.5 miles from Pettijohn Trail. You'll find several campsites near the water that offer southward views of looming Black Rock Mountain, another hike destination.

North Yolla Bolly Lake Trail. This lake is both more attractive and more secluded than Black Rock Lake. It also requires a bit more effort to reach. Take the trail on the left off Pettijohn Trail 1.2 miles from the trailhead. Climb 0.7 mile to the ridge, then look for a rock outcrop with vistas to the east, north, and west. From here, descend 0.4 mile to the lake, which offers good swimming, good campsites, and a view of a 1,000-foot cliff stretching up to the south.

North Yolla Bolly Mountain Trail. The trail goes left from Pettijohn Trail 2.5 miles from the trailhead—look for a sign directing you to North Yolla Bolly Station Spring. Head east 0.5 mile to the spring, where you'll find a lush meadow, a campsite, and ice-cold water flowing from a pipe, the ridge's only reliable source of water. Continue east 0.1 mile, then head cross-country uphill (southeast) where the trail fades. Reach a ridge, then turn left (northeast) for the final climb to the 7,900-foot summit, 1 mile from Pettijohn Trail. Note that you began the climb in the company of red fir, but at the summit you'll find primarily foxtail pine, a hardy species that can withstand extreme conditions of wind and cold. Most people, however, climb this mountain for the spectacular panoramic vistas: the Trinity Alps and the rest of the Klamath mountain range to the north; Mount Shasta, Lassen Peak, and the rest of the Cascades to the northeast; the Sacramento Valley and the Sierra Nevada to the east and southeast; and row upon row of Coast Range mountains stretching south and west.

Black Rock Mountain Trail. This 1.8-mile path on the right also leaves Pettijohn Trail 2.5 miles from the trailhead. It initially travels west along the open, lupine-covered ridge and allows good views to the north and south, including Mount Linn and the Ides Cove area (hike 33, Ides Cove Loop Trail). After 1.2 miles, it begins a relatively gentle climb to the summit. Once at the top of the 7,755-foot peak, you'll have views similar to those of North Yolla Bolly Mountain.

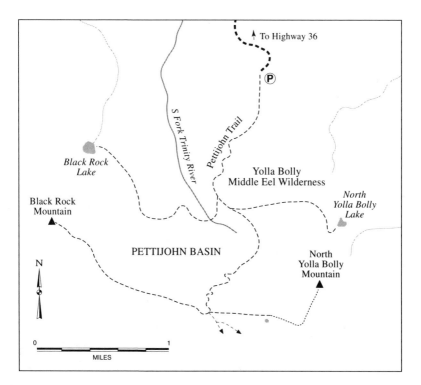

45 MILL CREEK/TOWER HOUSE HISTORICAL DISTRICT

Length: 5.2 miles round trip
Hiking time: 3 hours
High point: 2,050 feet
Total elevation gain: 800 feet
Difficulty: easy
Season: year-round

Water: available from Mill Creek
Map: USGS 7.5' French Gulch
Information: Whiskeytown-
Shasta-Trinity National
Recreation Area

This hike initially takes you through an area rich in Northern California's pioneer history and then enters a nature lover's paradise as it travels through mixed pine/fir forest and riparian habitat along Mill Creek, a year-round stream that courses in cool shade over granite boulders.

The parking area is on the south side of Highway 299, just east of the highway's bridge across Clear Creek. The bridge is 0.1 mile east of Trinity Mountain Road (signed for French Gulch) and 1.3 miles west of the Carr Powerhouse turn off.

Take the footbridge across Clear Creek, then do the same for Willow Creek. The sandy path heads northwest along Willow Creek through the heart of the Tower House Historical District. Camden House and smaller outlying buildings to your right were built in the 1850s. The caretaker house and barn across the meadow to your left were built around 1913. The path reaches Levi Tower's shady grave site after a level 0.25 mile. From here, turn left and follow the Camden Water Ditch, which brought water from nearby Crystal Creek to the meadow's former orchard and garden. After another 0.25 mile, bear right and join a dirt road that leads you to the El Dorado Mine at 0.7 mile. This gold

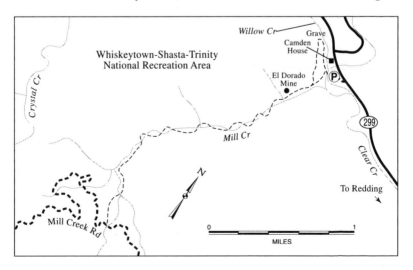

mine, in operation until 1967, still has much of the original machinery, and you can walk a short distance into one of the shafts.

As you continue up the dirt road paralleling Mill Creek, all signs of civilization drop away. A small swimming hole on the left just beyond the mine allows you to cool your body on hot days. At 1 mile take the path to the right, and walk in the shade provided by ponderosa pine, incense cedar, and Douglas fir. The trail follows very near the creek, and makes you rock-hop on granite boulders at nineteen creek crossings. At 2 miles you'll reach the second and best swimming hole: 15 feet in circumference, 5 feet deep, and fed by a 5-foot waterfall.

After you've absorbed the beauty of this spot, follow the trail as it bends ninety degrees to the left, passes through a dogwood grove, and then crosses Mill Creek at 2.2 miles. The path now follows

Hikers explore the dark recesses of a gold-mine shaft near Mill Creek.

a seasonal tributary uphill until finally reaching Mill Creek Road at 2.8 miles. If you wish to extend your hike, walk this seldom-traveled dirt road in either direction. When you do return, note that you can follow the road past the El Dorado Mine all the way to the parking area.

46   CANYON CREEK LAKES AND BOULDER CREEK LAKES

Length: 23.2 miles round trip
Hiking time: 3 to 4 days
High point: 6,350 feet
Total elevation gain: 4,500 feet
Difficulty: strenuous
Season: mid-June to early October

Water: available from lakes and creeks
Maps: USGS 7.5' Mount Hilton, USFS Trinity Alps Wilderness
Information: Weaverville Ranger District, Shasta-Trinity National Forest

Surround yourself with steep, jagged granite peaks. Sunbathe on flat, house-sized granite slabs. Wander through lush meadows. Swim in deep, cool lakes. This trip offers all this and more as it takes you deep into the Trinity Alps.

Take Highway 299 to Junction City, 8 miles northwest of Weaverville, then turn east on an unsigned road 75 yards southeast of the Junction City bridge. Drive 13.2 miles on the mostly paved road that follows Canyon Creek to the Canyon Creek trailhead.

The trail starts level amidst ferns, dogwoods, bigleaf maples, madrones, Douglas firs, and canyon live oaks. It crosses Bear Creek at 0.3 mile and then steepens. Pass a madrone tree at 0.8 mile, then gently climb through a forest of ponderosa pine, black oak, incense cedar, and more madrone. Take the 10-yard spur trail to the left at 2.4 miles for a commanding vista of the sprawling basin, which contains a white-water stretch of Canyon Creek far below high granite peaks. At 2.8 miles consider the 0.2 mile side-trail option to The Sinks, a series of swirling pools in Canyon Creek. Otherwise, bear right, climb past a lichen-carpeted granite rock wall, then ascend a series of switchbacks that crosses the same tributary three times. Watch for a campsite on the left at 3.9 miles, where you can admire a small waterfall cascading into a round, clear pool. Also, look for Lower Canyon Creek Falls crashing into a deep pool a short distance downstream.

The trail gently climbs past a fern community for 0.8 mile and then enters a small corn lily field in Canyon Creek Meadow at 4.9 miles. Cross several tributaries, and climb through forest to a trail fork at 6.1 miles. The left trail goes 2.4 miles to Boulder Creek Lakes (described later).

Go right to the more-visited Canyon Creek Lakes. Climb through a 0.6-mile stretch of open forest, followed by magnificent, misty Upper Canyon Creek Falls. The final leg to Lower Canyon Creek Lake gradually switchbacks between granite boulders and across granite slopes before reaching the lake itself at 7.5 miles.

Crossing Canyon Creek near Lower Canyon Creek Lake's mouth can be difficult in early summer, especially in the late afternoon; you might

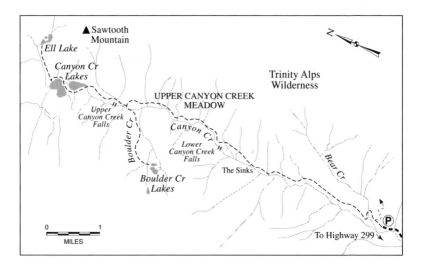

have to wade thigh-deep across the narrow mouth of the lake instead. Once on the west side, you'll find several campsites with good eastward views of Sawtooth Mountain. On hot days, this clear, deep lake offers chilly refreshment to swimmers.

To get to the less-visited Upper Canyon Creek Lake, follow the rock ducks (cairns) past the campsites on the west side, travel a faint path through forest, then reach several campsites near Upper Canyon Creek Lake's south shore. The path continues, crossing at 8.2 miles the stream linking Upper Canyon Creek Lake with its lower sibling. From

Eastward view of the Canyon Creek drainage and Sawtooth Mountain from above the Boulder Creek lakes

the lake's east shores, you'll have magnificent views of the meadow surrounding the higher reaches of Canyon Creek and the high granite peaks and ridges to the north, including Thompson Peak, the highest mountain in the Trinity Alps at 9,002 feet.

Continue northeast to Ell Lake from Upper Canyon Creek Lake's north side. The moderate 1.0-mile-long climb requires following rock ducks that lead directly to the lake, which is tucked into a narrow, glacier-carved slot bordered by steep granite. Seldom-visited Ell Lake offers a few campsites on the west side. Explore the meadows next to the north shore that encompass a circular pond.

For the 2.4-mile climb to Boulder Creek Lakes, retrace your steps to the earlier mentioned trail junction at 6.1 miles. Wade Canyon Creek, then go left. (The spur trail on the right leads to a campsite.) The trail heads southwesterly past a marsh and then ascends moderately through ceanothus and manzanita chaparral and a few stands of sugar pine, western white pine, ponderosa pine, and incense cedar. It eventually carves steeply through a thicket on the south-facing mountainside, routing you to a sheer, black cliff. Pick up the rock ducks here that head right of the cliff for another 0.3 mile to the lakes.

Boulder Creek Lakes, nestled in a glacial bowl and surrounded by high granite peaks, feature moist meadows, red mountain heather, yarrow, dwarfed western white pines, red firs, mountain hemlocks, and the rare weeping spruce. Tiny pools and small brooks surround the small lower lake on the southeast section of the basin. Look for powerful waterfalls that pour from the large Boulder Creek Lake's outlet and topple off a granite cliff.

You'll find a few campsites near the eastern shore of the larger Boulder Creek Lake and a couple of makeshift spots near three ponds. The shallow lakes and ponds receive a lot of summer sun, making long swims in the warm water very pleasurable.

47 FOUR LAKES LOOP

Length: 23.9 miles round trip
Hiking time: 3 to 4 days
High point: 7,500 feet
Total elevation gain: 5,700 feet
Difficulty: moderate
Season: early July through
  September

Water: available from lakes and
  year-round streams
Maps: USGS 7.5' Siligo Peak,
  USGS 7.5' Covington Mill,
  USFS Trinity Alps Wilderness
Information: Weaverville Ranger
  District, Shasta-Trinity
  National Forest

Glacial cirques, high mountain passes, and panoramas of the Trinity Alps and other mountain ranges await you on this hike, as do clear streams and flower-ringed, subalpine lakes.

From Weaverville drive northeast on Highway 3 for 14 miles, then turn left onto a dirt road signed "Stonewall Pass," which is 0.7 mile

Deer Lake and Caribou Mountain from Deer Creek Pass

east of the bridge across Stuart Fork Creek. Follow this dirt road 6.2 miles to the spacious trailhead.

The trail begins its steady climb up Stoney Ridge through a mixed forest of ponderosa pine, incense cedar, Douglas fir, white fir, and sugar pine. The trees part occasionally to allow views of Trinity Lake and the mountains to the south as well as glimpses of Granite Peak and Red Mountain just to the north. At 2.5 miles you'll pass through a chaparral thicket and then, at 3.7 miles, bear left at a trail fork. At 4 miles you'll reach the first decent campsite, located under a western white pine in Red Mountain Meadows. Nearby Stoney Creek has water year-round.

Stonewall Pass, 4.8 miles from the trailhead, features a magnificent vista: to the south lie Trinity Lake, Shasta Bally, and the Sacramento Valley; to the north, you're treated to views of granitic Sawtooth Mountain and Thompson Peak and nearer metamorphic summits such as Siligo Peak and Seven Up Peak.

The trail then descends for 1 mile as it skirts the upper edges of Van

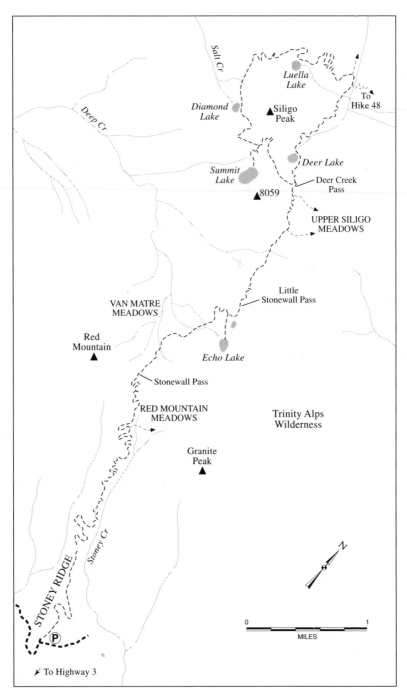

Salt Cr

Luella
Lake

To
Hike 48

Deep Cr

Diamond
Lake

▲Siligo
Peak

Deer Lake

Summit
Lake

Deer Creek
Pass

▲8059

UPPER SILIGO
MEADOWS

Little
Stonewall Pass

VAN MATRE
MEADOWS

Red
Mountain
▲

Echo Lake

Stonewall Pass

RED MOUNTAIN
MEADOWS

Trinity Alps
Wilderness

Granite
Peak
▲

N

STONEY RIDGE

Stoney Cr

Ⓟ

0   1
MILES

⚡ To Highway 3

Matre Meadows and then climbs another 1 mile to Little Stonewall Pass. Just below the pass, a sign points the way to Echo Lake, only 250 yards to the right off the main trail. This flower-ringed lake, surrounded by metamorphic, red-tinged mountains, offers open vistas of the western Trinity Alps. You can camp by the lake's south side or on the ridge to the west.

From Little Stonewall Pass, the main path descends steadily past western white pine, foxtail pine, and white fir for 0.7 mile to the edge of Lower Siligo Meadow. Cross the meadow and a year-round Deep Creek tributary, and pick up the trail on the other side.

Bear left at a trail fork 0.3 mile from the meadow, then climb through Upper Siligo Meadow's multihued display of lupine, yarrow, and other wildflowers to another trail fork 0.5 mile farther. Bear left again and climb the last few yards to 7,500-foot Deer Creek Pass, from which you'll see Siligo Peak towering high above Deer Lake.

After you catch your breath, begin the clockwise loop of the four lakes by heading downhill for 0.2 mile and turning left at the trail fork. The way then gently switchbacks uphill to another trail fork 1 mile from Deer Creek Pass. Turn left here and follow the trail 0.5 mile to the deep blue waters of Summit Lake, snugly situated under the protective shoulder of Peak 8059. Several good campsites lie near the west shore, and near the south shore you'll have open views of the Stuart Fork valley, Monument Peak, and forested mountains marching westward to the coast.

Back on the main trail, hike 0.2 mile to an impressive alpine view at a small saddle. If you wish, follow any of several faint trails along this 0.2-mile stretch up to the top of Siligo Peak, where you'll have a 360-degree view over all of far Northern California, including Mount Shasta and Lassen Peak.

From the saddle walk 0.9 mile down a dozen switchbacks to the inviting waters of Diamond Lake, the crown jewel of the Four Lakes Loop. The lake rests on a shelf overlooking the Salt Creek and Stuart Fork valleys, but the most impressive sight is undoubtedly the jagged granite spires of Thompson Peak, Wedding Cake, Mount Hilton, and Sawtooth Mountain piercing the skyline to the west. A large western white pine near the lake's north edge guards the only decent campsite.

The trail then climbs 0.7 mile north to an open, grassy saddle with more stunning vistas and then drops via several switchbacks another 0.7 mile to Luella Lake. This lake offers views of Seven Up Peak, Deer Creek Canyon, and the mountains ranging east and north but, alas, has no good campsites.

The path continues its descent 0.8 mile to a trail fork near Deer Creek, where you turn right. After a 0.2-mile walk, you'll see a trail on the left climbing 1.1 miles up to Seven Up Gap and then on to Granite, Horseshoe, and Ward lakes (see hike 48, Granite Lake and Seven Up Gap, and hike 49, Horseshoe and Ward Lakes). The main trail ascends another 1.1 miles to Deer Lake. This deep, mountain-ringed lake lies at the base of Siligo Peak and offers meadow camping at its southeastern edge. To get back to Deer Creek Pass, follow the trail 0.3 mile uphill and then go left at the fork.

48 GRANITE LAKE AND SEVEN UP GAP

Length: 15.6 miles round trip
Hiking time: 3 days
High point: 7,600 feet
Total elevation gain: 3,850 feet
Difficulty: moderate to strenuous
Season: late June through mid-October

Water: available from Swift and Granite creeks
Maps: USGS 7.5' Covington Mill, USGS 7.5' Siligo Peak, USFS Trinity Alps Wilderness
Information: Weaverville Ranger District, Shasta-Trinity National Forest

This trip takes you along the madly rushing waters of Swift and Granite creeks, both blessed by the sweet fragrance of azalea blossoms in early summer. After visiting cool, clear Granite Lake, you'll climb to Seven Up Gap for a panoramic vista over the heart of the Trinity Alps. From here, you have the option of adding hike 47 (Four Lakes Loop) and hike 49 (Horseshoe and Ward Lakes) to your backpacking trip.

Turn left off Highway 3 at the Swift Creek sign, which is 0.2 mile north of the main turnoff for the town of Trinity Center. Bear left at two main road intersections, then park in the upper lot when you reach the Swift Creek trailhead, 6.9 miles from Highway 3.

The raucous roar of surging Swift Creek emanates from the left as you begin a steady climb under the shade of incense cedars, Douglas firs, sugar pines, and Jeffrey pines. A good campsite nestled above the creek awaits at 0.5 mile, then you'll encounter three small, azalea-

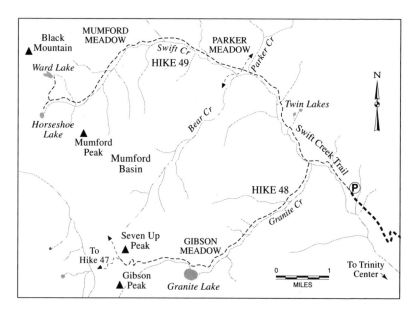

Snow-ringed Gibson Peak rises steeply above the deep waters of aptly named Granite Lake.

lined creeks. The trail then travels atop a steep canyon wall, from which you can see one of Swift Creek's cacophonous waterfalls crashing over a 40-foot drop into a deep pool. Go left at a trail junction at 1.3 miles (the right-hand trail is discussed in hike 49, Horseshoe and Ward Lakes), pass by another large campsite, and then cross Swift Creek on a large metal bridge at 1.5 miles.

You now trade Swift Creek for Granite Creek. After climbing a ridge, you'll encounter the first of numerous alder- and fern-bordered streams. At 2 miles the trail switchbacks away from the creek but rejoins it for a good view of a waterfall at 3 miles. As you continue up the trail, white fir replace Douglas fir, and yellow and blue lupine brighten the landscape, along with five-petaled white, pink, and red azalea flowers.

A good campsite sits to the left just before the trail enters an area of downed trees at 3.3 miles, where the first good views of the granitic ridge to the south await. Over the next 1.5 miles, you'll climb past another waterfall, enter a small lush meadow, encounter yet another waterfall, then enter expansive Gibson Meadow.

After another 1 mile of climbing, reach Granite Lake, elevation 6,000 feet. Several campsites, shaded by incense cedar, western white pine, sugar pine, red fir, white fir, and mountain hemlock, lie near the trail on the lake's alder-enshrouded north side. You may, however, prefer to cross the outlet creek on a log and head up to the campsites atop the granite hump on the lake's open east side. Besides easy swimming access, the best views of the clear, deep lake await you here. You'll see the granite ridge on the south and west, which soars 2,400 feet from the lake's surface to the top of multispired, 8,400-foot Gibson Peak, and also the reddish metamorphic mountains that make up the north side of Granite Lake's glacial cirque.

If you aren't traveling over to the Four Lakes Loop (hike 47), consider making the trip to Seven Up Gap a day hike, because climbing the steep trail takes a lot of energy. The path climbs above the north shore of Granite Lake and then crosses three small streams as it travels close to Granite Creek. At 6.4 miles enter a meadow, from which you have excellent views of the entire head of the Granite Creek drainage. Igneous granitic rocks rise skyward on the left, while jagged metamorphic rocks stretch upward on the right. Just 100 yards into the meadow, you'll see one of the several small, shallow ponds across the creek. It's possible to camp on the flat granite slabs, a good option if the Granite Lake sites are crowded.

The trail eventually leaves the creek to rise steeply past numerous wildflowers to Seven Up Gap. Hardy foxtail pines join a few red firs and mountain hemlocks at the 7,600-foot saddle; however, it's the extensive views that will command your attention. To the east you'll see the northern portion of Trinity Lake, and far beyond the forested Klamath Mountains rise the massive volcanic cones of the Cascades' Mount Burney, Magee Peak, and Lassen Peak. To the west you'll look far down to the Deer Creek Valley and then above it to Siligo Peak, which rises just south of the metamorphic ridge housing Luella Lake. Farther in the distance, Sawtooth Mountain punctures the skyline, joined by its jagged siblings Mount Hilton, Wedding Cake, Thompson Peak, and Caesar's Peak. Granitic Gibson Peak forms the south side of the Seven Up Gap saddle, and metamorphic Seven Up Peak the north side.

To join the paths of hike 47 (Four Lakes Loop), take the trail that switchbacks down the ridge for 1.1 miles to an intersection. You can then head left for Deer Lake or right for Luella Lake.

49 HORSESHOE AND WARD LAKES

Length: 21.4 miles round trip
Hiking time: 3 to 4 days
High point: 7,100 feet
Total elevation gain: 3,600 feet
Difficulty: moderate to strenuous
Season: mid-June through late September
Water: available from lakes and streams

Maps: USGS 7.5' Covington Mill, USGS 7.5' Siligo Peak, USGS 7.5' Caribou Lake, USGS 7.5' Ycatapom, USFS Trinity Alps Wilderness
Information: Weaverville Ranger District, Shasta-Trinity National Forest

Powerful Swift Creek, miles of meadows, displays of Trinity Alps peaks, and two peaceful mountain lakes highlight this backpacking trip.

On Highway 3 by Trinity Center, turn west at the Swift Creek Trail

Exploring the shoreline of Horseshoe Lake

sign. Drive 6.9 miles, following all signs indicating Swift Creek trailhead along the mostly dirt road.

Swift Creek Trail stays mostly level to the first visual attraction—granite slabs plunging into cascades and clear pools of rushing Swift Creek at 0.7 mile. A sign on an incense cedar at 1.3 miles marks the trail fork to Granite Lake (hike 48, Granite Lake and Seven Up Gap), but you bear right, staying on Swift Creek Trail. From 1.3 to 3 miles, the route climbs gently past western azalea, Douglas fir, ponderosa pine, and incense cedar.

Hike across a wide basin, carefully negotiate the tricky crossing of Parker Creek at 4.2 miles, then note the debut of the towering Trinity Alps mountains to the southwest. Bear right 0.1 mile farther at the sign that says "Fosters Cabin," go left at another trail fork just beyond, then reach Parker Meadow at 4.7 miles. Note that you can choose from plenty of campsites along Swift Creek for the next 4 miles in Parker and Mumford meadows. Fosters Cabin hides in the meadowy yellow pine forest at 5.1 miles. It contains a pot-bellied wood stove and several bunks and offers shelter during a thunderstorm.

Cross Landers Creek at 6 miles, then begin a 2 mile stroll through Mumford Meadow amid huge ponderosa pine and incense cedar. The path stays nearly level to 8.3 miles, traveling briefly into forests to return to the corn lily fields, marshes, and deer pastures of Mumford Meadow. Plan on frequent tributary crossings, and keep an eye on Mumford Peak as it looms on the left.

At 8.5 miles duck into a small forest, then begin the steep part of the hike to Horseshoe Lake across loose talus. The narrow path borders dwindling Swift Creek at 9.3 miles, reaches a signed trail junction 0.1 mile farther (stay left), then leads you past three campsites to Horseshoe Lake, the creek's origin, at 9.7 miles.

A mix of western white pine, mountain hemlock, and red fir grow in between the lake's rock outcrops, and a couple of small ponds hide near the willow-choked outlet. Scamper up the rock outcrops for a picturesque view featuring previously visited meadows and Mumford Peak to the southeast.

To get to Ward Lake, retrace your steps 0.3 mile, then bear left. You'll immediately traverse across stepping stones next to marsh marigolds. At 10.8 miles, look down into the meadow below Ward Lake, and look behind for a wide open display of major Trinity Alps mountains, including Siligo, Gibson, and Seven Up peaks.

Reach Ward Lake and its several campsites at 11 miles, where you'll enjoy small meadows and views of stark Black Mountain to the northwest.

If you want an extended trip, consider trekking to Granite Lake (hike 48) and beyond to the Four Lakes Loop (hike 47).

CARIBOU, EMERALD, AND SAPPHIRE LAKES

Length: 30.6 miles round trip
Hiking time: 5 to 7 days
High point: 7,600 feet
Total elevation gain: 4,000 feet
Difficulty: strenuous
Season: early July through mid-October

Water: sporadically available; have at least a quart on hand at all times
Maps: USGS 7.5' Caribou Lake, USGS 7.5' Thompson Peak, USFS Trinity Alps Wilderness
Information: Salmon River Ranger District, Shasta-Trinity National Forest

Take a long backpacking trip deep into the heart of the Trinity Alps, where you'll find expansive views, vertical granite mountain faces, deep glacial lakes, and numerous clear streams.

Drive west on Coffee Creek Road, which leaves Highway 3 about 8 miles north of the town of Trinity Center. Bear left at a road fork 19 miles from Highway 3 where a sign directs you to Big Flat Campground. Turn right 0.6 mile farther, then park near the outhouses.

Follow the Caribou Lake signs as you head downhill to a log crossing of the South Fork of the Salmon River, then take the left trail that heads up the bank. After a brief climb, hike 200 yards through a meadow, then bear right at a trail junction. From here, you begin a series of long switchbacks under the shade of white and Douglas fir, with a few open areas dominated by huckleberry oak, manzanita, and some tobacco brush. As you climb the gentle grade, occasional views of Preacher's Peak and Red Rock Mountain open up to the east, and you'll also see the long, granite ridge of Caribou Mountain to the south.

The saddle containing Caribou Meadows, and a waterless campsite, awaits 3.4 miles from the trailhead. Just past the campsite, the trail crosses the old Caribou Lake Trail, which travels over a 7,400-foot ridge on its way to Caribou Lake. This trail, about 2 miles shorter than the new trail, may be difficult to follow because of lack of use and maintenance. From Caribou Meadows the new trail passes some small, seasonal creeks and then gives a good view up a polished, glacial, granite slope to the cirque that houses Little Caribou Lake. As you contour around a mountainside, the northern ranges of the Klamath Mountains appear on the right.

A small campsite sits just below the trail by a stream at 4.6 miles. From here, you travel past patches of red and white fir forest broken up by manzanita chaparral. At 5.4 miles you enter Brown's Meadow, which is guarded by a steep wall of granite. These grass fields stretch up the mountainside and offer two campsites and a year-round stream.

As the trail climbs steeply, be sure to look eastward for a good view of Brown's Meadow and snowy Mount Shasta. The trail levels at 6.6 miles, where gaps between red fir trees allow expansive westward views of Caesar's and Thompson peaks rearing their high heads skyward. The long, granite spires of 8,575-foot Caribou Mountain appear as the trail undulates south, and eventually you'll see rock-ringed

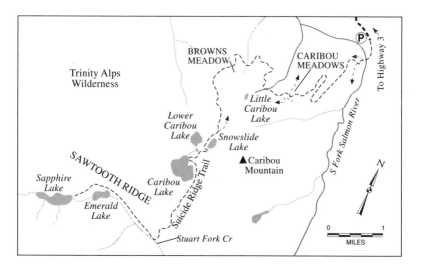

Caribou and Lower Caribou lakes. At 8.2 miles the old trail merges from the left just before your trail switchbacks down to Snowslide Lake.

The deep, cold waters of Snowslide Lake lie nestled under the steep slopes of Caribou Mountain, whose highest pinnacles reach more than 1,900 feet above the lake's surface. You'll find at least five good campsites by the trail on the lake's west side, most partially shaded by red fir, lodgepole pine, and mountain hemlock. As you continue south across sheets of granite toward Caribou Lake, several faint paths head down to Lower Caribou Lake, which offers good swimming but only one campsite.

Continue up to Caribou Lake, which, at 72 acres, ranks as the Trinity Alps' largest body of water. Nestled in a glacial cirque 10 miles from the trailhead, it also makes a strong claim as the prettiest. Its deep blue waters reflect the metamorphic ridge crest to the south and west as well as the steep granite ridge to the east. To the north the Klamath Mountains stretch clear to Oregon. If you're brave, take a chilly swim out to the two rock islands off the north shore. Several campsites lie near the north and east edges.

The trail, usually marked with rock ducks (cairns), continues along Caribou Lake's east shore and then climbs south up to jagged Sawtooth Ridge at 11.2 miles. From this aptly named point, you have a bird's-eye view of the territory hiked earlier; however, steep-sided Sawtooth Mountain towering over Stuart Fork valley will most likely capture your attention. The green of Morris Meadows glows downstream, and upstream you'll spy the crown jewels of the Trinity Alps: Emerald and Sapphire lakes. Thompson Peak and Caesar's Peak dominate the skyline to the west.

The next portion of your hike involves a 2-mile chaparral trek down the ninety or so switchbacks of Suicide Ridge Trail, which loses 2,100 feet of elevation. Be sure you have plenty of water for this dry section, both going down and especially coming back up, and make sure you don't lose the sometimes faint trail.

At the bottom you'll reach the cool shade of Portuguese Camp and also have easy access to Stuart Fork Creek. Head upstream under fir shade past a few small streams and several campsites. At 14.7 miles you'll see the sparkling surface of Emerald Lake, where you'll find a few campsites in the trees just below the dam.

The last stretch of trail borders Emerald Lake's north shore and then heads through chaparral to reach Sapphire Lake, a hefty 15.3 miles from the trailhead and this trip's final destination. Though Sapphire Lake receives far fewer visitors than its sister, it has only one good campsite, located near the outlet. However, the lake and its surroundings will transfix you with awe. The lake's depth is over 200 feet (the exact figure isn't known) and its waters gleam with deep blue glints. A glacier carved the valley holding Emerald and Sapphire lakes, leaving behind the steep sides of granitic Sawtooth Ridge, which forms a beautiful reflection in the lakes' waters.

Opposite: *The Sawtooth Ridge and one of several ponds just north of Caribou Lake*

51 BIG BEAR LAKE

Length: 10 miles round trip
Hiking time: 8 hours or over-
night
High point: 5,800 feet
Total elevation gain: 2,850 feet
Difficulty: moderate
Season: mid-June through mid-
October

Water: plentiful along most of the
route
Maps: USGS 7.5' Tangle Blue
Lake, USFS Trinity Alps
Wilderness
Information: Weaverville Ranger
District, Shasta-Trinity
National Forest

Granite-ringed Big Bear Lake makes a good overnight backpack trip: a variety of plants line the trail on the way up, you'll love the lake's clear waters and steep glacial cirque, and it's easily accessible from Highway 3.

Take Bear Creek Loop Road, which leaves the west side of Highway 3 15 miles north of Trinity Center. Follow this dirt road 1.2 miles to the signed trailhead.

The trail begins the long climb to Big Bear Lake in a forest of in-cense cedar, Douglas fir, and ponderosa pine and travels close to Bear Creek for the first mile. At 0.9 mile you'll see a signed stock trail head-ing to the right. A footbridge across the creek 200 yards farther up the main trail is no longer safe, so unless it's rebuilt by the time you take this hike, follow the stock trail. After you boulder-hop across the creek, follow this path as it winds uphill to eventually rejoin the main trail just after crossing a year-round stream.

The trail then switchbacks steeply up a ridge between Bear Creek and the smaller stream you just crossed. Manzanita and huckleberry oak, two common chaparral shrubs, line and occasionally intrude onto the path, while numerous black oak and an occasional stand of knob-cone pine provide some shade. Approach the creek again at 2.1 miles, then begin alternating between a mixed white fir and western white pine forest and lush open patches with numerous fern. The first open views of the glacial granite cirques harboring Big Bear Lake, your des-tination, and cousins Little Bear Lake and Wee Bear Lake, appear at 3.1 miles.

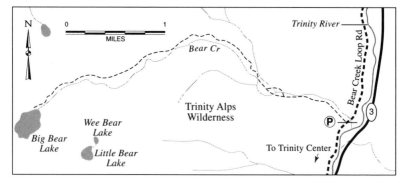

Twin western white pines just below Big Bear Lake point to a cloud-enshrouded Mount Shasta.

From here, the occasionally steep route passes through numerous moist areas inhabited by mountain alder, ferns, and some western azalea. At 4.6 miles the trail crosses granite outcrops, where rock ducks (cairns) guide you. Be sure to look back for an exquisite eastward view of Mount Shasta.

At 5 miles you finally reach Big Bear Lake, where steep granite walls tower over 1,000 feet on the south, west, and north sides. You'll find good deep spots for swimming by walking to the steep granite on the east shore. Several adequate campsites, most shaded by mountain hemlock, western white pine, and red fir, sit above the lake on both sides of the outlet creek.

52   CAMPBELL, CLIFF, AND SUMMIT LAKES

Length: 13.3 miles round trip
Hiking time: 10 hours or over-
  night
High point: 6,200 feet
Total elevation gain: 2,800 feet
Difficulty: moderate
Season: early June through late
  October

Water: plenty
Maps: USGS 7.5' Boulder Peak,
  USGS 7.5' Marble Mountain,
  USFS Marble Mountain
  Wilderness
Information: Scott River Ranger
  District, Klamath National
  Forest

Take a leisurely backpacking trip to three of the Marble Mountains' prettiest lakes. Along the way you'll be treated to the soothing sounds

This Cliff Lake beach offers easy swimming access and good views of steep metamorphic ridges.

of Shackleford Creek and obtain good views of multicolored metamorphic mountain ridges.

From the town of Fort Jones on Highway 3, head northwest on Scott River Road for 6.5 miles, then turn left onto Quartz Valley Road. Go 4 miles, then turn right onto Road 43N21 and go 7 miles to the trailhead.

The trail begins on the upstream side of the upper parking lot and climbs gently past Douglas fir, white fir, and occasional Jeffrey pine and incense cedar. After crossing two year-round streams, you'll reach a gate at 1.1 miles, a signal that you may encounter a few cattle ahead. After passing a good campsite at 1.4 miles, the trail crosses several small meadows filled with yellow sunflowers, purple daisies, and white-flowered yarrows. Bear right at a trail fork at 3 miles, then climb away from the creek.

Another trail fork awaits at 3.7 miles. Go left, then pass the aptly named Log Lake after a level 0.1-mile stroll. (A low ridge on the lake's south side houses several campsites.) The trail passes through more meadows strewn with bleached tree corpses before encountering yet another trail fork at 4.4 miles, where you go left.

The trail climbs moderately and eventually approaches Campbell Lake's outlet creek just before reaching the lake itself at 5.3 miles. Steep, rocky mountainsides border the east shore of Campbell Lake, nicely complementing the red fir and western white pine forest that surrounds the other three sides. Look for the two-needled lodgepole pine near the lake's edges. A 0.4-mile long trail leading to the outlet skirts the lake's north edge.

The main trail heads right for about 150 yards along the lake's west shore to a trail fork. Take the left-hand path south toward Cliff Lake. Almost immediately you'll bear right at a trail junction. (The left-hand trail of the first junction borders the southwest shore of Campbell Lake, where you'll find several campsites.)

From the edge of Campbell Lake, climb 0.9 mile to the northwest shore of Cliff Lake, one of the most beautiful bodies of water in the Marble Mountains. The lake's waters show shades of blue running from aquamarine to indigo and provide a perfect foreground for the glacially carved red and gray metamorphic cliffs to the east and south. The trail continues another 0.4 mile along the lake's west edge, where you'll find several campsites, and then finally peters out near talus slopes at the south shore.

Back on the main trail by Campbell Lake, head east at the signed junction toward Summit Lake. The path descends through a forest dominated by red fir and then passes through meadows. From here, head 0.9 mile to the shallow and marshy Summit Meadow Lake, then continue on to beautiful Summit Lake at 7.1 miles, where you'll find a couple of campsites. A trail junction at the west side of Summit Lake's outlet offers the opportunity to connect with the trails of hike 53 (Sky High Lakes and Summit Lake), allowing you to make a much longer trip if you can arrange a car shuttle.

To complete your loop trip, head downhill from Summit Lake 0.6 mile to a crossing of a small creek, then head right at a junction with a faint trail. Continue the downhill trek as you enjoy the open views of the Marble Mountains' rocky crags. At 8.9 miles you'll reach the end of this trip's loop, where you had earlier headed up to Campbell and Cliff lakes. Stay left and follow the familiar path 4.4 miles back to the trailhead.

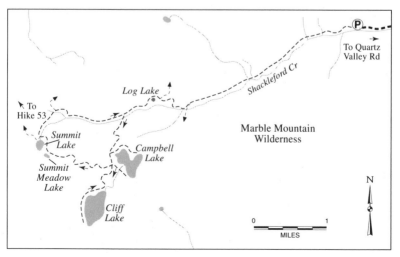

53 SKY HIGH LAKES AND SUMMIT LAKE

Length: 18 miles round trip	**Water:** available only from lakes;
Hiking time: 2 to 3 days	have plenty on hand
High point: 6,700 feet	**Maps:** USGS 7.5' Marble Moun-
Total elevation gain: 3,200 feet	tain, USFS Marble Mountain
Difficulty: moderate to strenuous	Wilderness
Season: mid-June to early	**Information:** Scott River Ranger
October	District, Klamath National
	Forest

This hike boasts a lot of variety: admire a white marble mountain, explore a big wildflower garden, swim in the attractive Sky High Lakes, and walk 5 miles along a high ridge with far-reaching views.

From Fort Jones on Highway 3, turn right on Scott River Road, then drive 13.5 miles to Indian Scotty Campground, where you turn left. For the next 5.4 miles, stay on Forest Road 44N45, then turn left onto Forest Road 43N45. Drive 1.7 miles farther to Lovers Camp, where you bear right and go 0.1 mile.

Black Marble Mountain from just below the Sky High Lakes

Climb gently for 0.2 mile to a dirt road, then pick up the trail proper at an information kiosk 100 yards farther. It weaves its way gently near Canyon Creek past dogwood, Douglas fir, sugar pine, and white alder. Go right on Canyon Creek Trail next to a large dogwood at 0.8 mile. The next 3 miles climb gently under shade above the creek. Cross a terraced tributary stream featuring a slender cascade and two tiny soaking pools at 4.2 miles, then bear left 0.1 mile farther at a trail intersection. Climb another 0.3 mile, then go left again at another trail junction.

The countryside opens into a green sloping meadow with a striking view of Marble Mountain's escarpment, which sports a vertical band of shiny white marble. The black schist protrusion on the northernmost marble rim is Black Marble Mountain.

At 5.1 miles look down on tiny, inaccessible Gate Lake, then reach Lower Sky High Lake at 6 miles, where ominous Peak 6817 towers high above the lime-green waters. You'll find two campsites 200 feet from the northeast shore. Nearby Upper Sky High Lake, just to the west, is a nice side trip but has no campsites.

The trail then leads to a handful of white fir and hemlock that dot the exposed, meadowy shoreline of shallow, swimmable Frying Pan Lake, From here it climbs to the lowest saddle on the western ridge at 7.1 miles, where you bear left twice onto the Pacific Crest Trail. Over a level, one mile ridge walk, enjoy open views of the surrounding Marble Mountains. Reach a signed trail fork at 8.2 miles, where you head left 0.4 mile to Shadow Lake. Obtain a view of Marble Mountain just a few footsteps from the lone campsite near the east shore and consider swimming near the boulder-strewn north shore.

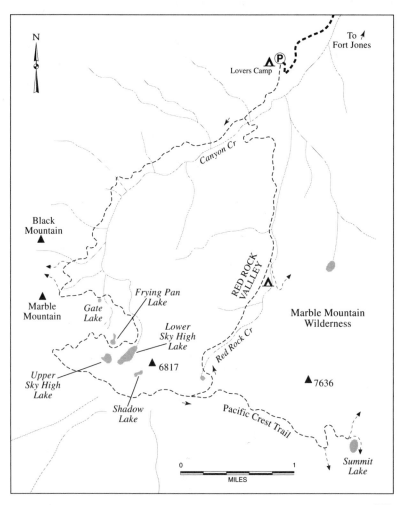

To continue the journey, double back, then go left on the Pacific Crest Trail. Make note of the left turn down Red Rock Valley at a four-way intersection at 8.8 miles (your return route), then go straight. The views instantly switch northward, with occasional glimpses of massive, orange-rocked Peak 7636 as you walk along the ridge.

Turn left at the double-signed junction at the gap at 10 miles. Your new trail descends toward Peak 7636 and then abruptly swings toward the Shackleford Creek basin at 10.3 miles.

Look carefully for the signed trail junction 0.3 mile farther, then head right to Summit Lake, where you'll find two campsites near the willow- and white fir–lined shore. Note that you can extend your trip by doing all or part of hike 52 (Campbell, Cliff, and Summit Lakes).

Retrace your steps for 2.2 miles, then turn right onto the signed Red Rock Valley Trail at 13.2 miles. The path plunges into a hemlock and Douglas fir forest to pass below a tiny lake at 13.6 miles and then crosses a tributary of Red Rock Creek.

The path stays above and west of the creek for a while and then crosses it at 15 miles. Go left at a trail fork near a campsite, then re-cross the creek at 15.1 miles. Depart the creek for good 0.7 mile farther, eventually crossing Canyon Creek at 17.2 miles. Bear right 100 yards farther onto Canyon Creek Trail for the last 0.8 mile to the trailhead.

54 PARADISE LAKE

Length: 15.2 miles round trip from Kelsey Camp, or 2.1 miles one way on Rye Patch Trail
Hiking time: 2 days
High point: 6,180 feet
Total elevation gain: 3,700 feet from Kelsey Camp, 1,400 from Rye Patch Trail
Difficulty: moderate to strenuous
Season: late June to mid-October

Water: plenty along Kelsey Creek Trail; none on Rye Patch Trail
Maps: USGS 7.5' Grider Valley, USGS 7.5' Marble Mountain, USFS Marble Mountain Wilderness
Information: Scott River Ranger District, Klamath National Forest

Hike along Kelsey Creek and through a long wildflower meadow to colorful Paradise Lake, where you'll have views of uniquely shaped Kings Castle, Cayenne Ridge, and other peaks in the Marble Mountains.

From Fort Jones on Highway 3, take Scott River Road. Drive 16 miles, then turn left at Kelsey Camp immediately following a bridge. Bear right at 0.2 mile, then park near the signed trailhead 0.2 mile farther.

Start your hike on Kelsey Trail, a major supply route constructed in the 1850s that stretched between nearby Fort Jones to the east and Crescent City on the north coast. The path initially climbs past sections of madly rushing water interspersed with serene pools and then reaches a sandy campsite with a makeshift table near a charred tree trunk at 2 miles.

The trail departs Kelsey Creek, only to return at 3 miles. It then gently climbs past a seasonal streambed and two of Kelsey Creek's numerous tributaries over the next 0.7 mile. The next 2 miles travel near the creek most of the time, steadily climbing through a Douglas fir forest that includes a few sugar pine and incense cedar. Canyon live oak dominate over the middle stretch, with an occasional black oak mixed in.

Packer's Valley Creek tumbles into Kelsey Creek at 5.8 miles, promptly followed by a campsite next to a rustic wooden fence. From 6.1 to 6.8 miles, two unsigned scant trails lead westward up the hillside. Bear left at these confusing cross trails, keeping close to Kelsey Creek.

A small grove of black cottonwood trees sways in the breeze 0.2 mile into a gently sloping meadow at 7 miles. From a small stream at 7.1 miles, the climb gets noticeably tougher as you pass a wildflower garden of blue lupine, white yarrow, orange Indian paintbrush, white angelica, western blue flax, and yellow meadow goldenrod. The escalation eases along the meadowy mountainside when you make the final crossing of Kelsey Creek at 7.5 miles. The trail finally crests at 7.6 miles at Paradise Lake's scenic meadow, which is decorated by stonecrop and lupine.

A splendid campsite beneath a white fir community lies 120 feet from the eastern shoreline of the lake, from which you have fantastic views of numerous ridges and peaks, including Kings Castle, which actually does resemble a rook in a chess game. A lone, grassy island invites you to wade out and sunbathe.

There's a backdoor shortcut to Paradise Lake via the strenuous Rye Patch Trail. It offers an excellent day hike option to the Cayenne Ridge

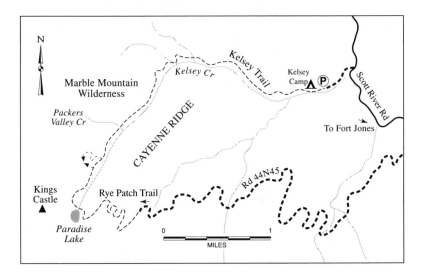

Angelica enhances a vista of Paradise Lake and the ridge just north of King's Castle from the Rye Patch Trail.

and Paradise Lake area, or it can serve as a 9.7-mile, one-way route to Kelsey Camp.

To reach this trailhead, travel 13.5 miles on Scott River Road from Fort Jones, then turn left onto Road 44N45. Go right at a road intersection 6.4 miles farther, then continue on Road 44N45 another 5.6 miles.

Rye Patch Trail climbs continuously and sometimes steeply in a well-shaded Douglas fir forest. The ascent finally eases when you reach a fern-covered hillside at 1.4 miles. Then, at 1.9 miles you'll reach the colorful, open slope near the southeast section of Paradise Lake.

55 BEAR LAKE

Length: 6 miles round trip
Hiking time: 4 hours or over-
  night
High point: 5,550 feet
Total elevation gain: 1,750 feet
Difficulty: moderate
Season: mid-June through mid-
  October

Water: available only at Bear
  Lake; bring your own
Map: USGS 7.5' Bear Peak
Information: Happy Camp
  Ranger District, Klamath
  National Forest

Hike into the heart of far Northern California's wild and remote Siskiyou Mountains; you'll visit the deep waters of Bear Lake and be treated to a panorama of high ridges and peaks.

Take paved Road 15N19, which is on Highway 96's west side 72 miles north of Willow Creek, 10 miles south of Happy Camp, and 0.4 mile south of the Highway 96 bridge over Clear Creek. Always stay on the best road at intersections, and follow signs for Bear Lake/Kelsey Trail. The pavement ends 6.5 miles from Highway 96. Drive 5 miles farther, then turn right at the sign for Bear Lake and climb the last 0.1 mile to the trailhead.

The path, a part of the nineteenth-century South Kelsey Trail that linked Fort Jones with the Pacific Coast, begins in a forest of Douglas fir, white fir, and incense cedar. It reaches the lush greenery of Elbow Spring at 0.2 mile and then climbs moderately past an understory of Sadler oak, huckleberry oak, manzanita, and tobacco brush. At 1.5 miles the trail nears a ridge and offers open views of the forested Siskiyou Mountains to the west and south.

As you continue in a northwesterly direction along the ridge, red fir, a few western white pine, and the relatively rare Brewer spruce line

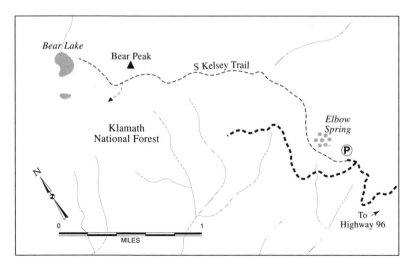

A mixed forest of pine and fir surrounds Bear Lake.

the path, which is occasionally punctuated by granite outcroppings. Look for a lone red fir on the right 2.1 miles from the trailhead and just east of Bear Peak. From here, you have spectacular vistas of the Siskiyou Mountains stretching north into Oregon and east toward Mount Shasta, the Marble Mountains rising skyward to the southeast, and farther southeast the rocky spires of the Trinity Alps climbing up to 9,000 feet. Note the Brewer spruce to the north just below.

Follow the trail another 0.2 mile to a Siskiyou Wilderness sign, where, in addition to the mountains seen from below the red fir tree, you can see Red Hill to the west, Twin Peaks and Rocky Knob to the northwest, and 7,309-foot Preston Peak (the tallest mountain in the region) to the north, with massive Cedar Crest guarding its southern flanks. Just below you'll spy the glacial cirque enclosing Bear Lake along with an upstream pond.

Go 10 feet past the Siskiyou Wilderness sign, take the unsigned trail on the right, and descend 750 feet over the next 0.7 mile to the shores of Bear Lake. Talus slopes border the deep lake's west side, and you'll find several campsites nestled in the forest that surrounds the other sides. If you want to hike more, take South Kelsey Trail west along the ridge toward Red Hill.

56 GRIDER CREEK

Length: 8 miles round trip
Hiking time: 4 hours
High point: 2,300 feet
Total elevation gain: 850 feet
Difficulty: easy
Season: year-round; occasional winter snow

Water: available from Grider Creek
Map: USGS 7.5' Seiad Valley
Information: Scott River Ranger District, Klamath National Forest

Hike a section of the Pacific Crest Trail along the tumbling waters of boulder-strewn Grider Creek, where you'll alternately walk through a diverse forest and then by riparian habitat near the creek's banks. Several swimming holes offer cool relief to those hiking during warmer months.

Turn south off Highway 96 at a sign for the Pacific Crest Trail and Grider Creek. This turnoff is 2 miles southeast of the town of Seiad Valley and 42 miles west of I-5. Go 100 feet, then turn right onto Grider Creek Road. Go left at a junction 2.6 miles from Highway 96, travel another 2.3 miles on the now-dirt road, then turn left at the sign for Grider Creek Campground. Park near the outhouses.

Walk toward Grider Creek, then head upstream on a dirt road for 100 feet to a wooden bridge. As you cross the bridge, you'll have your first views of Grider Creek's alder-lined, rushing waters, which originate in the high peaks of Marble Mountain Wilderness 10 miles to the south.

Turn right onto the Pacific Crest Trail and begin a gentle ascent. Tall Douglas fir compose the majority of the forest, but you'll also see dogwood, black oak, and bigleaf and vine maple. Tiny No Name Creek awaits at 0.5 mile, then at 0.7 mile you'll have the first views of the heavily forested slopes of Grider Ridge rising over 1,000 feet on the

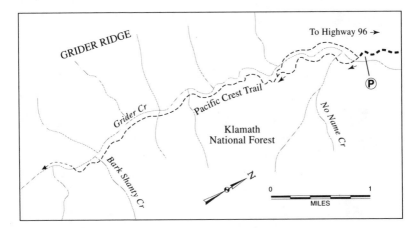

creek's west side. Shortly thereafter, you enter an area populated by madrone trees, interior live oaks, canyon live oaks, and occasional trailside poison oak. Note that some trees have blackened lower trunks, the only obvious evidence of a fire.

A trail fork awaits at 1.6 miles, just past a small creek. The right-hand Old Grider Creek Trail drops past two campsites to Grider Creek and offers an alternative way to get back to the trailhead. It crosses Grider Creek on a log, nears a swimming hole 100 feet farther, and

Douglas fir and dogwood border the Pacific Crest Trail above Grider Creek.

then follows the creek downstream 1.5 miles to the campground. Lush undergrowth partially occludes the trail in some spots near the creek, and the path occasionally climbs steeply up the hillside.

The Pacific Crest Trail continues a slight uphill climb as it takes you above a creekside flat area for the next 0.5 mile. At 2.5 miles you'll come close to the creek's small, cascading waterfalls and spy several swimming holes. The path eventually climbs well above the creek and through an area of metamorphic rock to reach year-round Bark Shanty Creek at 3.6 miles. It then passes just above an excellent campsite near good swimming holes and crosses Grider Creek on a wooden bridge at 4 miles. From here, the Pacific Crest Trail climbs to the Marble Mountain Wilderness, where you can eventually connect with hike 52 (Campbell, Cliff, and Summit Lakes), hike 53 (Sky High Lakes and Summit Lake), and hike 54 (Paradise Lake).

57 MOUNT EDDY AND THE DEADFALL LAKES

Length: 9.5 miles round trip
Hiking time: 6 hours or over-
  night
High point: 9,025 feet
Total elevation gain: 2,850 feet
Difficulty: moderate to strenuous
Season: early July through mid-
  October

Water: plenty from Deadfall
  Lakes and nearby streams;
  take at least a quart past
  Upper Deadfall Lake
Maps: USGS 7.5' Mt. Eddy, USGS
  7.5' South China
Information: Mount Shasta
  Ranger District, Shasta-Trinity
  National Forest

This hike features amazing wildflower displays plus stupendous views from Mount Eddy's summit. You'll also visit the Deadfall Lakes, each surrounded by colorful metamorphic rocks.

On I-5 drive north 3.4 miles beyond the Weed turnoff, then take the Edgewood/Gazelle Exit. Go under the freeway, turn right at the stop sign, then turn left onto unsigned Stewart Springs Road after 0.3 mile. At 4.7 miles turn right onto Forest Road 17, also known as Parks Creek Road. Park at the large trailhead clearing at Parks Creek pass, 13.7 miles from the freeway exit.

The Pacific Crest Trail stays mostly level at the onset and soon provides views of the Trinity Alps from a northeast vantage point. Red fir and white fir mix with Jeffrey pine and ponderosa pine to shade patches of dwarf larkspur and yarrow as you travel to a seasonal creek at 1.1 miles. Another stream gurgles down to scenic Deadfall Meadows at 1.8 miles, where yellow lupine and white-flowered angelica combine with sage for showy trailside color.

The wildflower displays keep coming, with corn lily and red colum-

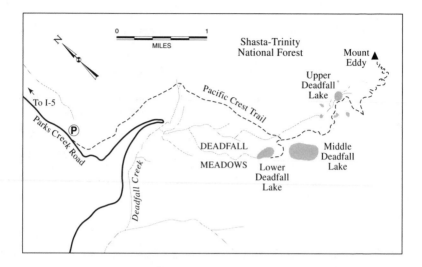

bine surrounding another brook at 2.1 miles. Western white pine dominates at 2.2 miles as you first sight Mount Eddy's southwest shoulder
along with the upper meadows where Deadfall Creek meanders. Go
right at the trail sign mounted on a huge western white pine at 2.3
miles, and soon reach swimmable Lower Deadfall Lake, which has a
few campsites. Back at the trail junction, continue southeast on
Sisson-Callahan Trail. You soon spot Middle Deadfall Lake on the
right. Big rocks on the shoreline make great tanning and dipping
spots, and you'll also find several campsites.

A marsh covered with marigolds empties into Middle Deadfall
Lake's north side. Rejoin Sisson-Callahan Trail near this colorful
marsh, then wander past a pure stand of western white pine on your
way to Mount Eddy. At 3.1 miles, just before the first of three alpine
ponds, foxtail pine appear. Three superb campsites exist at the first
pond, which reflects the orange metamorphosed rock of the west flank
of Mount Eddy.

Reach the meadow above Upper Deadfall Lake at 3.3 miles. A
sand-bottomed brook wanders through the meadow, where wild onion, buttercup, and bird's-foot grow next to a spring. The path escalates southwesterly, allowing numerous views of the Deadfall Lakes
and the Trinity Alps in the distance. At 4 miles you reach Mount
Eddy's pass. The trail momentarily grows faint: Head straight for
Mount Eddy and soon regain the path. The way then climbs relentlessly for the next 0.7 mile, graced by displays of Lake Siskiyou to the
east and Castle Crags to the southeast and a mix of shiny metamorphic stones and alpine wildflowers at your feet.

An excellent vista of Mount Shasta awaits at Mount Eddy's summit,
where an abandoned lookout still stands. In addition to all previously
encountered views, you'll also see Black Butte (described in hike 60).

An eastward view from Mount Eddy's summit shows Black Butte below Mount Shasta.

CASTLE DOME

Length: 4.8 miles round trip
Hiking time: 3 hours
High point: 4,700 feet
Total elevation gain: 1,950 feet
Difficulty: strenuous
Season: early April through mid-November

Water: bring your own
Maps: USGS 7.5' Dunsmuir, USFS Castle Crags Wilderness
Information: Castle Crags State Park

Castle Crags' steep granite spires entice many an I-5 traveler into the wilderness for a trek. On this hike you'll climb through the forest to Castle Dome, a massive stone bulwark that anchors the Crags and allows impressive views, including the brilliant white visage of Mount Shasta.

Leave I-5 at the Castle Crags State Park/Castella Exit, 48 miles north of Redding and 6 miles south of Dunsmuir, and follow signs west to the state park's headquarters. Turn right and take the paved main road through the campground for 0.3 mile, following signs for photography and vista point. It's another twisty mile from the campground to the trailhead.

The trail begins on the right, about 150 feet down the road from the parking area. A trail junction awaits after a flat 0.25 mile. Go left and

A view of Mount Shasta from the Castle Dome Trail

begin a climb under a pine/fir canopy that doesn't end until you reach Castle Dome.

At 0.5 mile you briefly join the Pacific Crest Trail and then take a signed trail to the right. Go right again at another trail fork at 1 mile. Tantalizing glimpses of vertical granite slabs lure you ever upward and help you forget the vigorous climb. At 2 miles a path heads left 0.2 mile to lush and shady Indian Springs, the hike's only sure source of water. Stay right for the final 0.9 mile. Over the last 0.5 mile, you'll enter the Crags proper, an area that's becoming increasingly popular with rock climbers.

Finally, at 2.9 miles, you reach the base of Castle Dome. Head to a chain-link fence at a small saddle on the dome's west side, where you'll

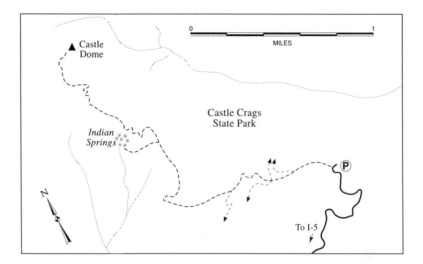

have the best view of the broad shoulders and summit of 14,162-foot Mount Shasta, the undisputed mountain king of Northern California. Girard Ridge and other forested mountains stretch eastward; Grey Ridge, Shasta Bally, and Bully Choop lie southward; and the Crags dominate the west.

You'll undoubtedly be tempted to climb to the top of Castle Dome. Do so only if you have rock-climbing experience, shoes with good tread, and dry rock. The least dangerous route begins on the dome's south side and then follows a crack around to the east. Be sure of your footing and the route, and remember that it's usually easier to climb up than down.

59 SULPHUR CREEK AND BURSTARSE FALLS

Length: 6.4 miles round trip
Hiking time: 4 hours
High point: 3,250 feet
Total elevation gain: 950 feet
Difficulty: moderate
Season: year-round; occasional winter snow

Water: available from creeks
Maps: USGS 7.5' Dunsmuir, USFS Castle Crags Wilderness
Information: Mount Shasta Ranger District, Shasta-Trinity National Forest

This hike offers solitude as you enjoy clear streams, a 40-foot waterfall, and extensive views of Castle Crags' steep granite spires.

Drive I-5 north of Redding 48 miles or south of Dunsmuir 6 miles, then take the Castle Crags/Castella Exit. Head west on Castle Creek

141

The Castle Crags rise high above the trail to Burstarse Falls.

Road for 3.2 miles, then turn into the large parking area on the right.

The trail begins on the northwest side of the parking area, quickly passes a grove of knobcone pine, then starts a steady climb through chaparral. Look south for views of Gray Rocks and Flume Creek Ridge on the other side of Castle Creek.

You reach the Pacific Crest Trail at 0.6 mile. Turn right and climb

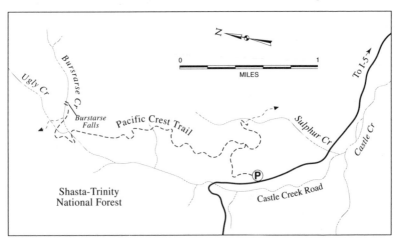

gently, then gain an exquisite northeasterly view of the massive granite bulk of Castle Crags. Continue downhill to the serene, shaded waters of Sulphur Creek at 1.2 miles, which originate in the high peaks above.

Retrace your steps and pass the previously encountered trail junction at 1.8 miles. The path now gently undulates under the shade of ponderosa pine, Douglas fir, incense cedar, and black oak and allows good views to the south and west. At 2.8 miles you reach Popcorn Spring, where bigleaf maple and black oak shade the small creek as it slides over smooth slabs of granite. The first meeting with Burstarse Creek occurs at 3.6 miles, but the waterfall awaits farther up the trail. Cross the misnamed Ugly Creek at 3.9 miles, then continue another 0.1 mile to where the trail makes a 180-degree turn just above Burstarse Creek.

Leave the path here, and carefully make your way down to the creek (watch for poison oak), taking note of a small wading pool as you cross to the creek's far side. Continue below the canyon wall 100 yards to Burstarse Falls. The greatest amount of water makes the 40-foot plunge in spring and early summer when snow melts, but the area at the falls remains lush, shaded, and cool even in late summer.

60   BLACK BUTTE

Length: 5.2 miles round trip
Hiking time: 4 hours
High point: 6,325 feet
Total elevation gain: 1,850 feet
Difficulty: moderate
Season: mid-May through mid-November

Water: bring your own
Map: USGS 7.5' City of Mount Shasta
Information: Mount Shasta Ranger District, Shasta-Trinity National Forest

To those traveling I-5 in far Northern California, Black Butte looms as a dark, impossibly steep visage rising 2,400 vertical feet, yet less than a mile away. Surprisingly, a moderately graded trail can take you to the summit of this young volcano, where spectacular views await.

Take the Central Mount Shasta Exit off I-5, head east through town for 0.7 mile on Lake Street, then curve left onto Everitt Memorial Highway. Drive 2.2 miles, then turn left onto the dirt road signed for Black Butte Trail. Turn right after 0.1 mile, drive 1 mile, then swing 90 degrees and head straight for Black Butte. Go right (north) at a road fork 0.3 mile farther. After another 1.2 miles, turn left at a powerline undercrossing, and continue the final 0.7 mile to the trailhead, which is a small turnaround in the road.

The path initially travels through a forest of Douglas fir, white fir, incense cedar, and ponderosa pine. Common trailside shrubs include bush chinquapin, huckleberry oak, and tobacco brush. As you continue the steady climb across talus slopes, the first of several sweeping vis-

Black Butte's summit offers an impressive panoramic view of Northern California that includes Mount Shasta.

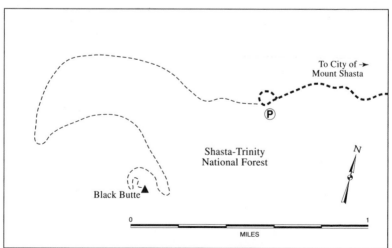

tas opens up to the north, where you'll see Shasta Valley and the town of Weed directly below and southern Oregon's Mount McLoughlin, a Cascade sibling of Mount Shasta. At 1.1 miles the path swings southwest, allowing views of Mount Eddy (hike 57, Mount Eddy and the Deadfall Lakes) and the Klamath Mountains to the west and Castle Dome (hike 58) and the rest of Castle Crags to the south.

At 1.6 miles the trail heads east, offering you the entrancing image of Mount Shasta, and eventually swings southeast past western white pine, mountain hemlock, and red fir. This is a good spot to search the far southeast horizon for Magee Peak and Lassen Peak, which lie near the Cascades' southern boundary.

You'll climb northwest and then southeast again before switchbacking up the last stretch to Black Butte's summit at 2.6 miles, where all the previously encountered views come together in a 360-degree panorama. Mount Shasta, though, will certainly demand most of your attention. This majestic peak, elevation 14,162 feet, is a stratovolcano formed by massive eruptions that began about one million years ago. Black Butte, a plug dome, formed from thick pasty lava extruded in four different eruptions about ten thousand years ago, making it quite young by geological standards.

61 WHITNEY BUTTE TRAIL

Length: 7 miles round trip
Hiking time: 4 hours
High point: 5,004 feet
Total elevation gain: 500 feet
Difficulty: easy

Season: early April through late
November
Water: none, bring your own
Map: USGS 7.5' Schonchin Butte
Information: Lava Beds National
Monument

Hike through an open landscape past chunks of recently extruded dark lava to the top of a small volcano, where you'll have sweeping views of Mount Shasta, Lava Beds National Monument, and other volcanic landforms of far northeastern California.

If coming from the north on Highway 139, turn right 5 miles south of the town of Tulelake. Follow Lava Beds National Monument signs for 24 miles, turn right (west) at the sign for Merrill Ice Cave, then go 0.6 mile to the trailhead. If coming from the south on Highway 139, turn left 26 miles northwest of Canby and follow Lava Beds National Monument signs 16 miles to the Visitor Center. From the Visitor Center, go north 1.2 miles, turn left (west) at the sign for Merrill Ice Cave, then drive the final 0.6 mile to the trailhead.

At the trailhead you'll see a short, paved trail to Merrill Ice Cave. Four tons of the roof collapsed in 1992, and at last report, safety concerns forced the closure of this cave. Check with the Visitor Center to see if it has reopened and what safety precautions are necessary.

Various bunchgrasses and wildflowers line the path, as do sagebrush, bitterbrush, mountain mahogany, and western juniper. These plants can tolerate the dry, desertlike conditions of northeastern California, a region that sees little rainfall.

Along the trail's first mile lies black basaltic rock, which once oozed as a hot liquid from nearby fissures to eventually cool into the twisted shapes you see around you. You'll also be treated to views of Tule Lake and the irrigated fields to the lake's north as well as 6,618-foot Mount Dome looming to the northwest and 9,495-foot Mount McLoughlin, a cousin of Mount Shasta, far off in southern Oregon.

The first sight of the steep, snow-clad slopes of 14,162-foot Mount Shasta awaits at 1.8 miles. Bear left at a trail fork at 2.2 miles, then border the north flank of Whitney Butte. At 3.3 miles you'll see the Medicine Lake highlands just to the south as well as the massive Black Lava Flow, a sheet of basalt covering several square miles. Your trail ends at the base of the Black Lava Flow, where you'll see lichens, sagebrush, and a few other plants gaining a tenuous foothold on the 20-foot-high sheet of inhospitable rock.

Be sure to climb to the top of Whitney Butte. Begin by a trailside ponderosa pine about 3.3 miles from the trailhead, where you get the

A stunted juniper on the summit of Whitney Butte frames a view of lava flows and Mount Shasta.

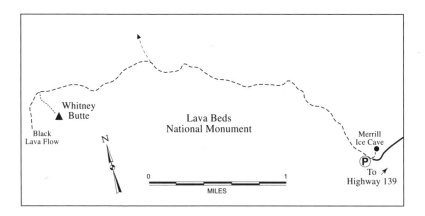

first good views of the edge of the Black Lava Flow. From the top you can view the small volcano's collapsed center and also enjoy a 360-degree view of the entire volcanic landscape.

Consider exploring some of the Lava Beds National Monument's lava caves before leaving. Inquire at the Visitor Center about the best caves and proper safety procedures.

62 PATTERSON LAKE AND SQUAW PEAK

Length: 18 miles round trip
Hiking time: 3 to 4 days
High point: 9,150 feet
Total elevation gain: 3,350 feet
Difficulty: moderate
Season: mid-June through late October
Water: generally available from lakes and streams, but none for the last 2.6 miles

Maps: USGS 7.5' Soup Creek, USGS 7.5' Eagle Peak, USGS 7.5' Warren Peak, USFS South Warner Wilderness
Information: Warner Mountain Ranger District, Modoc National Forest

This hike takes you through dense fir forest to lush meadows and eventually to high sagebrush desert country. Along the way you'll visit beautiful Patterson Lake and enjoy expansive views of the mountainous landscape of northeastern California, southern Oregon, and northwestern Nevada.

From the junction of Highways 395 and 299 in Alturas, head south on Highway 395 for 1.1 miles, then turn left onto County Road 56. Drive another 13.8 miles, then bear right at a major junction 0.3 mile past the point where the paved road changes to dirt. Follow this main dirt road another 10.4 miles, then turn left where a sign directs you the final 1.5 miles to "Pine Creek Trail," your trailhead. Avoid other signed roads taking off from the main dirt road that have destinations with the word "pine" in them.

The trail begins its steady uphill climb, usually within earshot of tributaries of the South Fork of Pine Creek, under the shade of white fir, Jeffrey pine, and quaking aspen. However, by the time you pass a small, shallow pond on the left side of the trail at 0.6 mile, the latter two trees have been replaced by whitebark pine, a hardy species that you'll encounter frequently from here on.

Reach a trail fork at 1.3 miles. The left-hand trail leads 50 yards downhill to a small but relatively deep lake with campsites at both the west and east ends. At 2.3 miles you'll pass another trailside pond on the right, also with campsites at the east and west ends. If other hikers have already claimed these, continue 100 yards due north of the pond to a lake with two sites on the east side.

Just past these two bodies of water, the trail leaves the white fir and whitebark pine forest. You now have the first open view of the Pine Creek Basin: a huge glacial bowl with 1,800-foot rock walls overlooking both sagebrush-covered slopes and lush, verdant meadows.

About 100 feet from the forest, the trail makes a ninety-degree turn to cross the creek and then a 50-foot stretch of meadow. Look carefully for two rock cairns on the other side of the meadow, just in case the trail is obscured.

Your way immediately leaves the meadow behind and starts a steady ascent of 1,600 feet over the next 2.4 miles. Initially you travel through a white fir forest and then pass through an aspen grove. At 0.5 mile from the creek crossing, leave most of the trees behind and walk along the sagebrush-dotted open slope with mule ear, lupine, Indian

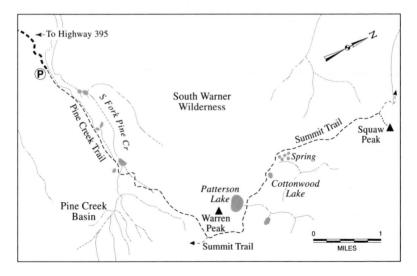

Warren Peak's volcanic rim guards the glacial cirque that holds Patterson Lake.

paintbrush, and other flowers keeping you company. Be sure to look for the numerous antelope and deer that call this paradise home. You'll also encounter several small creeks along the way, but these can dry up by late summer.

After enjoying the spectacular view of the Pine Creek Basin as you climb, you'll be rewarded with even more stupendous views at 4.7 miles when you reach the ridgecrest junction with Summit Trail, which runs north–south along the crest of the South Warner Mountains. Look south to the commanding summit of 9,892-foot Eagle Peak, the highest mountain in the Warners. To the east lie the irrigated green fields of Surprise Valley, along with three large, dry alkaline lakes. The desolate stretches of Nevada's basin and range dominate the landscape farther east. To the immediate north rise the steep sides of Warren Peak, and to the west and southwest Mount Shasta and Lassen Peak punctuate the skyline.

Once you've recovered from both the climb and the awe-inspiring view, head left up to a saddle frequented by numerous Clark's nutcrackers. Look northward for views of final-destination Squaw Peak, the North Warner Mountains, part of Goose Lake, and tall mountains stretching into southern Oregon. Also, note the sedimentary rock layers here, which are overlain by volcanic basalts. The Warner Mountains were largely formed by volcanic eruptions over sediments that were then pushed up along faults as adjacent valleys, such as Surprise Valley, dropped down.

From the saddle the trail descends to the deep, cold, and clear waters of Patterson Lake at 5.5 miles. This beautiful body of water sits in a glacial cirque surrounded by 600-foot-high walls of basalt, crowned by 9,710-foot Warren Peak. You'll find several good campsites near the lake's west side.

The trail continues downhill 0.7 mile to the shallow waters of Cottonwood Lake. This small lake offers two campsites and good views of cliffs to the west.

Consider doing the last 2.8 miles to the summit of Squaw Peak as a day hike, using one of the two lakes as a base camp. The path enters a meadow filled with corn lilies and then passes a spring 0.2 mile past Cottonwood Lake, your last source of water for the remainder of the hike. Ascend briefly from here, then walk along the crest of the South Warner Range past mountain mahogany, sagebrush, and numerous wildflowers as you enjoy the wide, open views to the west and east.

Once beside Squaw Peak, located 9 miles from the trailhead, you can easily pick a cross-country route to the top. From here, you'll take in a breathtaking 360-degree view over all of northeastern California and large sections of southern Oregon and northwestern Nevada.

63 BURNEY FALLS

Length: 4.9 miles round trip
Hiking time: 3 hours
High point: 3,000 feet
Total elevation gain: 300 feet
Difficulty: easy
Season: year-round; occasional
    winter snow

Water: available near the
    Visitor's Information Center,
    in campgrounds, and from
    Burney Creek
Map: USGS 7.5' Burney Falls
Information: McArthur–Burney
    Falls Memorial State Park

This state park offers a relatively easy family hike that's doable year-round. Burney Falls is breathtaking, and everyone enjoys Burney Creek's lush coolness and the soothing sound of wind through the pine and fir.

From the junction of Highways 299 and 89, take Highway 89 north for 6 miles, then turn left and follow signs for McArthur–Burney Falls Memorial State Park. Park in the lot just beyond the check-in station.

First, buy a brochure that explains what you'll see at the twenty-four numbered posts along Falls Trail. Then follow your ears in the direction of roaring water, which brings you to the falls overlook. Springs from a vast underground reservoir feed Burney Creek a daily supply of 200 million gallons of clear, cold water, which then crashes 129 feet over Burney Falls into a deep aqua-blue pool.

From the falls overlook, head downhill on the paved trail. After 300 feet it bends left, taking you to the edge of the huge pool at the falls'

Burney Falls fascinates all viewers, especially the youngest ones.

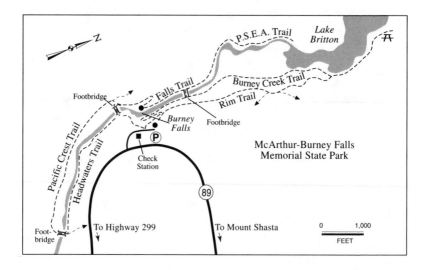

base, where cool mists from the pounding water caress your face.

Follow the path downstream. Just before Falls Trail turns left and crosses a footbridge, stay straight and begin Burney Creek Trail, which follows Burney Creek downstream 0.8 mile to Lake Britton. After passing through a forest of ponderosa pine, Douglas fir, and incense cedar, the trail skirts the edge of Lake Britton and then reaches a trail fork 0.5 mile from the bridge. Go left and walk 0.3 mile down to the lake's shore, where you'll find a picnic area and swimming beach. (If you desire, take the right-hand Rim Trail, which climbs up to the canyon rim and then back to the falls overlook.)

Return to the footbridge just below Burney Falls, then cross it, pausing at the center to admire the cold water rushing below your feet. Turn right on the other side of the bridge onto P.S.E.A. Trail. This path, well-shaded by Douglas fir, white alder, and dogwood, stretches a level and peaceful 0.5 mile along Burney Creek. The trail ends at a gate, near where you'll find some tranquil spots to picnic and watch the water flow.

When you're ready to continue, go back to Falls Trail and follow it uphill, enjoying a view of the falls along the way. A trail fork awaits at the top; go right, then immediately left onto the Pacific Crest Trail. Travel the famous PCT for 0.7 mile through the forest to a bridge across Burney Creek. Note that Burney Creek has very little water here; most of the springs that feed Burney Falls enter downstream. Turn left just past the bridge onto Headwaters Trail, which travels near the creek and reaches a trail fork after 0.5 mile. Turn left to a bridge, where you'll see the now-rushing waters of Burney Creek just before the big plunge. When you're finished, go back to Headwaters Trail, turn left, and walk 0.1 mile back to the falls overlook and the parking lot.

64 MAGEE PEAK AND THE THOUSAND LAKES WILDERNESS

Length: 12.6 miles round trip
Hiking time: 2 days
High point: 8,550 feet
Total elevation gain: 3,200 feet
Difficulty: moderate to strenuous
Season: mid-June through October; zillions of mosquitos in June and July
Water: available only from Everett and Magee lakes; bring your own
Map: USGS 7.5' Thousand Lakes Valley
Information: Hat Creek Ranger District, Lassen National Forest

This trip takes you to two beautiful, cirque-surrounded, subalpine glacial lakes much less visited than lakes in nearby Lassen Park, and then continues to the summit of Magee Peak, where you'll have a panoramic view that encompasses most of Northern California.

To reach the trailhead, turn west off Highway 89 onto Road 26,

Fallen whitebark pine and Lassen Peak from Magee Peak summit

153

which begins 0.4 mile north of the Hat Creek Work Center and 10 miles south of Highway 299. Follow this road 7.5 miles through several junctions with lesser roads, as indicated by signs for Road 26, Thousand Lakes Wilderness, and Cypress Camp. At 7.5 miles turn left onto Road 34N60 for the last 2.6 miles to the parking area, marked by a "Thousand Lakes Wilderness–Cypress Camp" sign.

Walk up the rough road, bearing right and then left at two intersections within the first 200 yards, then cross seasonal Eiler Gulch Creek. From here, the trail climbs southeast at a moderate grade under the partial shade of white fir, Jeffrey pine, and the occasional western juniper and then levels at 1.7 miles upon reaching the Thousand Lakes Wilderness boundary.

You'll reach a trail fork 0.25 mile farther. Bear right, then right again, at two other trail forks within the next 0.7 mile. The path then climbs gently through a forest of red and white fir and lodgepole and western white pine. Pinemat manzanita covers the ground, but you'll also see greenleaf manzanita, bush chinquapin, tobacco brush, and numerous wildflowers.

Forest-encircled Everett and Magee lakes lie 1.8 miles past the last trail junction at an elevation of 7,200 feet. Both boast good views of the misnamed, though magnificent, Red Cliff to the south and the rest of the glacial cirque to the west, and offer excellent swimming opportunities in late summer. You can camp at either lake, though Magee has more sites.

For the final 1.8-mile push to Magee Peak, bear right at the trail fork by Magee Lake. As you climb steadily and enjoy increasingly open views of the surrounding mountains, the red fir disappear as mountain hemlock and whitebark pine, which can better handle winter's fierce

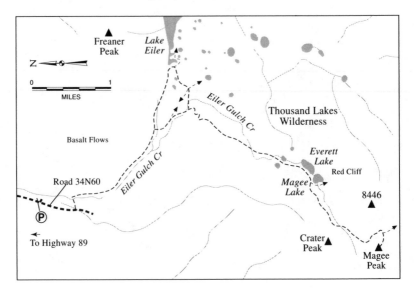

winds and heavy snowloads, take over. Note the various basaltic and other types of multicolored volcanic rocks.

You'll crest the ridge 1.5 miles from the lake. From here, take the faint path on your right 0.3 mile to Magee Peak summit, elevation 8,550 feet. You're standing on the rim of an ancient volcano that encompassed 8,683-foot Crater Peak (0.5 mile north) and Peak 8446 (0.3 mile southeast), among others. Glaciers sculpted most of the Thousand Lakes Wilderness, which stretches east to the Hat Creek valley.

The 360-degree, long-range view, however, will demand most of your attention. Lassen Peak (hike 70) dominates the skyline to the southeast. Swinging northward, you'll see Lassen Park, the Fall River Valley, and Mount Shasta. West of Mount Shasta lie the Klamath Mountains, which stretch south to the Coast Range.

If you wish to extend your trip on the way back, turn right at the first trail fork 1.8 miles below Everett Lake. Follow this path 0.7 mile through a trail junction and past a lily pond and other lush scenery to the shores of Lake Eiler, located at Freaner Peak's base. The lake, often visited by both hikers and mosquitos, offers numerous campsites. From the water's western edge, follow the trail signed for Cypress Camp for 1 mile past the massive black basalt flows, then turn right for the downhill roll to the trailhead.

65 CINDER CONE, SNAG LAKE, AND BUTTE LAKE

Length: 14-mile loop
Hiking time: 2 days
High point: 6,900 feet
Total elevation gain: 1,700 feet
Difficulty: moderate
Season: late June through October

Water: available only from Snag Lake, Grassy Creek, and Butte Lake
Maps: USGS 7.5' Prospect Peak, USGS 7.5' Mount Harkness
Information: Lassen Volcanic National Park

Cinder Cone's volcanic wonderland combines with a gently undulating trail around two of Lassen Park's largest lakes to make a good overnight backpacking trip. The journey offers open views of Lassen Peak and other prominent mountains from Cinder Cone's summit and the shores of both Butte and Snag lakes.

To reach the trailhead, drive Highway 44 for 11 miles east of its junction with Highway 89. Turn right at the sign for Butte Lake, go 6 miles to the Butte Lake Campground, then park in the lot by the lake's north shore.

The trail begins 100 yards up the road by the ranger station. Grab the nature trail brochure from the trailhead box; it explains in detail the natural history of the route's first 2.4 miles. Also, start the trip with plenty of water; there's none trailside until you reach Snag Lake.

At the trip's beginning, you'll join Nobles Immigrant Trail, a route used by thousands of California-bound pioneers in the 1850s and 1860s. Follow this historic path as it parallels the edge of the brooding black basalt hillocks of the Fantastic Lava Beds and passes by Jeffrey pine and the occasional lodgepole pine.

The trail forks 0.4 mile from the trailhead. Bear left and gently ascend 1 mile to another fork. (Some backpackers may want to leave their packs at this trail fork before exploring the top of Cinder Cone. After returning, they can go right, then left, to continue the hike.) Bear

Painted Dunes, Fantastic Lava Beds, and Snag Lake from the top of Cinder Cone

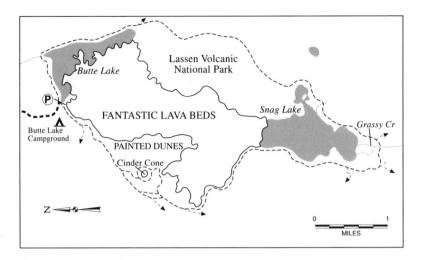

left again, and gain 750 feet of elevation during the steep climb to Cinder Cone's sparsely vegetated 6,900-foot summit.

Formed by at least five eruptions over the last 500 years, Cinder Cone last erupted in 1851. Massive basalt flows from the cone's base spread for several square miles to the south and east, creating the Fantastic Lava Beds. Hydrothermally altered ash accounts for the gray and orange Painted Dunes on the cone's southern edges.

When you're done exploring, head down the trail on the south side. Once you leave the cone's flank, turn left at two successive trail junctures within 50 yards, then head south 0.4 mile to another trail fork. Go left along the Fantastic Lava Beds 1.5 miles through a mixed forest of lodgepole pine, Jeffrey pine, and white fir to Snag Lake, which formed about 300 years ago when lava flows from Cinder Cone dammed Grassy Creek. You can camp at any of the numerous sites near the lake's west and east shores.

After reaching Snag Lake, the trail travels 1.6 miles to a trail junction. Turn left here and again 0.3 mile farther. The way now heads east along the lake's south shore, crossing Grassy Creek and passing through a lush area of springs and flowers to reach yet another trail fork after 0.5 mile. Turn left and walk 1.8 miles along the lake's east shore, where you'll have good views of the Fantastic Lava Beds and Cinder Cone.

From Snag Lake's northeast shore, you'll initially travel by hundreds of aspen as the trail gently rises, levels, then descends through 3 miles of forest. Then you'll encounter a trail fork (go left) just before reaching Butte Lake.

The trail then goes 1.6 miles along Butte Lake's shore, where you'll find aspen, black cottonwood, and willow that frame views of the Fantastic Lava Beds, Cinder Cone, Lassen Peak, and Prospect Peak. From the lake's outlet, climb steeply 150 feet, then gently descend the last 0.6 mile to the parking lot.

66 TERRACE, SHADOW, AND CLIFF LAKES

Length: 8.4 miles round trip
Hiking time: 5 hours
High point: 7,900 feet
Total elevation gain: 1,900 feet
Difficulty: moderate
Season: early July to mid-October

Water: available from lakes and streams
Maps: USGS 7.5' West Prospect Peak, USGS 7.5' Reading Peak
Information: Lassen Volcanic National Park

Hike through a dense forest by a rushing stream to a large, lush meadow, then continue to three of Lassen Park's most beautiful lakes. Along the way you'll be treated to impressive views of Lassen Peak and numerous other high peaks and ridges.

From the junction of Highways 44 and 89, drive 10.2 miles on Highway 89, then turn left into the parking lot across the road from the Hat Lake sign. Alternatively, reach the trailhead by driving 24 miles on Highway 89 from the junction of Highways 36 and 89.

The signed trail begins just east of what is left of Hat Lake. A large mudflow swept down from Mount Lassen in 1915 and dammed the West Fork of Hat Creek, creating Hat Lake; however, the lake quickly filled with stream sediments, and now only a small pond remains, which will eventually turn to meadow. Such a fate befalls most lakes but usually takes much longer.

After allowing a brief glimpse of Lassen Peak, the trail begins its climb to Paradise Meadows through a mixed forest of western white pine, red fir, and mountain hemlock. At 1.3 miles a 20-foot, multistep waterfall awaits on the right.

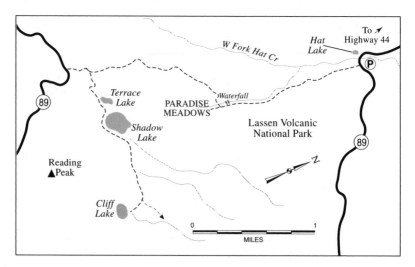

Two park rangers hike past Terrace Lake.

Continue to a trail fork just past the waterfall and then bear left for the level 100-yard stroll to expansive Paradise Meadows. Here the swift waters of a tributary of the West Fork of Hat Creek slow to a lazy meander through grasses and a variety of wildflowers. The talus-sloped heights that house Terrace and Cliff lakes stretch upward to the south, with Reading Peak rising even higher in the distance.

After absorbing the pleasant ambience of Paradise Meadows, go back to the trail fork, cross the creek, and head uphill. The trail eventually offers excellent views of Mount Lassen looming to the west from gaps in the mountain hemlock forest. At 2.7 miles you'll reach a trail fork. The right fork heads 0.3 mile uphill to post 27 on Highway 89. Head downhill to the left for 0.3 mile to Terrace Lake, where a grassy beach area offers easy swimming access for those willing to brave the chilly waters. The much larger and deeper Shadow Lake lies 0.1 mile east. From the eastern shore, you'll see its aquamarine waters reflecting a shimmering visage of Lassen Peak.

About 0.6 mile after leaving Shadow Lake, an unsigned path heads south on the right. Follow it 0.15 mile to the aptly named Cliff Lake. The namesake talus shoulders keep watch over the shallow corn lily– and red mountain heather–ringed waters. Note the red fir and mountain hemlock growing on the lake's island. This hike's final destination is an excellent spot for a quiet picnic.

67 TWIN LAKES, HORSESHOE LAKE, AND GRASSY SWALE

Length: 15.2 miles round trip
Hiking time: 2 days
High point: 7,800 feet
Total elevation gain: 1,800 feet
Difficulty: easy to moderate
Season: early July through early October

Water: available from creeks and lakes
Maps: USGS 7.5' Reading Peak, USGS 7.5' Mount Harkness, USGS 7.5' Prospect Peak, USGS 7.5' West Prospect Peak
Information: Lassen Volcanic National Park

A long stroll through meadows, opportunities to explore six lakes, and a visit to a waterfall highlight this long day hike or easy backpack trip.

From the intersection of Highways 44 and 89, drive 12.9 miles on Highway 89 and turn east (at marker 36) into Summit Lake's north shore campground. From the intersection of Highways 36 and 89, drive 20.2 miles on Highway 89. Park near Summit Lake's north shore.

Cross the wooden footbridge that leads to a trail sign, then turn left. Gain 500 feet over the first mile in an open forest blanketed by pinemat manzanita. Look left to inspect Hat Mountain, and gaze behind to observe the east faces of Lassen Peak, Crescent Crater, and Chaos Crags. Typical Lassen Park conifers abound here, including mountain hemlock, red and white fir, and lodgepole and western white pine.

At 1 mile you reach a broad plateau and bear right at the signed junction. The trail begins a moderate descent at 1.3 miles and then reaches driftwood-lined Echo Lake at 1.8 miles (no camping allowed). The path climbs away from the lake at 2 miles, leads gently down to a pea-green, algae-laced pond on the right at 2.4 miles, and then, after another 0.3

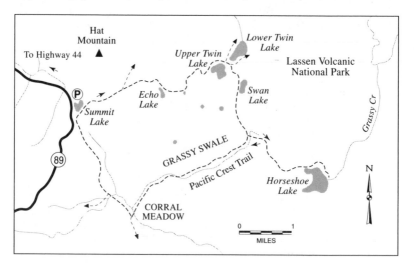

mile, borders the right side of a long, skinny pond lined with grass.

Reach the shore of Upper Twin Lake at 3.2 miles, and enjoy a scenic stroll past several campsites. The trail departs this forest-surrounded lake after 0.4 mile, then leads to Lower Twin Lake a mere 100 yards farther. Bear right and pass by a number of flat spots suitable for camping.

Go right at the signed trail intersection at 4 miles, where the route promptly steepens, allowing views of aqua-colored Lower Twin Lake on the right. The dry, open, hillside trail flattens 0.2 mile farther, staying mostly level to the attractive, secluded Swan Lake, off the trail to the left at 4.5 miles. You can camp on all sides of this shallow lake.

Enjoy easy hiking along a broad plateau, then turn left at the signed trail intersection 0.3 mile beyond Swan Lake. Reach a signed trail junction at 5.6 miles and bear left toward Horseshoe Lake. The next 1.4 miles are on level forest trail. Horseshoe Lake ranks as the biggest lake on this trip and has ample camping. To complete your trip, retrace your steps 1.4 miles, then go left at the trail marker at 8.4 miles.

Slender stretches of Grassy Swale's meadow appear intermittently over the next 3.5 miles. Numerous flowers persist here into early October, and camping is permitted in the neighboring lodgepole pine forest.

The path crosses the meadow at 9.1 miles, where you bear left at a signed trail junction. Descend to a crossing of Grassy Swale Creek at 10.5 miles. The trail eventually topples into Kings Creek at 12.4 miles. Cross carefully, then bear right at the signed trail junction near a cluster of campsites at Corral Meadow.

A steep climb ensues, rewarding you after 0.2 mile with an excellent view of a waterfall plunging 50 feet into Kings Creek. The trail then negotiates two consecutive stream crossings, followed by a signed trail junction at 13.1 miles, where you bear right.

A steady climb through forest takes you into a corn lily–covered minimeadow at 14.8 miles. The trail becomes the Summit Lake south campground road 0.2 mile farther. Head north to the lake, then choose either of two scant paths around Summit Lake's east and west shores to return to the north shore parking area at 15.2 miles.

68 KINGS CREEK FALLS AND SIFFORD LAKES

Length: 5.3 miles round trip
Hiking time: 3 hours
High point: 7,200 feet
Total elevation gain: 500 feet
Difficulty: easy

Season: late June through
    October
Water: available from Kings
    Creek and Sifford Lakes
Map: USGS 7.5' Reading Peak
Information: Lassen Volcanic
    National Park

Hike through verdant, flower-filled meadows bordering the cascading waters of Kings Creek to a 50-foot waterfall, then escape the crowds by hiking up to the Sifford Lakes, where tranquility and good swimming await. You can camp overnight at the lakes, but get a back-country permit from park headquarters.

Drive to post 32 on the Highway 89, which is 16.7 miles from the intersection of Highways 44 and 89 and 17.5 miles from the intersection of Highways 36 and 89, and park in the lot on the north side of the road.

The trail leaves from the road's south side and immediately parallels the meadow that borders the clear waters of Kings Creek. As you pass under the branches of mountain hemlock, red fir, western white pine, and lodgepole pine, look out into the meadow for grazing deer. Go left at a trail fork at 0.4 mile and then right at another fork at 0.6 mile. The gentler left trail rejoins your trail before reaching the falls.

The path now descends a rocky stretch next to a series of small cascades: Watch your step. The route levels after leaving the cascades behind and then meets the trail to Sifford Lakes at 1 mile. Go left for the last 100 yards to the top of Kings Creek Falls. Here you'll see the roaring water tumbling 50 feet from a lush meadow to the rocks below.

After steeping yourself in the beauty of this spot, retrace your steps and cross the creek on a wooden bridge at the above-mentioned trail fork for Sifford Lakes. After a stiff initial climb, the path passes under a talus cliff with two small caves near the top and then, 0.6 mile from Kings Creek, reaches shallow Bench Lake, which usually dries up by late summer. Ascend gently to a trail fork 0.4 mile past Bench Lake; go right and climb 0.3 mile to another trail fork. Go left for the final 0.4 mile to the first of the Sifford Lakes. This lake has a camping site on the north side and is deep enough for swimming. A faint trail continues along the lake's edge and heads 0.4 mile northwest to the other Sifford Lakes. The next lake encountered offers excellent swimming

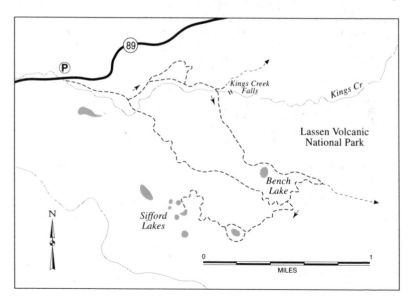

Kings Creek above Kings Creek Falls

and two campsites. You can easily visit the other small, shallow lakes in the flat basin by walking cross-country.

Once you've finished exploring the Sifford Lakes, head back down the main trail 0.4 mile below the first Sifford Lake to the trail fork. Go left, and hike downhill 0.9 mile to Kings Creek. Cross the creek and rejoin the previously traveled path for the last 0.4 mile to the trailhead.

69 CRUMBAUGH LAKE AND BUMPASS HELL

Length: 6 miles round trip
Hiking time: 4 hours
High point: 8,350 feet
Total elevation gain: 1,500 feet
Difficulty: moderate
Season: late June through October

Water: bring your own
Maps: USGS 7.5' Reading Peak, USGS 7.5' Lassen Peak
Information: Lassen Volcanic National Park

This walk takes you in the back way to Bumpass Hell, thus avoiding the crowds that reach this entrancing volcanic landscape from the other end of the trail near Lake Helen. Along the way you'll visit Cold Boiling Lake, which lives up to its name, and Crumbaugh Lake, which offers the opportunity for a quiet picnic with scenic views.

Get to post 30 on Highway 89, which is 17.5 miles from the intersection of Highways 44 and 89 and 16.6 miles from the intersection of Highways 36 and 89. Turn onto the road signed for Kings Creek Picnic Area, then drive 0.3 mile to the trailhead parking lot.

The trail begins from the lot's south side. After a brief climb, it stays fairly level through a forest of mountain hemlock, lodgepole pine, and red fir, tree species present for most of the hike. Stay straight at a trail fork at 0.5 mile, then, at 0.7 mile, reach Cold Boiling Lake, where gasses bubble up from far below the lake's bottom.

The trail splits at Cold Boiling Lake. For now, take the left-hand path and descend gently. After a pleasant 0.5-mile stroll, you'll reach a trail fork just above Crumbaugh Lake. Take either path to reach the shore, where you can explore or take a relaxing rest and enjoy the southward view of Mount Conard.

When you've had your fill of Crumbaugh Lake, return to Cold Boiling Lake and take the path signed for Bumpass Hell. As you begin the ascent to this hike's final destination, you'll have views of Bumpass Mountain, Cold Boiling Lake, Crumbaugh Lake, Mount Conard, and many other outstanding topographical features of Lassen Park. You'll also cross a small, flower-bordered stream.

The path reaches a saddle at 2.3 miles, which offers an excellent view of Bumpass Hell, and then descends the final 0.2 mile. Plan to spend a lot of time exploring the steam vents, fumaroles, and mud pots. This hydrothermal activity probably results from groundwater percolating deep underground to a hot magma chamber, which heats it

A boardwalk safely guides hikers through Bumpass Hell's surreal volcanic landscape.

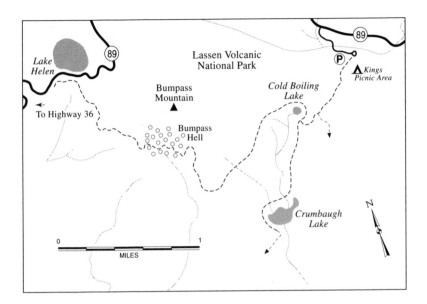

and forces it back up to the surface at Bumpass Hell. Note that for your own safety you must stay on the boardwalk. Watch all young children carefully.

If you want to arrange a car shuttle, leave a vehicle at the Bumpass Hell Nature Trail parking lot, which is on the south side of Lassen Park Road by Lake Helen 23.2 miles from the junction of Highways 44 and 89 and 11 miles from the junction of Highways 36 and 89. To reach the parking lot from Bumpass Hell, hike 1.5 miles northwest and enjoy magnificent views of Lassen Peak (hike 70), Brokeoff Mountain (hike 71), and many other high summits.

70   LASSEN PEAK

Length: 5 miles round trip
Hiking time: 4 hours
High point: 10,453 feet
Total elevation gain: 2,000 feet
Difficulty: moderate

Season: mid-July through
   October
Water: none, bring plenty
Map: USGS 7.5' Lassen Peak
Information: Lassen Volcanic
   National Park

Along with its cousin Mount Shasta, Lassen Peak dominates the skyline of inland Northern California. Climb this massive volcano, which last erupted in 1917, and enjoy panoramic views ranging over 100 miles in every direction.

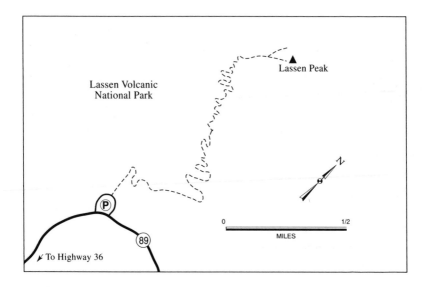

Note that conditions on the summit often differ dramatically from those at the trailhead. Prepare for high winds and snow-reflected sunlight by bringing layers of warm clothes, a hat, sunglasses, and sunblock. Also, don't begin the climb in threatening weather: there's nowhere to hide from lightning strikes.

To reach the signed trailhead, drive 12 miles north on Highway 89 from Highway 36 or 22 miles south on Highway 89 from Highway 44.

After getting the nature brochure at the trailhead, begin the steady ascent and enjoy good views. As you climb, the mountain hemlock trees decrease in size and eventually disappear as whitebark pine, which can better tolerate the harsher weather conditions prevalent at higher elevations, increase in number.

Once you reach the summit at 2.5 miles, the topography of Northern California spreads in all directions: to the north, Mount Shasta, second highest of the Cascade volcanos, reigns in white splendor; the broad Modoc plateau and steep-sided Warner Mountains lie to the northeast; the mighty Sierra Nevada range extends from Lake Almanor south; across the vast extent of the Sacramento Valley, the Coast Range marches westward; and north of the Coast Range, the rocky peaks of the Trinity Alps punctuate the Klamath Mountains.

In the near vicinity of Lassen Park, you can see numerous natural features, including examples of the four major volcano types. Plug dome volcanos, such as Lassen Peak, extrude thick, pasty, andesitic lava. Shield volcanos, such as Prospect Peak 10 miles to the northwest, emit liquid basalt, which can spread for miles. Cinder cones, such as the aptly named "Cinder Cone" 2 miles southwest of Prospect Peak, eject ash, cinders, and larger rocks. Stratovolcanos, such as Mount Shasta, contain layers of andesitic lava, cinders, and ash and are thus called composite volcanos.

The path to Lassen Peak's summit offers good southward views of Mount Diller and Brokeoff Mountain.

Be sure to hike around Lassen Peak's summit and see how the volcanic activity from 1914 to 1917 dramatically altered its topography; much of the snow-encrusted, chunky rock on the top was extruded during that time. One eruption sent an ash cloud 33,000 feet into the air and caused mud and rock to course down the mountain's northeast flank, destroying several square miles of forest now known as the Devastated Area.

71 BROKEOFF MOUNTAIN

Length: 7.2 miles round trip
Hiking time: 5 hours
High point: 9,235 feet
Total elevation gain: 2,550 feet
Difficulty: moderate
Season: mid-July through
   October

Water: available only for the first
   2 miles
Map: USGS 7.5' Lassen Peak
Information: Lassen Volcanic
   National Park

This hike offers two rewards. First, you'll travel through several plant habitats with a variety of multicolored wildflowers. Second, you'll gain an excellent view of Lassen Park and Northern California that rivals that of nearby Lassen Peak (hike 70), but you'll share it with far fewer people. Do, however, read the warning in hike 70, which also applies to this journey.

Find the trailhead at post 2 on Highway 89, which is 4.8 miles from the intersection of Highways 36 and 89 and 29.2 miles from the intersection of Highways 44 and 89.

The path begins near a willow- and alder-lined tributary of Mill Creek. After climbing through a mixed forest of lodgepole and western white pine, it reaches a marshy pond at 0.8 mile. Towering red fir begin dominating the forest as you ascend past several small meadows. For a pleasant side trip, follow the creek at 1.3 miles north 250 yards to the shallow waters of Forest Lake.

The trail then offers increasingly open views as it heads up Brokeoff's south ridge. The final 1.1 miles, a mild ascent to the summit, pass through a weather-tortured subalpine zone, where a few stunted red fir eke out an existence among whitebark pine and mountain hemlock.

The summit of Brokeoff Mountain offers unobstructed views. To the immediate northeast, a ridge punctuated by Mount Diller, Pilot Pinnacle, and Eagle Peak stretches to Lassen Peak's flanks and beyond to Chaos Crags. Long-distance views encompass the Warner Mountains in the far northeast, Lake Almanor to the east, the Sierra Nevada marching southward, the Coast Range and Klamath Mountains to the west and northwest, and the snow-clad slopes of mighty Mount Shasta gleaming to the north.

Brokeoff Mountain, along with nearby Mount Diller, is a remnant of ancient Mount Tehama, which once soared to an elevation of 11,000 to 11,500 feet and boasted a 5.0-mile diameter. A combination of numerous eruptions from its sides and the action of ice-age glaciers slowly

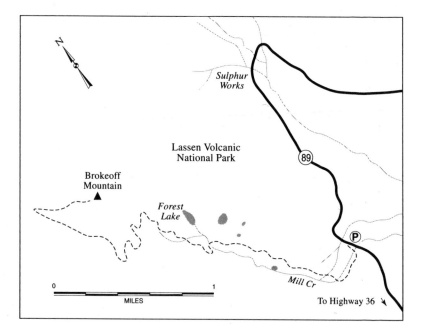

View of Lassen Peak from the top of Brokeoff Mountain

destroyed the mighty volcano. Sulphur Works, part of Mount Tehama's vent, lies 2,400 feet below and 1.0 mile east of Brokeoff's summit. After you finish this hike, walk the short nature trail through this hydrothermally active area (located 1.5 miles north of the Brokeoff Mountain trailhead on Highway 89).

72 BOILING SPRINGS LAKE AND DEVIL'S KITCHEN

Length: 6.2 miles round trip
Hiking time: 3 hours
High point: 6,020 feet
Total elevation: 800 feet
Difficulty: moderate

Season: late May through October
Water: bring your own
Map: USGS 7.5' Reading Peak
Information: Lassen Volcanic National Park

This hike offers impressive geothermal activities; you'll see the multi-colored shoreline of Boiling Springs Lake and watch steam rise from bubbling Hot Springs Creek in Devil's Kitchen.

From Highway 36 in Chester, turn north onto Feather River Drive

Hot Springs Creek at Devil's Kitchen

and follow all signs to Drakesbad. Bear left at 0.7 mile at a road fork, then veer right at another road fork at 6.2 miles onto Warner Valley Road. Turn left onto a signed dirt road at 13.5 miles, then at 13.8 miles go right. Drive 0.3 mile past Warner Valley Campground, and park at the trailhead at 16.9 miles.

Grab the self-guiding nature leaflet from a box by the trailhead. At

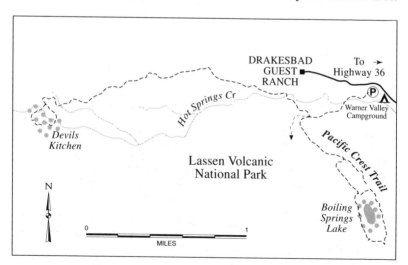

0.1 mile you'll reach Hot Springs Creek, partially fed by Boiling Springs Lake and Devil's Kitchen. Walk above a marsh and alongside a tall stand of lodgepole pines, then cross the creek on a bridge next to a huge white fir.

Note the thermal pool at the Drakesbad Guest Ranch at 0.3 mile. Look for a large, double-trunked incense cedar 0.1 mile farther, which measures 22.5 feet in circumference, then bear left at two trail forks. You'll ascend gently in an open forest of Jeffrey pine and red and white fir, then bear right at 0.7 mile at a signed junction.

After another 0.2 mile, your nose will definitely note the rotten egg odor of hydrogen sulfide emanating from Boiling Springs Lake's steam vents, just prior to actually spotting the lake. Steam escapes through underground vents and fissures, keeping the lake's temperature a hot 125 degrees. A suspension of clay, opal, and iron oxide particles gives the water its yellowish tan color. After circling the lake, retrace your steps 0.5 mile back to the signed marker for Devil's Kitchen.

Bear left upon returning to the meadow next to the above-mentioned double-trunked incense cedar. At 2.1 miles the trail crosses Hot Springs Creek and winds through the Warner Valley's Drakesbad Meadow.

Step into the forest at 2.7 miles as the path gradually climbs to Devil's Kitchen at 3.5 miles. Always stay on the self-guided paths as you explore the 0.5 mile of spur trails to fumaroles, steam vents, boiling springs, and tiny mineral brooks.

73 MILL CREEK

Length: 26 miles round trip
Hiking time: 3 to 4 days
High point: 4,400 feet
Total elevation gain: 2,900 feet
Difficulty: moderate
Season: mid-April through November

Water: available from Mill Creek and numerous trailside streams and springs
Maps: USGS 7.5' Mineral, USGS 7.5' Onion Butte, USGS 7.5' Barkley Mountain
Information: Almanor Ranger District, Lassen National Forest

Mill Creek Trail offers backpackers an ideal spring trip. While trails at higher elevations still lie under several feet of snow, you can enjoy views of a 1,000-foot-high canyon rim, a bounty of wildflowers, and fresh green leaves on deciduous trees. And in autumn, when the first snows cloak distant peaks, those same deciduous tree leaves turn to vibrant shades of pink, orange, and yellow.

Drive to the intersection of Highways 89 and 172, which is located 9 miles east of Mineral and 9 miles northwest of the junction of Highways 32 and 89. Go 3 miles down Highway 172 to the town of Mill Creek, then turn left 0.3 mile past Mill Creek Resort onto an unsigned

Mill Creek begins near Lassen Peak and empties into the Sacramento River south of Red Bluff.

dirt road. Go straight at an intersection 2.8 miles farther, then continue another 3.3 miles to the trailhead.

The journey begins at the far end of the parking area. Douglas fir dominate the forest here and along most of the length of Mill Creek Trail. These stately trees, along with a few incense cedar and large-coned sugar pine, provide ample shade as you gently descend 2.2 miles to a bluff that allows the first views of the rapids and waterfalls of Mill Creek.

The trail then undulates uphill as you pass by numerous dogwood trees (with large, white, six-petaled "flowers" in spring) and cross several streams. After slowly descending back to Mill Creek, you'll find

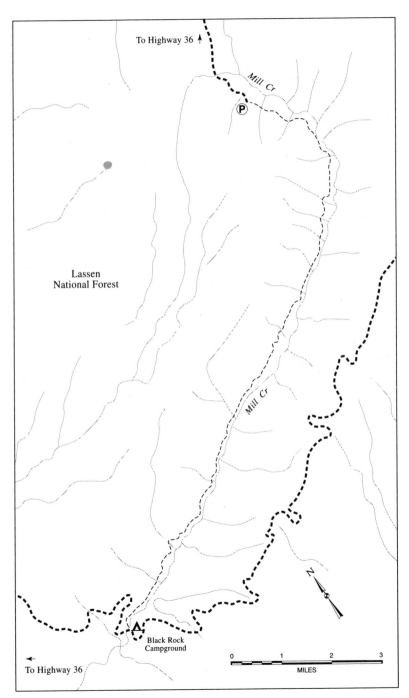

To Highway 36

Mill Cr

P

Lassen
National Forest

Mill Cr

N

Black Rock
Campground

To Highway 36

0   1   2   3

MILES

the first good campsite at 4.5 miles. Spacious, well-shaded, and situated by the water, it makes a good first-day stopping point.

The path again climbs, and at 5.5 miles you'll encounter the relatively rare California nutmeg tree. It sports dark green, stiff, sharp needles; a gentle squeeze of a branch is all that is necessary to identify it. You'll notice dozens of others farther along the trail.

At 6.5 miles the trail begins traveling along a dry, exposed, south-facing slope punctured by volcanic rocks. Chaparral shrubs such as buckbrush and whiteleaf and greenleaf manzanita dot the hillside, and white popcorn flowers, purple brodiaea, and numerous other wildflowers grow amid the grasses. This is also where you'll see the first open views of the steep, rock-studded mountain slope on the other side of Mill Creek.

An increasing number of ponderosa pine and numerous canyon live oak and black oak line the trail as you again descend to another rendezvous with Mill Creek at 8.1 miles. An obvious campsite lies just to the left, and as the trail travels near the creek for the next 1.7 miles, you'll find several other flat areas suitable for camping.

At 10 miles the trail passes through a flat area populated with ponderosa pine, climbs to a lush spring, then descends to a large, wet meadow at 11.4 miles, where you can find a camping spot near the creek. After crossing through the meadow, hike 1 more mile to Black Rock Campground.

It is possible to do this hike one-way with a car shuttle. To reach Black Rock Campground, take Highway 36 to the town of Paynes Creek. Then take Paynes Creek Road and turn right 0.3 mile farther onto Plum Creek Road. After 8 miles, turn right onto Ponderosa Way. Travel this dirt road for 20 miles to the trail, following signs for Black Rock and Mill Creek at all intersections. Note that the road is occasionally rough (though still passable for two-wheel-drive vehicles), and crossing Antelope Creek may be difficult during periods of high water flow.

74 CHAMBERS CREEK FALLS

Length: 7.6 miles round trip
Hiking time: 5 hours
High point: 4,950 feet
Total elevation gain: 2,800 feet
Difficulty: strenuous
Season: mid-April to late November

Water: available from Chambers Creek
Maps: USGS 7.5' Storrie, USFS Bucks Lake Wilderness
Information: Quincy Ranger District, Plumas National Forest

Hike up the steep and scenic trail to Chambers Creek Falls, then continue on to a viewpoint that offers vistas of the North Fork of the Feather River and its surrounding mountains.

Drive Highway 70 either 30 miles northeast of Oroville or 34 miles west of Quincy. The parking area, with a sign for Chambers Creek Trail at the back, lies on the northwest side of Highway 70, directly across from James Lee Campground and just north of a school.

Begin on a dirt road for the first 100 yards, then turn right and cross aptly named Granite Creek, which is shaded by bigleaf maple and white alder. The path now heads uphill, paralleling the North Fork of the Feather River. Three oak tree species—black, canyon live, and interior live—border the trail and are soon joined by ponderosa pine, incense cedar, and Douglas fir.

At 0.5 mile the path turns away from the river, snakes through several switchbacks, and continues its steady climb high above the tumbling waters of Chambers Creek. Bigleaf maple and dogwood soon provide deciduous greenery to the forest understory.

The frenetic crash of rushing water provides the energy to continue the ascent, and you are am-

Footbridge across the lower portion of Chambers Creek Falls

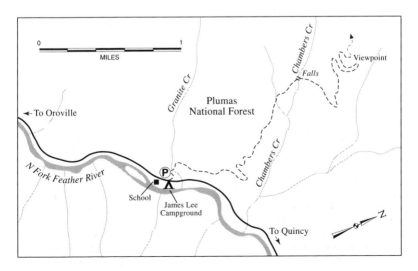

ply rewarded at 2.1 miles when you reach the bridge across Chambers Creek. Here you'll see a series of waterfalls dropping 200 feet, with a deep pool fed by a 20-foot waterfall just below the bridge. You can picnic atop the granite at the creek's edge as you dip your feet into the cool waters.

Continue on the ever-upward path as it offers better and better views from beneath black oak. The first of several switchbacks awaits at 2.6 miles; continue climbing past ponderosa pine and incense cedar. At 3.1 miles look for the foot-long cones of the stately sugar pine on the forest floor.

At 3.8 miles the path makes a sharp switchback just to the left of a small, open, level area, this hike's final destination. Those willing to carry a backpack this far can camp (bring enough water) and should have the place to themselves. Here white fir join the previously encountered sugar pine, ponderosa pine, and incense cedar; all of these trees tower over numerous diverse shrubs, including whiteleaf and greenleaf manzanita, bush chinquapin, and tan oak.

The views, however, will command most of your attention. The North Fork of the Feather River flows far below, with its steep canyon walls rising 5,000 feet to the top of Bald Eagle Peak. To the west 6,093-foot Chambers Peak towers above Chambers Creek, and numerous other forested Sierra peaks stretch in all directions.

75   BIDWELL PARK TRAILS

Length: 8.2-mile loop
Hiking time: 4 hours
High point: 1,100 feet
Total elevation gain: 750 feet
Difficulty: easy
Season: year-round

Water: bring your own
Maps: USGS 7.5' Richardson Springs, USGS 7.5' Paradise West
Information: City of Chico Parks Division

Chico's Bidwell Park packs a lot of beauty into a relatively small area. Hike high atop a canyon rim with expansive vistas, then walk along the shaded banks of Big Chico Creek, a year-round stream that offers solitude in winter and swimming in summer.

If heading north on Highway 99 to Chico, take the Highway 32 Exit, go right, then take an immediate left onto Fir Street. Cross westbound Highway 32, turn right onto East Eighth Street, go 1.7 miles, then turn left onto Bruce Road. After 1.2 miles turn right at the Bidwell Park sign onto Wildwood Avenue. If heading south on Highway 99 to Chico, take the East Avenue Exit, then go east on East Avenue for 2.5 miles to the above-mentioned Bidwell Park sign. Once on Wildwood Avenue, go 1.7 miles, and just before reaching a road gate, turn into the lot on the left and park.

Two trails leave from the parking lot's north side. Take the one farthest west, then follow it north. It quickly crosses two other trails and then gently switchbacks to join Rim Trail at 0.5 mile.

Hikers leave blue oaks and gray pines behind as they descend from the Rim Trail to the parking area.

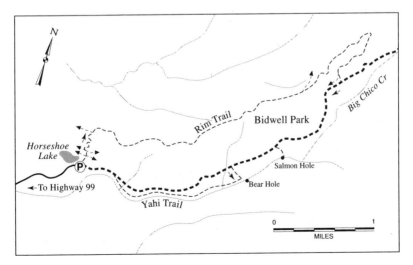

Turn right and begin a long gentle ascent. You'll certainly notice the dark rock in and around the trail that forms the huge, lichen-encrusted cliffs lining Big Chico Creek's canyon. Numerous large flows of lava and mud from the Cascade Mountains deposited this rock several million years ago. If you look closely, you'll see many different types of rock cemented together. Common tree species in this dry area include blue oak and interior live oak as well as the twisted, multitrunked gray pine. At 1.5 miles look for an unusually large number of buckeye trees growing on the trail's north side.

As you continue to gain elevation, pause to enjoy the views. To the south you'll see Big Chico Creek and its canyon, with the Sutter Buttes thrusting out of the valley floor beyond. To the west lies Chico and the fertile flatlands of the Sacramento Valley, with the Coast Range marking the far horizon. To the north are several canyons, with Shasta Bally and Bully Choop rising in the distance to the west of Redding.

Turn right at a trail fork at 2.7 miles and gently descend, first in a northeasterly direction, then southwesterly. Pass through a California laurel grove at 4.1 miles, then reach a trail fork at 4.4 miles. Turn left, go 100 feet, then turn right onto the park's main road.

Follow the road 1.2 miles to parking area N, then take a trail to the left 100 yards down to your first encounter with Big Chico Creek at famous Salmon Hole. Here you'll find a large and deep swimming area bounded on the south by high basalt cliffs and large canyon live oak.

Back on the dirt road, continue past a lush area fed by springs where willow, cattails, and even a few wild roses grow. You'll reach parking area K at 6.2 miles. Turn left and head down to Bear Hole, another swimming spot with scenery similar to that at Salmon Hole.

Look for the signed Yahi Trail, which leaves from Bear Hole, and follow it downstream. It leads you to other, smaller swimming places, if you're so inclined. In addition to the tree species previously encountered, you'll see California sycamore, white alder, cottonwood, and valley oak, trees that thrive in the richer, wetter soil near the creek. At 7.8 miles Yahi Trail meets the park road. Turn left and walk the last 0.4 mile to the trailhead.

76 FEATHER FALLS

Length: 7.6 miles round trip
Hiking time: 5 hours
High point: 2,400 feet
Total elevation gain: 1,100 feet
Difficulty: moderate
Season: year-round

Water: available from Frey Creek and Fall River
Maps: USGS 7.5' Forbestown, USGS 7.5' Brush Creek
Information: La Porte Ranger District, Plumas National Forest

This hike offers a smorgasbord of natural delights. You'll walk through tall stands of incense cedar and ponderosa pine, along streams

shaded by bigleaf maple and dogwood, and past a multitude of spring
and early summer wildflowers to Feather Falls, where the clear waters
of Fall River drop 640 feet into a granitic gorge.

Take Highway 70 to Oroville, exit onto Oro Dam Boulevard, head
northeast, then turn right after 1.5 miles onto Olive Highway. Go 6
miles, then turn right onto Forbestown Road. Go another 6 miles, then
turn left onto Lumpkin Road. Follow Lumpkin Road 10 miles, then
turn left at a Feather Falls sign for the final 1.6 miles to the trailhead.

For the first 200 yards, the path travels past dozens of madrone
trees, easily recognizable by their large, shiny green leaves and the
peeling red bark. Near the 0.5-mile marker, look for the relatively
scarce California nutmeg tree, which has long, sharp needles.

Reach the cool canyon shade of Frey Creek at 1.1 miles. As you
gradually descend near the gurgling water, look for a swimming hole
at the bottom of a two-stage waterfall to the left at 1.4 miles.

Views through the trees of the Middle Fork of the Feather River and
its steep canyon walls appear at 1.5 miles: look for the smooth granite
head of Bald Rock Dome looming above the river's west bank. From
here, you descend for 1 shady mile and then begin a moderate climb to
a trail fork at 3.2 miles. Stay left and follow the safety railings to another trail fork. Go left again to reach the overlook.

From the overlook you have a magnificent view of Feather Falls,
where the aptly named Fall River drops 640 vertical feet past sheer
granite cliffs to the canyon far below before joining the Middle Fork of
the Feather River and Lake Oroville.

After imbibing this broad view of the United States' sixth highest
waterfall, go back to the last trail fork, turn left, and walk 0.2 mile to
where a small trail leads to granite boulders at the lip of the falls.
Those not afraid of heights can lean against a chain-link fence and
watch the water plummet all the way to the bottom of the canyon.

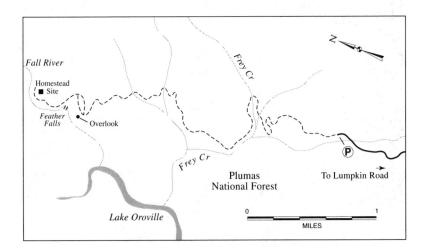

The trail continues another mile upstream along Fall River. Summer swimmers will find good swimming holes, and overnighters will find several campsites. Near the end of the trail, you'll see some old fruit trees and an old water ditch, which are all that remains of an old homestead.

The overlook allows unimpeded views of Feather Falls's 640-foot plunge.

77 SMITH LAKE TO WADES LAKE

Length: 13.8 miles round trip
Hiking time: 2 days
High point: 6,600 feet
Total elevation gain: 1,600 feet
Difficulty: moderate
Season: mid-June through October

Water: available from numerous creeks and lakes
Map: USGS 7.5' Gold Lake
Information: Beckwourth Ranger District, Plumas National Forest

This hike takes you past the cascading waters of clear mountain streams as you travel through pine and fir forests. You'll also visit five of the Sierra's northernmost glacial lakes and enjoy fine alpine views of rocky ridges.

Turn onto Gray Eagle Lodge Road, which is on the west side of Gold Lake Road 11 miles north of Highway 49 and 5 miles southwest of Highway 89. Drive 0.6 mile, bear right at a fork, then go another 0.2 mile to the trailhead.

The path climbs gently north, first through open chaparral and then under forest shade. Just after crossing Smith Creek at 0.6 mile, bear left at a trail fork. As you continue to follow Smith Creek upstream, stay right at another trail junction.

Reach Smith Lake at 1 mile. This lake, with its two good campsites along the southern shore, makes a good destination for those getting a late afternoon start. Note that camping (except in campgrounds) is forbidden in the Lakes Basin except at this hike's five lakes.

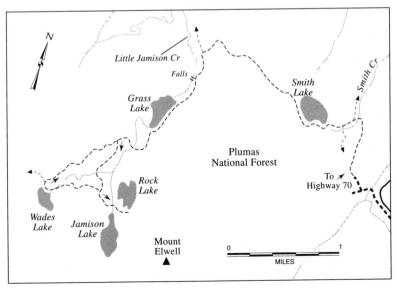

Lodgepole pines shade the south shore of Rock Lake.

The trail ascends west of Smith Lake and then gradually descends through a red fir forest to a trail fork at 3.7 miles. Turn left and head uphill, paralleling Little Jamison Creek. At 3.9 miles your ears will guide you to 40-foot-high Jamison Falls to the right of the trail.

Campsites abound on all sides of Grass Lake at 4.2 miles. Western serviceberry surrounds much of the lake, as do Jeffrey pine, lodgepole pine, and red fir. You'll have views of the rocky ridges to the north and west, and you can also search the lake's surface for ducks and beaver.

Large numbers of quaking aspen populate the moist area along the trail just south of Grass Lake as you climb to cross Little Jamison Creek at 5 miles. Hike under the shade of red fir, incense cedar, and Jeffrey pine, and go left at trail junctions at 5.4 miles and 6.2 miles.

Jamison Lake, at 6.4 miles, has two campsites, one near the northeast shore, the other near the northwest shore. Rock Lake, 0.2 mile farther, offers more picturesque surroundings. The rock-rimmed lake, much deeper than Jamison, allows much better swimming opportunities and also has several campsites at its south end. At both lakes you'll see rock striations and other evidence of the glaciers that both carved the wide valley through these mountains and scooped out the lakes.

To reach Wades Lake, return to the trail fork 0.2 mile below Jamison Lake and turn left. For the first 0.5 mile, the path climbs west over a rocky ridge and can be a bit difficult to follow. Begin climbing south next to the lake's outlet stream at 0.7 mile, then reach Wades Lake 0.9 mile from the last trail fork. Rimmed by willow, mountain alder, lodgepole pine, and red fir, this lake offers the best mountain ridge views of all the lakes on this hike. You'll find two good campsites along the south shore.

Take the trail that begins by a sign giving Wades Lake's elevation and follow it downhill, initially through an open meadow. Bear right at a trail junction 0.25 mile from the lake, and then enjoy increasingly open views of Mount Elwell towering over Rock and Jamison lakes to the east and Grass Lake and the distant mountains to the north and northeast. You'll reach a trail junction 0.9 mile from Wades Lake, which is the same one encountered at mile 5.4. Head left to return to the trailhead.

78 MOUNT ELWELL

Length: 8.2 miles round trip
Hiking time: 5 hours
High point: 7,818 feet
Total elevation gain: 1,600 feet
Difficulty: moderate to strenuous
Season: mid-June through
  October

Water: available from lakes and
  streams, except for the last 1.5
  miles
Map: USGS 7.5' Gold Lake
Information: Beckwourth Ranger
  District, Plumas National
  Forest

This trip takes you past numerous rock-encircled, high Sierra lakes to the top of Mount Elwell, a peak that offers panoramic views over all the Lakes Basin and northern Sierra Nevada. Note that camping outside of official campgrounds is prohibited in this area.

The dirt road to the trailhead lies on the west side of Gold Lake Road, 8 miles northwest of Highway 49 and 8 miles southeast of Highway 89, and is just south of the Sierra–Plumas county line. Go 200 feet, then park.

Follow a dirt road (on the right as you drive in) marked by a sign for Grass Lake. Go right at 0.2 mile onto a trail, then descend gently past two small ponds. Reach Big Bear Lake at 0.7 mile. The large lake's deep waters, surrounding forest, and rocky crest tie it with the upcoming Long Lake for the most picturesque body of water in the Lakes Basin.

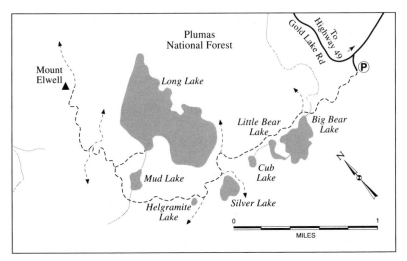

Storm clouds gather over Long Lake and Mount Elwell.

Go left at the trail fork just beyond Big Bear Lake's outlet, and walk under the shade of red fir, lodgepole pine, and Jeffrey pine. At 1.1 miles you'll encounter Little Bear Lake. The trail then climbs to a rendezvous with Cub Lake at 1.3 miles and then to a trail junction at 1.5 miles. Turn left and enjoy the magnificent view of your destination—the summit of Mount Elwell, towering above the broad expanse of Long Lake.

Silver Lake, another deep and beautiful lake nearly on par with Big Bear Lake, awaits at 1.7 miles. Go right at a trail junction at the lake's shore, then right again at 2.2 miles. After passing small and shallow Helgramite Lake, the trail descends to Mud Lake, crossing its inlet creek at 2.7 miles. Note that this is your last sure source of water.

At 2.9 miles you'll see an unsigned spur trail that travels 0.3 mile down to the shore of Long Lake, an excellent side trip. The main path now climbs in earnest up an open, moist slope before encountering a double trail junction at 3.3 miles. Go right, then immediately left, following signs for Mount Elwell.

The path ascends steeply for the last 0.8 mile, initially past pink, purple, white, and blue phlox and large blue lupine, and later past pinemat manzanita and bush chinquapin. Stately red fir clad in coats of green lichen provide occasional shade.

After the vigorous workout, you finally reach the rocky summit of Mount Elwell, elevation 7,818 feet. To the immediate south lies the Lakes Basin, with Long Lake directly below. Farther south the sharp-edged Sierra Buttes puncture the sky, and to the southeast rise the vast, high ridges of the Tahoe Sierra region. Rock, Jamison, and Wades lakes inhabit the valley just to the west (see hike 77, Smith Lake to Wades Lake), while to the north and farther west forested mountains stretch to the skyline.

79 CROOKED LAKES TRAIL TO PENNER LAKE

Length: 6 miles round trip
Hiking time: 3 hours
High point: 6,900 feet
Total elevation gain: 500 feet
Difficulty: easy
Season: mid-June through October

Water: available from trailside lakes
Maps: USGS 7.5' Graniteville, USGS 7.5' English Mtn.
Information: Nevada City Ranger District, Tahoe National Forest

Take Crooked Lakes Trail past a bounty of large and small bodies of water, where you'll have ample opportunity to picnic, swim, and fish. Gentle climbing and numerous campsites make this hike an excellent family backpacking trip.

From its junction with I-80, drive Highway 20 west 4 miles, then turn right (north) onto Bowman Lake Road (Forest Road 18). Follow this paved road 8.4 miles, then turn right at a sign for Carr Lake, your destination. Stay on the main road and bear right at all road junctions as you drive the last 2.7 miles of a somewhat rough dirt road to the trailhead at Carr Lake Campground.

Take the campground road east, where it crosses a creek before turning into the trail. The path initially travels along the shores of Feely Lake, a favorite spot for fishing, and offers good views of Fall Creek Mountain to the north. Begin a gentle ascent at 0.5 mile, then level off by a small, shallow pond.

Turn left at 1 mile onto the Crooked Lakes Trail just after encountering an unnamed lake (hike 80, Sand Ridge and the Five Lakes Basin, travels to the right). You now pass between the unnamed lake on the left and the much larger and deeper Island Lake on the right. Granite-encased Island Lake, with its clear waters and small islands, rivals your final destination, Penner Lake, for swimmability and the most scenic beauty of the hike. Several campsites line the west shore of Island Lake and the east shore of the lake on the left.

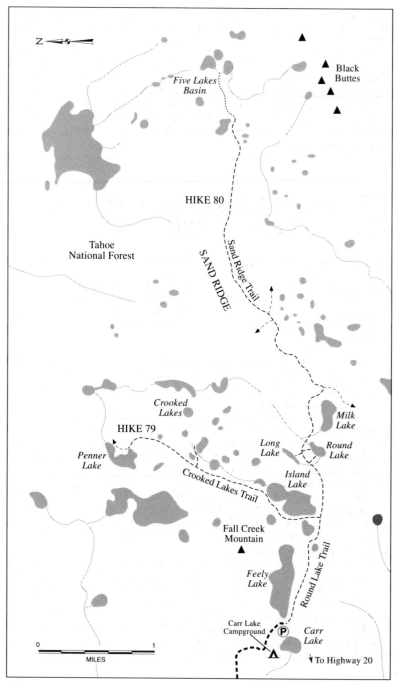

Leave Island Lake behind at 1.5 miles, then travel through a red fir forest. Look for a small waterfall on Island Lake's alder-lined outlet creek at 1.8 miles. The first of the Crooked Lakes lies to the right at 2 miles, but press past its shallow, marshy waters to the better lakes to come.

As the path descends at 2.3 miles, take a small side trail on the right just before reaching a small lake. Follow it across the creek to the best of the Crooked Lakes, a large, deep lake rimmed by granite. You'll find a good campsite right where the trail ends, and from the lake's shore you'll have open views of the Black Buttes to the east.

Back on Crooked Lakes Trail, climb steadily for the next 0.5 mile over rocky tread past pinemat manzanita and huckleberry oak. At 2.8 miles crest a ridge and see the rocky shores of expansive Penner Lake below. Follow the trail the final 0.2 mile down to the lake, where you'll find excellent swimming spots but few campsites.

Be sure to enjoy the open views of the surrounding mountains as you hike back to the trailhead, and also consider adding part of hike 80 (Sand Ridge and the Five Lakes Basin) to your journey.

A lodgepole pine and a Jeffrey pine front a view of Penner Lake and Bowman Mountain.

80 SAND RIDGE AND THE FIVE LAKES BASIN

Length: 12 miles round trip
Hiking time: 7 hours or over-night
High point: 7,420 feet
Total elevation gain: 1,400 feet
Difficulty: moderate
Season: late June through October

Water: available from lakes and streams
Maps: USGS 7.5' Graniteville, USGS 7.5' English Mtn.
Information: Nevada City Ranger District, Tahoe National Forest

A series of beautiful lakes lines the trail on this hike, and most have campsites and deep sections suitable for a summer swim. You'll also enjoy a panoramic 360-degree view over much of the northern Sierra from the spine of Sand Ridge.

From the junction of Highways 20 and 80, drive 4 miles west on Highway 20, then turn right (north) onto Bowman Lake Road (Forest Road 18). Go 8.4 miles on this paved road, then turn right at a sign for Carr Lake, your destination. Stay on the main, somewhat rough, dirt road, and bear right at all road junctions for the last 2.7 miles to the trailhead at Carr Lake Campground.

Follow the road, which becomes Round Lake Trail after crossing a creek. The path borders the shores of fisherman-festooned Feely Lake and offers good views of Fall Creek Mountain. After 0.5 mile begin a gentle climb past red fir and western white pine. Reach an unnamed lake on the left at 1 mile with several campsites on its eastern edge, then immediately reach a trail junction. Go right (the left-hand trail is covered in hike 79, Crooked Lakes Trail to Penner Lake), and ascend above the granite-lined shores of Island Lake, the prettiest lake in the region. At least two campsites lie among lodgepole pine near the water's edge down to the left. If others have already claimed these, try one of the several sites along the lake's west shore.

You'll reach a crest at 1.2 miles with good views of Island Lake and the serrated Sierra Buttes to the north. The trail then descends 0.2 mile to a creek that runs from Round Lake to Long Lake. On the creek's far side, take a footpath to the right for the short streamside stroll past mountain heather to Round Lake. Granite and metamorphic rock stretch steeply upward on the lake's southeast side, and red fir and lodgepole pine clothe the rest of the lake's shore. Camp at one of the sites near the northwest shore if you find Island Lake too crowded.

Back on the main trail, at 1.5 miles you'll see a faint path traveling through a shallow gully on the left. It leads to Long Lake, which has two campsites on its east shore and, like Round Lake, sees few visitors. One hundred yards past the Long Lake turnoff, you'll see another spur trail to Round Lake on the right. Stay left and climb gently to a spur trail on the right heading down to Milk Lake at 2.1 miles. This shallow lake has a good campsite underneath a two-trunked fir tree near the

The Black Buttes rise beyond an unnamed lake just above the Five Lakes Basin.

water's edge. Note that this is your last sure source of water for the next 2.7 miles.

At 2.2 miles you reach a trail junction. Go left and travel under the shade of the red fir forest. A trail fork awaits at 2.8 miles. Go right and then left 100 yards farther for Sand Ridge Trail, where your path initially passes through a grove of young lodgepole pine.

Sand Ridge Trail gains most of its elevation over 0.3 mile and then levels out at 3.5 miles. You now walk along the open ridge that's covered with mule ear, phlox, purple lupine, and other components of a multicolored floral display. Western white pine, red fir, and an occasional mountain hemlock grow here and there in the exposed landscape but rarely hinder views of the imposing peaks of Black Buttes to the southeast, Stoddard Lake and the Sacramento Valley to the southwest, Fall Creek Mountain to the west, the Sierra Buttes and numerous other mountains to the north, and English Mountain to the northeast.

The trail eventually descends from the ridge and reaches a shallow, though swimmable, lake at 4.8 miles. A faint trail runs near the south shore, where you'll find several campsites.

From the lake's east side, you'll see the Five Lakes Basin, the hike's final destination, about 0.5 mile east and 250 feet below. Choose your own cross-country route over the gently sloping granite slabs. Most of the lakes offer several campsites and good swimming. Consider adding hike 79 (Crooked Lakes Trail to Penner Lake) to your itinerary on the way back to the trailhead.

81 LOCH LEVEN LAKES

Length: 7.2 miles round trip
Hiking time: 5 hours or overnight
High point: 6,850 feet
Total elevation gain: 1,350 feet
Difficulty: moderate
Season: mid-June to late October

Water: available from streams and lakes
Maps: USGS 7.5' Cisco Grove, USGS 7.5' Soda Springs
Information: Nevada City Ranger District, Tahoe National Forest

This hike takes you to three granite-ringed lakes and serves equally well as a good day hike or an easy overnight backpacking trip. An added bonus is its easy access from I-80.

The trailhead and parking area lie 100 yards east of the Big Bend Visitor Information Center on Hampshire Rocks Road, which is off I-80 about 75 miles northeast of Sacramento. If going east on I-80, take the Big Bend Exit off I-80, then turn left onto Hampshire Rocks Road. If going west on I-80, take the Cisco Grove Exit and bear right onto Hampshire Rocks Road.

The signed trail begins on the south side of the road, follows a dirt road for 50 feet, then turns left. Jeffrey and lodgepole pine and some western juniper provide intermittent shade as you make your way up-

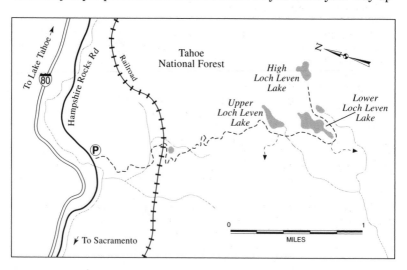

Numerous granite islands dot the Loch Leven Lakes.

hill past outcroppings of granite. Pass a pond at 0.6 mile, continue along a hillside covered by white-flowered red cherry bushes, then reach a bridge across an alder-lined creek at 1.1 miles.

You'll eventually cross railroad tracks at 1.3 miles and then continue the uphill push as western white pine and the occasional quaking aspen join the forest cover. Be sure to look north for good views of forested mountains and the South Yuba River. At 2.2 miles the trail levels and passes through a red fir forest before starting the descent to the lakes at 2.5 miles.

Upper Loch Leven Lake, surrounded by granite and pine, awaits at 2.7 miles. You'll find numerous campsites near the water, along with several good swimming spots. A trail fork lies at the lake's south end. Head left 150 yards to Lower Loch Leven Lake, which is prettier than its upper cousin. The path, bounded by purple lupine and huckleberry oak, travels by the lake's shore, where you'll find several campsites.

Bear left at another trail junction at 3.1 miles, then follow the occasionally faint path for the last 0.5 mile as you enjoy good views of Snow Mountain to the south. High Loch Leven Lake is both the least visited and most beautiful of the Loch Leven Lakes. Granite slabs surround most of the island-dotted waters, while red fir, lodgepole pine, and western white pine provide shoreline shade for the south-side campsites. Spend most of your time here.

82   FIVE LAKES

Length: 4.6 miles round trip
Hiking time: 3 hours or over-
   night
High point: 7,550 feet
Total elevation gain: 1,100 feet
Difficulty: moderate
Season: late June to mid-October

Water: at the lakes only; bring at
   least a quart
Maps: USGS 7.5' Tahoe City,
   USGS 7.5' Granite Chief
Information: Truckee Ranger
   District, Tahoe National Forest

A short climb past ever-changing, gorgeous High Sierra scenery brings you to the Five Lakes, where you can swim, picnic, and camp while enjoying views of surrounding peaks.

From I-80's Highway 89 exit in Truckee, drive south for 10 miles, then turn west on Alpine Meadows Road. Or drive 31 miles north of the junction of Highways 89 and 50 to Alpine Meadows Road. Park on the side of this road 2.1 miles farther, near the turnoff to Deer Park Drive.

Low-lying huckleberry oak and green leaf manzanita initially escort you up the wide path, followed by an impressive community of mule ear at 0.4 mile. Note the contrasting rock faces on the right, then look left at the posh log castles by Alpine Meadows ski bowl.

Bear right at an unsigned junction at 0.6 mile, then engage in even steeper climbing 0.2 mile farther amid pinemat manzanita and Jeffrey pine. The trail levels slightly and becomes sandy at 1.2 miles as it crests a mountain shoulder.

Enter a multicolored rocky stretch at 1.4 miles as the trail snakes upward past a lone Sierra juniper and a Jeffrey pine. The way then travels westerly past huckleberry oak, red fir, and tall western white pine.

The trail noticeably levels at 1.9 miles near the Granite Chief Wilderness boundary sign as it passes through a white fir forest. You soon step into a small garden of mule ear and corn lilies and then go left at a trail junction.

The path gently descends 0.1 mile farther to the first and biggest of the Five Lakes. Tall white fir and the occasional western white pine

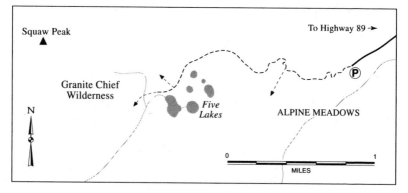

Boulders and stunted western white pines decorate the first of the Five Lakes.

shade a handful of campsites near the big lake's scenic shoreline, where you obtain views of nearby lower-elevation peaks and taller Squaw Peak to the west.

Take any of the faint side trails that escort you around the other small, shallow, swimmable lakes to the east, where you'll find secluded campsites beneath mountain hemlock. All the lakes share common highlights, including grassy marshes and ground cover consisting of red mountain heather, pinemat manzanita, and huckleberry oak.

83 CRAG LAKE AND RUBICON LAKE

Length: 16.2 miles round trip
Hiking time: 2 days
High point: 8,200 feet
Total elevation gain: 2,100 feet
Difficulty: moderate
Season: early July through early October

Water: available from lakes and streams
Maps: USGS 7.5' Rockbound Valley, USGS 7.5' Homewood, USFS Desolation Wilderness
Information: Lake Tahoe Basin Management Unit

This backpack trip features both peaceful, easy walking near delightful Meeks Creek and visits to six different High Sierra lakes.

On Highway 89 drive 0.1 mile southwest of Lake Tahoe's Meeks Bay Resort (11 miles south of Tahoe City and 16 miles from the interchange of Highways 89 and 50), and park at the signed trailhead. Day hikers can fill out self-issue wilderness permits here.

Walk around the locked gate, then stroll along the level dirt road to

Crag Lake and its outlet

the signed trail junction at 1.3 miles, where you bear right on Meeks Creek Trail. Watch closely for an eye-catching handful of rare, red snow plants (protected by law) that decorate the dry chaparral hillside, and then at 1.7 miles climb to a view of Lake Tahoe.

White yarrow and red wavy-leafed paintbrush border Meeks Creek at trailside at 2 miles, then you pass through a field lined with mysterious, dead, white-limbed trees at 2.3 miles. The steady sound of Meeks Creek accompanies a 0.5-mile trek into a wide basin where huckleberry oak prospers in the sunny sections and thimbleberry thrives beneath the shade of western white pine and Jeffrey pine.

Cross the wooden bridge over Meeks Creek at 3.3 miles next to a couple of campsites. Swing away from Meeks Creek and into a white and red fir forest, then walk past pinemat manzanita to the welcome return of Meeks Creek at 4.2 miles.

A king-size campsite awaits at 4.7 miles near the north shore of Lake Genevieve, where the shallow lake's waters reflect Peak 9054. Keep left at the signed trail junction just past two campsites near the lake's eastern shore.

Another campsite awaits 0.3 mile farther at Crag Lake next to the dam's spillway. Peak 9054 also hovers above this lake, which features a peninsula on the south side. The trail skirts the eastern shore past several campsites nestled under red fir and western white pine.

The path now briefly climbs to pond lily–covered Shadow Lake, promptly followed by another mysterious stand of bare, rotting tree trunks at 6 miles. At 6.6 miles the main trail reaches the western shoreline of Stony Ridge Lake at 6.6 miles, which features two good trailside campsites. To the east Rubicon Peak towers above the lake, along with siblings Peak 9269 and Jake's Peak. Native fescue grasses abound, as do Sierra juniper and western white pine. Look for camping sites on the south side.

Climb gently through forest and meadow, cross a stream, then begin negotiating a series of steep switchbacks at 7.8 miles. Reach gorgeous

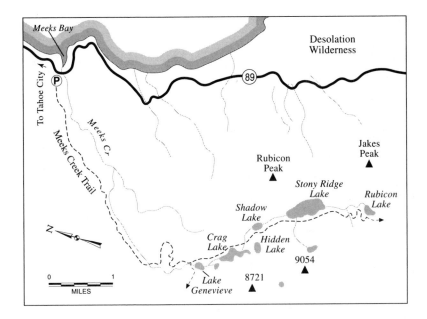

Rubicon Lake at 8.1 miles, where you'll enjoy refreshing swimming and mountain views. A good campsite is located close to the lake under lodgepole pine and mountain hemlock.

EMERALD BAY

Length: 10.8 miles round trip
Hiking time: 6 hours
High point: 6,700 feet
Total elevation gain: 1,200 feet
Difficulty: easy to moderate
Season: late May through early
October

Water: bring your own
Maps: USGS 7.5' Emerald Bay,
USFS Desolation Wilderness
Information: D. L. Bliss–Emerald
Bay State Park

Get great views of Mount Tallac, Lake Tahoe, and Emerald Bay's Fannette Island on this scenic shoreline excursion.

From the junction of Highways 28 and 89, drive Highway 89 south for 19 miles to Emerald Bay. From the Highway 50 junction with Highway 89, travel north on Highway 89 for 10 miles to Emerald Bay, then park at either the Vikingsholm parking lot on the east side or the Eagle Lake trailhead on the west side.

Pick up the old dirt road off the east side of Highway 89. It drops 0.7 mile to Vikingsholm Castle past ponderosa pine, Jeffrey pine, incense

Common mullein grows on Emerald Point, which separates Lake Tahoe and Emerald Bay.

cedar, and quaking aspen. At 0.6 mile you'll find three sturdy, hand-carved wooden chairs and a signed junction. Bear right here, and walk the 0.1 mile to the exquisite castle, then continue 0.2 mile farther to impressive Eagle Falls.

After your castle and falls visit, head north on Vikingsholm Beach 0.1 mile until you gain Rubicon Trail proper. The sandy tread leads

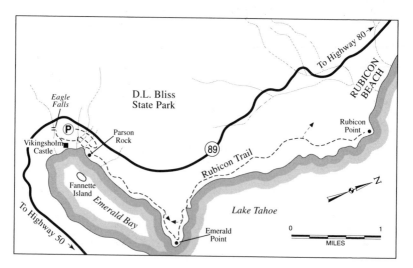

past beachside views of Emerald Bay and decorative Fannette Island. At 1.3 miles choose between two side trails that escort you to Parson Rock for open scenery of Emerald Bay, Lake Tahoe, and surrounding Sierra mountains.

Travel through forest, then pass the boaters' campground at 2.1 miles. Good views of beach and bay continue as you reach a signed trail junction at 2.6 miles and go right. Gain a good southward view of 9,735-foot high Mount Tallac from Emerald Point at 3.1 miles, along with broad vistas of the lake and other mountains.

The trail continues close to the shoreline and into an open forest featuring sugar pine. Keep right at 3.5 miles at a signed trail junction. The path escalates 100 feet at 3.9 miles, providing a prime view atop boulders of Lake Tahoe between white fir. The path then gradually descends to a seasonal creek and then starts a longer climb at 4.5 miles. Keep right at 4.7 miles when you spot an old dirt road. Bear right at another trail junction at 5.3 miles, then reach Rubicon Point at 5.6 miles. Take the spur trail here, and climb the rocks for good views of Lake Tahoe.

The final 100 yards brings you to Rubicon Beach in D. L. Bliss State Park, another good spot to picnic and beachcomb.

For those arranging a car shuttle, reach this end of the trail by driving 2.5 miles north of the trailhead, turning right into D. L. Bliss State Park, then continuing another 2.3 miles.

85 EAGLE LAKE AND THE VELMA LAKES

Length: 9.2 miles round trip
Hiking time: 6 hours or over-
night
High point: 8,300 feet
Total elevation gain: 2,100 feet
Difficulty: strenuous
Season: late June to early
October

Water: available only from the
lakes; have at least a quart on
hand
Maps: USGS 7.5' Rockbound
Valley, USGS 7.5' Emerald Bay,
USFS Desolation Wilderness
Information: Lake Tahoe Basin
Management Unit

This trip gives great views of Lake Tahoe and several Sierra peaks as it travels to several of the Desolation Wilderness's most beautiful lakes, where swimming and camping opportunities abound.

From the junction of Highways 89 and 28, drive south on Highway 89 for 19 miles to Emerald Bay. From the junction of Highways 89 and 50, drive north on Highway 89 for 10 miles to Emerald Bay. Park at either the Vikingsholm parking lot or the Eagle Lake trailhead. Day hikers can fill out the required visitor's permit at the Eagle Lake trailhead.

Red fir shades the continuous climb past alder, thimbleberry, and a

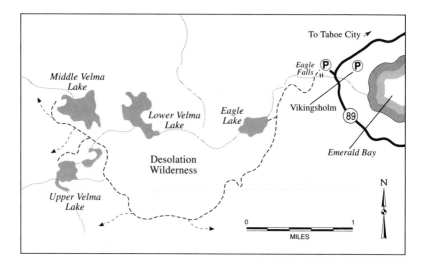

waterfall to a rocky clearing at 0.4 mile, which features an exquisite view of deep blue Lake Tahoe. At 0.5 mile huge granitic outcrops and twisted, gnarled Sierra juniper hint of the more stark alpine conditions to come. After another steep 0.4 mile, reach the Eagle Lake turnoff. This very popular lake, encased by rigid rock cliffs, has a few campsites and offers good swimming and picnicking. Explore the lake's lightly forested shoreline, then return to the main trail and observe the lake from afar as you bear south for the Velma Lakes.

Vistas of Lake Tahoe beyond Sierra junipers highlight the trail to Velma Lakes.

Climb steadily to 1.3 miles, where the view of Eagle Lake vanishes, then enter a forest of mountain hemlock, western white pine, and red fir. The path grows faint from 1.5 to 1.7 miles, so follow the rock ducks (cairns) closely.

At 2.2 miles reach a crest where lodgepole pine predominate, signaling an end to most of the strenuous climbing. At 2.5 miles start a modest ascent amid mountain hemlock and red fir alongside a seasonal stream. When you reach another crest at 2.8 miles, head right at the signed trail junction and enjoy a long stretch of nearly level strolling past pinemat manzanita, red fir, western white pine, and Jeffrey pine, highlighted by an inspiring panorama of Lake Tahoe and scenic Sierra peaks.

Keep right at another trail junction at 3.5 miles, then view Middle Velma Lake ahead as you begin a gradual descent. At 4.2 miles the path skirts a grass-lined lake on the left. Cross the outlet stream of Upper Velma Lake 0.1 mile farther, proceed past a small open field featuring lupine and aster, then head right at a signed trail junction (the left fork goes to Upper Velma Lake).

At 4.6 miles continue right at another trail junction, enter a hemlock forest, then reach picturesque Middle Velma Lake 0.2 mile farther. Although peak views diminish, campsites abound here for the many backpackers, and numerous rock islands make good swimming destinations. Scout the many side trails that lead to the other Velma Lakes nearby for more campsites and slightly more seclusion. Although not as picturesque as Middle Velma Lake, Upper Velma Lake has just as many campsites and a little more seclusion. Note that you can extend your trip by doing all or part of hike 86 (Dick's Lake, Gilmore Lake, and Lake Aloha).

86 DICK'S LAKE, GILMORE LAKE, AND LAKE ALOHA

Length: 30 miles round trip
Hiking time: 4 days
High point: 9,280 feet
Total elevation gain: 4,700 feet
Difficulty: moderate
Season: late July to early October

Water: available from lakes and streams
Maps: USGS 7.5' Emerald Bay, USGS 7.5' Pyramid Peak, USGS 7.5' Rockbound Valley, USFS Desolation Wilderness
Information: Lake Tahoe Basin Management Unit

Camp near clear mountain lakes, hike past beautiful wildflower displays, and gaze at expansive vistas of high Sierra peaks on this journey through the heart of Desolation Wilderness.

From the intersection of Highways 89 and 28, drive south on Highway 89 for 20 miles to Bayview Campground. From the intersection of

Half Moon Lake from Dick's Pass

Highways 89 and 50, take Highway 89 north for 9 miles to the campground. Turn into Bayview Campground, then drive 0.2 mile through the campground to the trailhead.

Begin climbing steadily through a mixed conifer forest past tobacco brush to a vista point at 0.6 mile of Emerald Bay and the stark, steep, south-facing slopes of Peak 9195. The deep waters of gray-green Granite Lake appear at 1.1 miles. Look for several white fir– and lodgepole pine– shaded campsites near the alder-clogged outlet stream.

Continuous views of Granite Lake, Emerald Bay, and Lake Tahoe accompany the steep climb to the boulder-strewn pass that splits the twin Maggies Peaks at 1.9 miles. From here you can admire white firs framing Lake Tahoe to the east. Eagle Lake shimmers to the northwest, and there are impressive views of Peak 9263 to the west.

Stroll level trail as statuesque Sierra juniper and shapely western white pine foreground numerous views, especially that of Mount Tallac's jagged walls to the south. Go left at a trail fork 1.2 miles past the gap as you briefly join the trails of hike 85 (Eagle Lake and the Velma Lakes), then turn left again 0.7 mile farther. At 4.5 miles note an attractive, unnamed, grass-lined lake stashed at the bottom of granitic Peak 9190. Look for dwarf western white pine decorating the lake's numerous rock islands.

The trail then switchbacks past mountain spiraea and red mountain heather while showing off the Velma Lakes to the north. From a gap at 5 miles, look back for the best vista yet of scenic Lake Tahoe, then scurry westward up Peak 8619 for great views of Fontanillis Lake.

Regain the gap, find the trail fork, and bear right for a quick descent down to Dick's and Fontanillis lakes, two of the most beautiful bodies of water in Desolation Wilderness. The high-usage campsites at Dick's Lake lie on the outskirts of a small meadow on the north shore. More exposed sites sit on a granite outcrop overlooking the lake above the east shoreline.

Although the east shore of Fontanillis Lake sports many campsites, more secluded spots rest amid granitic rock outcrops above the lake's

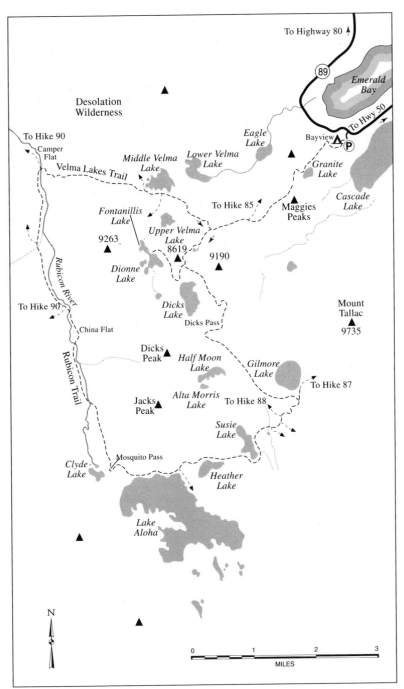

southwest section. You can dip into the chilly, gray-blue waters from an array of boulders on the southeastern shore. Farther west, a separate unnamed lake sits invitingly above Fontanillis Lake; a slim creek connects the two.

Back at the gap, note the prominent wildflowers nestled in the rocks on the climb to Dick's Pass. Yellow ivesia and sulphur flower are soon replaced by aster, orange Indian paintbrush, and red mountain heather. After numerous switchbacks, the last portion through an open forest of mountain hemlock and whitebark pine, you reach view-filled Dick's Pass at 7.2 miles.

From this 9,280-foot vantage point, Dick's and Fontanillis lakes gleam to the north, Dick's Peak towers to the west, and farther south sit Jack's Peak, Pyramid Peak, and the distant southern Sierra. For better views walk to each of the four corners of this football-size field and marvel at Half Moon and Susie lakes and Lake Aloha to the south. The south-facing slope of Dick's Pass features an inspiring array of wildflowers: look for ivesia, sulphur flower, sunflower, paintbrush, bitter brush, and big sage.

Continue for an open 1.6 miles past sloping wildflower gardens highlighted by blue lupine. You'll also enjoy previously mentioned views of southward lakes and mountains most of the way. Go left at a trail fork to scenic and secluded Gilmore Lake, which takes on the same deep blue hue of Lake Tahoe. Look for numerous campsites in the flower-covered meadow above the south shore. Note that you can climb Mount Tallac (hike 87), which towers to the east, by taking the trail from the lake's southeast shore.

From the trail fork just south of Gilmore Lake, go left down the wildflower-bordered trail and note Pyramid Peak jutting to the southwest during the 0.4-mile stretch to an intersection with the trail to Half Moon and Alta Morris lakes (see hike 88, Half Moon Lake). Go straight, turn right 0.3 mile farther, then reach deep gray Susie Lake. From this attractive lake's rock-lined shore, you can look north to the lofty heights of Dick's Peak and Dick's Pass. You'll find good campsites near the east shore by the outlets. Heather Lake, 0.5 mile past Susie Lake, shares similar scenic qualities with her sister and also has east-shore campsites. Look nearby for a 20-foot waterfall.

Reach a trail fork 0.4 mile past Heather Lake and go right. (The trails of hike 89, Lake Aloha, Lake of the Woods, and Ropi Lake, lie 1.5 miles to the left.) You now walk 0.7 mile along the shore of island-rich Lake Aloha, the largest lake in Desolation Wilderness, and then climb up to Mosquito Pass for inspiring, previously described southward views. From the pass turn left down to Clyde's Lake, which hosts suitable campsites between the lake and two small bodies of water just to the north.

Back on the main trail, head north on Rubicon Trail. Meadow camping among lodgepole pine awaits after 2.5 miles at China Flat. Reach a trail fork 0.4 mile farther. The trails of hike 90 (Maud, Lois, and Zitella Lakes) lie to the left; you, however, go right and walk near the Rubicon River for 2.7 miles to Camper Flat, another popular meadow loaded with campsites. (Note that you can also connect with hike 90 trails here.)

From Camper Flat, go right onto Velma Lakes Trail for a 1.8-mile gradual climb to the Velma Lakes (described in hike 85, Eagle Lake and the Velma Lakes). Go right at a trail fork just before Middle Velma Lake, then go left at another fork 0.3 mile farther. From here it's another mile to reach previously encountered paths and the route back to the trailhead.

87 MOUNT TALLAC

Length: 11 miles round trip
Hiking time: 7 hours
High point: 9,735 feet
Total elevation gain: 3,500 feet
Difficulty: strenuous
Season: early July through mid-October

Water: available at Floating Island and Cathedral Lakes; little to none along the last 2.7 steep miles
Maps: USGS 7.5' Emerald Bay, USFS Desolation Wilderness
Information: Lake Tahoe Basin Management Unit

This hike challenges even the most physically fit, but the reward of a panoramic view over Lake Tahoe, Desolation Wilderness, and the rest of the northern Sierra Nevada make the exertion worthwhile. Be sure to bring warm clothing and protection from the sun. Also, check the weather: you don't want to get caught in a thunderstorm on Mount Tallac's exposed ridges and summit. Hardy backpackers can climb Mount Tallac and then head down to Gilmore Lake and the trails of hike 86 (Dick's Lake, Gilmore Lake, and Lake Aloha).

From the junction of Highways 89 and 50 in South Lake Tahoe, go northwest on Highway 89. Do not take the road on the left after 3.9 miles that's signed for Mount Tallac. Instead, continue another 0.7 mile, then turn left onto paved Spring Creek Road (Road 13N07). Follow this road, ignoring lesser

A hiker rests at Cathedral Lake.

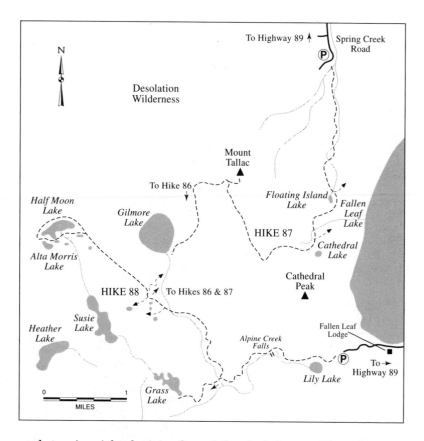

roads turning right, for 0.8 mile, and then look for a small wooden sign on the left.

The trail immediately crosses Tallac Creek and begins a gentle 1.9-mile climb under white fir, quaking aspen, and towering Jeffrey pine along Floating Island Lake's outlet stream to the lake itself. Here you'll find a few campsites and good swimming in relatively shallow waters.

Follow the trail nearest the lakeshore, then climb through a mixed red fir–lodgepole pine forest, with occasional views of Mount Tallac. Look for a small, rocky knob that's ringed by western juniper just east of the trail at 2.4 miles: from its top are excellent views of Fallen Leaf Lake, Lake Tahoe, and the steep Sierra peaks to the east. Back on the trail, cross Cathedral Creek, go right at a trail fork, then reach Cathedral Lake, which is guarded by steep-walled Cathedral Peak. The lake's waters offer good swimming in late summer.

So far your path has climbed very gently; now it becomes very steep, testing your leg strength and aerobic conditioning. As you leave Cathedral Lake, look for views of Fallen Leaf Lake, Lake Tahoe, and its surrounding mountains. Lodgepole pine, mountain hemlock, and stunted Jeffrey pine dot the landscape, and numerous wildflowers help you forget your pounding heart. At 3.5 miles the trail begins switchbacking west up a glacially carved bowl. Go left at an unmarked trail junction, and reach the ridge at 4 miles. From here, your eyes take in nearly the whole of Desolation Wilderness, with westward views of Pyramid Peak, the Crystal Range, and numerous lakes.

Savor this fantastic scenery as you climb northwest just below the ridge's crest. A stone cairn at 5.2 miles marks a trail junction. A 1.5-mile downhill walk brings you to Gilmore Lake (see hike 86, Dick's Lake, Gilmore Lake, and Lake Aloha). Head uphill for the final rocky 0.3 mile to your lofty goal.

Plan to spend a lot of time perched on metamorphic Mount Tallac's 9,735-foot summit. You'll have fantastic views over all of the northern Sierra Nevada and some of Nevada's basin and range topography.

88   HALF MOON LAKE

Length: 12 miles round trip
Hiking time: 8 hours or over-
   night
High point: 8,200 feet
Total elevation gain: 2,000 feet
Difficulty: moderate
Season: mid-July through early
   October

Water: available from lakes and
   streams
Maps: USGS 7.5' Emerald Bay,
   USGS 7.5' Rockbound Valley,
   USGS 7.5' Echo Lake, USFS
   Desolation Wilderness
Information: Lake Tahoe Basin
   Management Unit

The huge glacial cirque that holds Half Moon and Alta Morris lakes rates among the most gorgeous areas in the northern Sierra. Swim, sun, and admire steep peaks and high ridges.

Drive 3 miles northwest on Highway 89 from the junction of Highways 50 and 89, then turn left on Fallen Leaf Road. Go 4.6 miles to the former Fallen Leaf Lodge, and continue past it as far as possible before parking.

The hike begins paved and level past swampy Lily Lake, where day hikers can fill out a self-issue wilderness permit. Skirt several summer cottages at 0.6 mile, then pass one of Glen Alpine Creek's many scenic falls, flanked by Cathedral Peak to the north and Angora Peak to the south. Step into a shaded forest at 1.8 miles at a reunion with Glen Alpine Creek, then bear right 0.1 mile farther at a signed trail junction. (The left trail travels 0.7 mile to Grass Lake, which offers good swimming and camping.)

Sections of strenuous climbing ensue past scattered ferns, sage, red-flowered mountain spiraea, and huckleberry oak, and then Sierra juniper, Jeffrey pine, pinemat manzanita, and ceanothus. Bear right at a signed trail junction at 3.6 miles, then 0.2 mile farther note a spectacular display of Indian pond lilies dotting a black pond on the left. A few more footsteps connect you with hike 86 (Dick's Lake, Gilmore Lake, and Lake Aloha) at a four-way trail intersection: the left fork heads for Susie and Heather lakes and Lake Aloha; the right fork goes to Gilmore Lake. You proceed straight. At 4.2 miles come to a rocky flat where Sierra junipers frame a view of Susie Lake, surrounded by numerous high peaks.

Continue up into a large glacial cirque, accompanied by mountain hemlock, juvenile lodgepole pine, and several ponds, to the lightly visited yet very beautiful Half Moon Lake, where the deep waters reflect the steep visages of nearby Jack's and Dick's peaks.

The scenic north shoreline trail escorts you past a mix of lodgepole and western white pine, sage, abundant corn lily, and sulfur flower. At 6 miles, cross an alder-choked inlet stream and a colorful meadow to Alta Morris Lake, where you'll spot a large campsite on the Dick's Peak side. Continue cross-country along Half Moon Lake's south side past several campsites to regain the trail back to the parking area.

89 LAKE ALOHA, LAKE OF THE WOODS, AND ROPI LAKE

Length: 17.5 miles round trip
Hiking time: 2 to 3 days
High point: 8,400 feet
Total elevation gain: 2,800 feet
Difficulty: strenuous
Season: early July to late September

Water: available from lakes and streams
Maps: USGS 7.5' Echo Lake, USGS 7.5' Pyramid Peak, USGS 7.5' Emerald Bay, USFS Desolation Wilderness
Information: Lake Tahoe Basin Management Unit

This hike offers extensive views of high Sierra peaks as it takes you to five beautiful lakes.

From the Lake Tahoe Visitor Center on Highway 89 (3.1 miles northwest of the junction of Highways 89 and 50), drive east 0.1 mile, then turn right (south) on Fallen Leaf Road. Go 4.6 miles to the former Fallen Leaf Lodge, then watch closely for the signed trailhead on the left, 0.1 mile past the lodge.

For the first 1.9 miles, the trail (17E10) often crosses Lily Lake's inlet streams as it steeply ascends up rocky switchbacks, which necessitate the use of occasional handholds. The next 0.5 mile, level or slightly downhill, passes sulfur flower and sage with great views to the left of rocky Angora Peak. At 2.4 miles head straight at a trail intersection.

At 2.8 miles you reach the highest elevation of this journey, 8,400 feet, which features a panorama of nearby High Sierra lakes and mountains, including Echo Lakes to the east and an open display of Desolation Wilderness scenery to the south and west. The next 0.4 mile reveals many odd-shaped Sierra juniper growing in exposed spots, with the steep Sierran slopes beyond. Tamarack Lake, Ralston Lake, and Ralston Peak lie to the south, and the upper 500 feet of Pyramid Peak rises to the west.

Reach the Pacific Crest Trail at 3.2 miles. A left turn leads to Tamarack, Ralston, and Echo lakes (see hike 95, Tamarack and Ralston Lakes via Echo Lakes). You go right and gently climb along a plateau sporting scattered sage, native fescue grasses, red fir, and tall western white pine for 0.3 mile to scenic Haypress Meadows. Bear right 0.1 mile farther at a signed trail intersection. Go right at 3.8 miles, left 100 yards farther, then look right for a view of a green pond and Lake Margery.

At 4.1 miles the path leads through a meadow highlighted by blue lupine and red mountain heather. Bear right at a trail fork 0.1 mile farther, shortly followed by your first full view of Pyramid Peak.

Reach a trail fork near the middle of Lake Aloha's eastern shoreline at 5.3 miles (a right turn leads to Heather and Susie lakes [see hike 86, Dick's Lake, Gilmore Lake, and Lake Aloha]). Go left for a scenic shoreline stroll. Note the western white pine and mountain hemlock thriving on the countless granite rock islands that highlight shallow Lake Aloha. Also, look for abundant campsites a short distance from the lake.

Bear right at 5.8 miles, then left 100 yards farther at an unsigned junction. Follow the faint trail as it skirts the northeastern flank of Peak 8383. At 5.9 miles a crest affords a view of aptly named Lake of the Woods, which rivals Lake Aloha in popularity because of the numerous campsites. The path drops to the north shore and two large campsites, then heads east.

At 6.2 miles note the return trail on the left at the northeast corner

Western white pines grow near Desolation Wilderness lakes.

of Lake of the Woods, then proceed straight. At 6.7 miles the trail departs Lake of the Woods and heads south 0.3 mile onto a flat. You soon cross Lake of the Woods's outlet stream and head due west, just south of a steep cliff. Arrive at rocky Ropi Lake at 7.6 miles. Loaded with plenty of campsites, this uniquely shaped, snag-covered lake invites a circumnavigating trek highlighted by views of Pyramid Peak. Consider easy cross-country walks to Toem Lake (west) and Avalanche Lake (south).

To return to the trailhead, retrace your steps to the above-mentioned junction at the northeast tip of Lake of the Woods. Turn right here and climb for 0.5 mile, then go straight at a trail intersection. Hike down into Haypress Meadows, then head right 0.2 mile farther at the signed trail junction onto previously trekked trails.

90 MAUD, LOIS, AND ZITELLA LAKES

Length: 24.7 miles round trip
Hiking time: 3 to 5 days
High point: 8,650 feet
Total elevation gain: 5,400 feet
Difficulty: moderate to strenuous
Season: late July to early October

Water: plenty at the lakes, but bring water to Maud Lake
Maps: USGS 7.5' Rockbound Valley, USGS 7.5' Pyramid Peak, USFS Desolation Wilderness
Information: Eldorado National Forest Information Center

Journey deep into one of Desolation Wilderness's more remote sections and visit numerous high lakes and vista points.

Take the signed Wrights Lake Road from the north side of Highway 50 about 46 miles east of Placerville and 17 miles west of the junction of Highways 50 and 89. This paved road, initially signed 11N26, reaches a dirt road after 4 miles (see hike 94, Sylvia and Lyons Lakes). Go straight here and at another road junction 2 miles farther. After another 1.9 miles, bear left at a three-way junction, then go 0.5 mile to the trailhead, 0.2 mile south of Dark Lake.

The trail skirts the west and north shores of Beauty Lake at 0.5 mile, followed by a left turn at a signed trail fork 0.1 mile farther. Teasing views of Mount Price become more prominent when the ridge crests from 0.9 to 1.1 miles. Go left at the trail sign at 1.8 miles, break into open, granite boulder country, then bear left again 0.4 mile farther. (The right fork leads to Gertrude and Tyler lakes [see hike 91, Tyler and Gertrude Lakes]).

Walk past quaking aspen, white fir, lodgepole pine, and mountain hemlock to your first sighting of Rockbound Pass at 3.1 miles, then cross Silver Creek 0.2 mile farther. Head straight at an unsigned junction just outside a lodgepole pine and white fir forest at 4.1 miles.

Massive Sierra juniper shrubs appear just prior to your arrival at

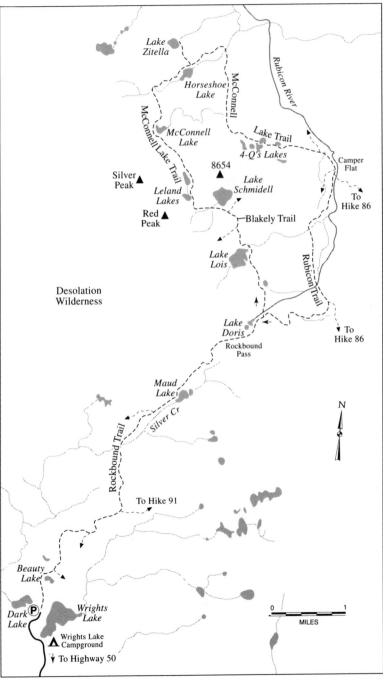

Lake Zitella

Horseshoe Lake

McConnell

McConnell Lake

Silver Peak

McConnell Lake Trail

8654

Lake Trail

4-Q's Lakes

Rubicon River

Camper Flat

To Hike 86

Leland Lakes

Lake Schmidell

Red Peak

Blakely Trail

Lake Lois

Rubicon Trail

Desolation Wilderness

Lake Doris

To Hike 86

Rockbound Pass

Maud Lake

Silver Cr

N

Rockbound Trail

To Hike 91

Beauty Lake

Dark Lake

Wrights Lake

Wrights Lake Campground

To Highway 50

0   1

MILES

shallow and slightly muddy Maud Lake. The numerous campsites here frequently fill up on late summer weekends, but other overnight spots are readily available in the wide, open basin above the lake.

Switchback 1.1 miles and climb past profuse alpine wildflowers to splendid views east and west atop often windy Rockbound Pass. Hardy whitebark pine survive in this stark environment as wide-growing shrubs, and a lone, weathered mountain hemlock bears the sign of the 8,650-foot pass.

Drop 0.5 mile to Lake Doris, where a series of unprotected campsites borders the south and east sections of the sky-blue waters. A couple of sheltered campsites rest in the more forested north area.

A sloping meadow leads gently down from Lake Doris to a trail sign 0.2 mile away, where you bear left on Blakely Trail at 6 miles. The level tread rounds a bend, heads into a lupine-covered field by a pond, and reaches scenic Lake Lois at 6.7 miles. A few adequate campsites exist around this deep and clear lake, which is bound by chunks and walls of metamorphic rock.

After a brief climbing burst past Lake Lois, the trail levels to a signed junction, where you continue straight at 7.3 miles. The path then offers magnificent northerly views, including an inaugural

sighting of Lake Schmidell. Plunge into a western white pine and mountain hemlock forest, then go left onto McConnell Lake Trail 0.3 mile farther. A brief scamper to the right, however, leads down to roundish Lake Schmidell, which offers plenty of campsites and views of steep cliffs to the west and north.

Back on McConnell Lake Trail, you'll cross one of the lake's inlet creeks and then begin a climb with numerous vantage points for viewing Lake Schmidell. Reach a mountain hemlock–covered saddle at 8.4 miles, a good perch for eagle's-eye views of Leland Lakes. The trail then winds by the eastern shoreline of both Leland Lakes, revealing an array of good campsites. Eastward, gently sloping rock mounds culminate in Peak 8654. The western walls are decidedly steeper, climaxed by

Lake Lois

8,930-foot Silver Peak due west and 9,307-foot Red Peak to the southwest.

Leave the Leland Lakes behind at 9.6 miles, then gently descend for 1 mile in open forest. Pay close attention to the rock ducks (cairns) that guide you the final 0.2 mile to the west side of shallow, marshy McConnell Lake. Following the countless rock ducks from this lake on the mile-long journey to Horseshoe Lake is tricky, so be alert. A small island highlights this grassy lake at 11.4 miles, where two campsites nestle underneath the pines on the northwest side.

Just beyond Horseshoe Lake, turn left at the signed trail junction for Lake Zitella. Rock ducks lead you 0.4 mile to this beautiful spot, where you can admire tiny islands decorating the surface. A campsite awaits on a ledge on the lake's south side, and you'll discover a couple of hidden sites in the woods on the north side.

If you prefer the more scenic return, retrace your steps to the trailhead. For a more diversified round trip, return to the signed junction near Horseshoe Lake, then head left (northeast) and drop 0.5 mile through open forest to a flat at 13.4 miles. The trail goes south upon crossing Horseshoe Lake's outlet and remains mostly flat to the shallow 4-Q's Lakes at 15.2 miles.

Bear right 0.5 mile farther onto the signed Rubicon Trail, proceed into denser forest, cross the sometimes dry Lake Schmidell outlet, then hike through Camper Flat, where you'll find good campsites and the opportunity to connect with the trails of hike 86 (Dick's Lake, Gilmore Lake, and Lake Aloha). Stay left at a junction at 16.2 miles (unless you choose to climb 1.4 miles west to Lake Schmidell), then go right 0.1 mile farther.

The following mile stays level and just above the Rubicon River. At 17.4 miles bear right onto Rockbound Trail, then climb steadily for 1.3 miles to Lake Doris. From here, it's a 6-mile hoof to the trailhead.

91 TYLER AND GERTRUDE LAKES

Length: 8 miles round trip
Hiking time: 6 hours or overnight
High point: 8,200 feet
Total elevation gain: 1,400 feet
Difficulty: moderate to strenuous
Season: late July to mid-October
Water: bring your own
Maps: USGS 7.5' Rockbound Valley, USGS 7.5' Pyramid Peak, USFS Desolation Wilderness
Information: Eldorado National Forest Information Center

Attain seclusion while admiring rugged and scenic alpine back-country on this trek to two small lakes that rate among the most pristine in the High Sierra. Choose from several lake campsites that allow good views of steep rocky ridges.

Drive Highway 50 about 46 miles east of Placerville and 17 miles

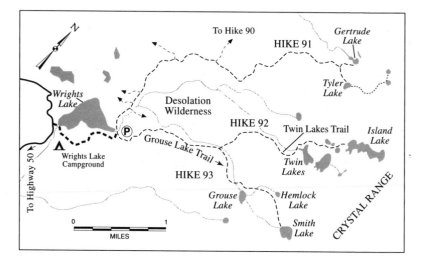

west of the junction of Highways 50 and 89. Take paved Wrights Lake Road (initially signed 11N26), and reach a dirt road after 4 miles (the trailhead for hike 94, Sylvia and Lyons Lakes). Go straight here and 2 miles farther. After another 1.7 miles, note the wilderness area parking lot on the right. Backpackers leave vehicles here, but day hikers continue along the main road another 1.1 miles (go right at two road forks) to the trailhead (look for self-serve dayhike permits).

From the north side of the trailhead parking lot, cross the creek, then pass through the meadow as you enjoy eastward views of Mount Price. Walk through an open red fir and Jeffrey pine forest, and stay left at a trail junction at 0.4 mile. Bear right at two other trail forks shortly thereafter, then go right again on Rockbound Trail at 1.2 miles.

Take Tyler Lake Trail by making a right 0.5 mile farther (the left-hand trail is described in hike 90, Maud, Lois, and Zitella Lakes). Proceed past quaking aspen, huckleberry oak, and lodgepole pine, then watch for rock ducks (cairns) as you ascend a steep gully. The jagged mountaintops to the east come into view at 2 miles, after which the trail climbs steeply.

The trail levels at a saddle at 2.2 miles. From here, climb past a section of scattered Sierra juniper and Jeffrey pine at 2.6 miles, then pass a dark bog in a mountain hemlock forest 0.2 mile farther. Watch for the sign at 3.3 miles directing you to the Tyler grave site.

Arrow-shaped Gertrude Lake appears on the left at 3.9 miles. A mix of mountain hemlock and lodgepole pine adorn the shoreline of this shallow and swimmable lake. Two exposed campsites sit atop the rocky ledge above the north shore.

Plan on spending most of your time at the more scenic Tyler Lake. Retrace your steps 75 yards and locate the rock ducks that guide you 0.2 mile to the oval-shaped and comparatively deeper body of water, sided by steep granite on the south, east, and north sides. A superb campsite rests near the northwest shore beneath a large western white pine and smaller whitebark pine. Find other campsites part way up the smooth granite slabs that taper to the north shore. An easy 0.5 mile cross-country climb northwest to a bench just west of Peak 9441 lets you visit two large, clear alpine ponds. If you want more hiking, consider the trails of hike 90 (Maud, Lois, and Zitella Lakes), hike 92 (Twin and Island Lakes), and hike 93 (Grouse, Hemlock, and Smith Lakes).

92 TWIN AND ISLAND LAKES

Length: 6.2 miles round trip
Hiking time: 4 hours or over-
**   night**
High point: 8,150 feet
Total elevation gain: 1,200 feet
Difficulty: easy to moderate
Season: early July through mid-
**   October**

Water: available from streams
**   and lakes**
Maps: USGS 7.5' Pyramid Peak,
**   USGS 7.5' Rockbound Valley,**
**   USFS Desolation Wilderness**
Information: Eldorado National
**   Forest Information Center**

Twin and Island lakes offer numerous campsites, excellent swimming, and magnificent views of Desolation Wilderness's granitic Crystal Range.

Take the signed Wrights Lake Road from the north side of Highway 50 about 46 miles east of Placerville and 17 miles west of the junction of Highways 50 and 89. This paved road, initially signed 11N26, reaches a dirt road after 4 miles (the trailhead for hike 94, Sylvia and Lyons Lakes). Go straight here and at another road junction 2 miles farther. After another 1.7 miles, you'll see a wilderness area parking lot on the right. Backpackers must leave their car here, but day hikers can continue along the main road another 1.1 miles (go right at two road forks) to the trailhead, where you'll usually find self-serve dayhike permits.

The trail initially travels near the border of a lush meadow/marsh, which provides good eating for the cattle that inhabit the vicinity in late summer. You soon leave them behind, however, and enter a forest of red fir and lodgepole pine. The path crosses granite slabs (look for rock ducks [cairns]), meets a small stream, and then hits a trail fork at 1.1 miles. The right-hand trail is discussed in hike 93 (Grouse, Hemlock, and Smith Lakes). You go left.

From here to the shore of Twin Lakes, you'll be walking across a lot of granite. Carefully placed rocks often line the trail, or you'll see rock ducks. Pay attention: It's easy to lose the way. The main distraction is the high, stark, granite peaks of the Crystal Range looming straight ahead as you climb eastward toward the lakes. At 2.2 miles the trail skirts some small pools of Twin Lakes' outlet stream and then passes through a wet area.

The deep waters of the first Twin Lake await at 2.5 miles. Take a while to imbibe the grandeur of the surrounding mountains. Then, if it's late enough in summer, dive from granite ledges into the lake's deep waters. Look for a couple of campsites at the west end of the lake.

The path crosses a rock dam and then travels along the first Twin Lake's north shore. You'll eventually catch sight of the other Twin Lake to the east as you climb toward Island Lake. A deep pond on the left at 2.8 miles also offers good swimming; several other smaller ponds also line the trail farther on.

Aptly named Island Lake lies in a shallow glacial valley 3.1 miles from the trailhead and offers even better views of the Crystal Range than the Twin Lakes. You can swim in its cool waters or hike along its circumscribing granite. Camping options, however, are limited: look for a few mediocre sites near the west end of the lake.

The Crystal Range looms above the first Twin Lake.

93 GROUSE, HEMLOCK, AND SMITH LAKES

Length: 5.6 miles round trip
Hiking time: 4 hours or overnight
High point: 8,700 feet
Total elevation gain: 1,750 feet
Difficulty: moderate

Season: early July through mid-October
Water: available at the lakes
Maps: USGS 7.5' Pyramid Peak, USFS Desolation Wilderness
Information: Eldorado National Forest Information Center

Climb a forested trail to three magnificent lakes. Besides opportunities for swimming, picnicking, and camping, you'll be treated to expansive views of steep-sided granite Sierra peaks that pierce the sky at nearly 10,000 feet.

Take the paved road signed for Wrights Lake on the north side of Highway 50 about 46 miles east of Placerville and 17 miles west of the Highway 50/89 junction. Follow this road (initially signed 11N26), and go straight where a dirt road turns off to the right for Lyons and Sylvia lakes (hike 94, Sylvia and Lyons Lakes) 4 miles from Highway 50; stay straight again at another junction 6 miles from Highway 50. Look for a wilderness area parking lot on the right another 1.7 miles farther; you must park here if you will be backpacking. Day hikers follow the main road through the campground (bear right at two road forks) and continue another 1.1 miles to the signed trailhead, where there's often self-serve dayhike permits.

The path skirts a lush meadow surrounding a marshy area, which may be populated by cattle in late summer, and then begins a gentle climb. You'll hike past lodgepole pine, red fir, and an occasional Jeffrey pine as intermittent views tantalize you with northward vistas of rolling hills of forest and granite. After crossing some granite slabs (look for rock ducks [cairns]), the path encounters a small stream at 0.9 mile and then reaches a trail fork at 1.1 miles. Hike 92 to Twin and Island lakes goes left; you go right, as indicated by the sign for Smith Lake.

Cross more granite, then ascend an increasingly steep slope through the forest to reach the grass-lined shore of Grouse Lake at 1.8 miles, a good spot for a rest or perhaps a swim in the shallow waters. Several adequate campsites lie near the lake's east and south sides.

Once past Grouse Lake, the trail crosses a seasonal stream, passes through a wet area, and begins a stiff climb. Look for views down to Wrights Lake at 2.2 miles, just before reaching Hemlock Lake at 2.4 miles. Namesake mountain hemlock trees grow in abundance here, nicely complementing the steep granite rising from the north and east shores. The small lake offers two campsites.

However, the splendor of Smith Lake awaits. Continue up through a forest of mountain hemlock, then ascend bare granite slopes that require careful attention to the rock duck guides. Finally, 2.8 miles from the trailhead, you reach Smith Lake, where high walls of exfoliated

High Crystal Range ridges border Smith Lake on three sides, leaving open Sierra vistas to the northwest.

granite surround the lake's deep, cold waters on three sides, leaving open views to the north. This lake, one of the prettiest in the Sierra Nevada, is well worth the effort. Backpackers should search for a level stretch of granite to sleep on.

94 SYLVIA AND LYONS LAKES

Length: 10 miles round trip
Hiking time: 6 hours or over-
night
High point: 8,380 feet
Total elevation gain: 1,600 feet
Difficulty: easy to Lake Sylvia,
moderate to Lyons Lake

Season: early July through mid-
October
Water: available from lakes and
Lyons Creek
Maps: USGS 7.5' Pyramid Peak,
USFS Desolation Wilderness
Information: Eldorado National
Forest Information Center

This hike takes you along the waters of Lyons Creek to some of the most beautiful territory in Desolation Wilderness: the Crystal Range and Pyramid Peak, and also Lyons Lake.

Take the paved road signed for Wrights Lake, which is on the north side of Highway 50 about 46 miles east of Placerville and 17 miles west of the junction of Highways 50 and 89. Follow Wrights Lake Road (Road 11N26) 4 miles, then turn right at a dirt road signed for the Lyons Creek Trail for the final 0.4 mile.

The trail travels most of its length near the granite and mountain alder-lined banks of Lyons Creek. Lodgepole pine is the primary tree species, and as you continue you'll pass by several meadows and seasonal streams. Numerous wildflowers provide a multihued display in midsummer: look for corn lily, brodiaea, and lupine, among others.

Glimpses of 9,983-foot Pyramid Peak lead you onward. Bear right at a trail junction at 1.5 miles, then continue on to the Desolation Wilderness boundary at 2.8 miles. If you wish to cool off on a warm day, look for some small pools in the creek about 100 yards past the boundary. The path then climbs past granite boulders and hillocks to a crossing of Lyons Creek at 4 miles and then to a trail junction at 4.1 miles.

Sylvia Lake lies 0.4 mile down the right fork. Several campsites lie between lodgepole pine and mountain hemlock near the west shore. From the lake's edges you can see mighty Pyramid Peak and its accompanying granite ridges. Consider the 1-mile cross-country hike northeast along a small creek to granite-encased Noelle and Mozelle lakes. Here, nestled under Pyramid Peak's shoulder, you're much more likely to find solitude.

A left turn at the trail fork will take you 0.5 mile up a steep granitic ridge to Lyons Lake. This large, deep, granite-ringed body of water ranks as one of the prettiest anywhere. The Crystal Range's heavily exfoliated granite rises over 1,500 steep feet on the east side, and more moderately sloping granite lies to the north and west. Granite slabs and granite sand beaches surround the entire lake, making an invigo-

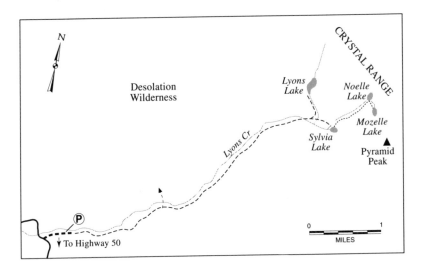

Sylvia Lake campsites offer unimpeded views of 9,983-foot Pyramid Peak.

rating swim into the deep cold water easy. Look for campsites on the southeast side of the lake, or search near the lake's perimeter for a level granite slab. An easy northwesterly cross-country scramble up the rock of at least 150 vertical feet will reward you with southward views of Round Top (hike 99, Winnemucca Lake and Round Top) and other peaks in Mokelumne Wilderness.

95 TAMARACK AND RALSTON LAKES VIA ECHO LAKES

Length: 8.4 miles round trip
Hiking time: 5 hours or over-
night
High point: 7,800 feet
Total elevation gain: 450 feet
Difficulty: easy

Season: early July to mid-
October
Water: available only at the lakes
Maps: USGS 7.5' Echo Lake,
USFS Desolation Wilderness
Information: Eldorado National
Forest Information Center

Take a long, leisurely hillside stroll just above the twin Echo Lakes, then admire windswept, twisted conifers and High Sierra mountain views on the way to island-dotted Tamarack and Ralston lakes.

From Highway 50's Echo Pass 12 miles southwest of South Lake Tahoe, drive west 0.8 mile, then turn right (north) on Johnson Pass Road. Turn left 0.5 mile farther on Echo Lake Road, then drive 0.9 mile to the large parking lot near Echo Lake Chalet.

Trek across Echo Lake's heavily visited spillway area to gain the trail on the far northeast side, and leave most of the hustle and bustle behind. The sandy, level trail keeps you close to sky-blue Echo Lake and whisks you past Sierra juniper, Jeffrey pine, ponderosa pine, and a dry chaparral understory of manzanita and huckleberry oak. You'll see exquisite lakeside summer cottages and notice the jagged rock outcrops hovering above you on the right. Then, at 1.7 miles, arrive at a vista point above Dartmouth Cove, which separates Lower Echo Lake from Upper Echo Lake.

At 2.1 miles the trail climbs noticeably away from Upper Echo Lake to allow eastward views at 2.5 miles of the alpine mountains neighboring the twin lakes. Pyramid Peak rises westward above stunted Sierra juniper as you continue up this exposed, rocky trail section. Reach the Desolation Wilderness boundary at 2.9 miles. The ascending path then ducks into an open forest dotted with orange wavy-leaved paintbrush,

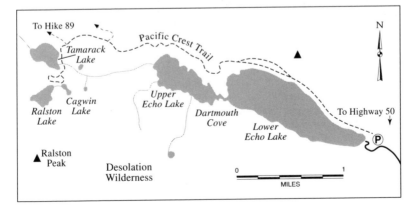

Lower Echo Lake

white yarrow, and blue lupine.

At 3.7 miles go left for the 0.2-mile stroll to Tamarack Lake. A granite wall, laced with communities of fir and western white pine, rises above the lake's far side, topped by the steepest flank of 9,235-foot Ralston Peak. Stands of slender western white pine dominate the shoreline and grow to equal 50-foot heights. The eastern shoreline offers an abundance of campsites.

The on again/off again trail skirts the eastern shoreline, crosses Tamarack Lake's outlet stream, and then passes twin campsites near the lake's marshy south side. Climb the faint trail 0.2 mile to overlook Ralston Lake, nestled below namesake Ralston Peak. This pristine, deep lake and neighboring Cagwin Lake offer excellent swimming and a few campsites.

Note that you can walk the trails of hike 89 (Lake Aloha, Lake of the Woods, and Ropi Lake) by traveling 0.5 mile northwest upon rejoining the Pacific Crest Trail.

96 DARDANELLES AND ROUND LAKES

Length: 8.4 miles round trip
Hiking time: 5 hours or over-night
High point: 8,037 feet
Total elevation gain: 1,400 feet
Difficulty: moderate
Season: late June to mid-October

Water: available from lakes and streams
Maps: USGS 7.5' Echo Lake, USGS 7.5' Freel Peak
Information: Lake Tahoe Basin Management Unit

This hike takes you through expansive meadows, across clear streams, and past numerous wildflowers to visit two magnificent, cliff-bordered lakes that offer good swimming and camping.

From the junction of Highways 50 and 89, drive south on 89 for 5.2 miles to the signed Big Meadow trailhead. Go 150 yards farther, and park in the lot on the left.

Walk down to the trailhead, then start climbing past Jeffrey and ponderosa pine and red and white fir. Lodgepole pine and quaking aspen flank a gate at 0.4 mile. Go right 75 yards farther at a signpost and promptly enter Big Meadow. Cross a wooden bridge and follow the path 0.4 mile through the middle of the green expanse. Resume gentle climbing at 0.8 mile through an open, dry forest, which provides ideal conditions for blue lupine, orange Indian paintbrush, and aster. At 1.6 miles the climb steepens as you notice a slender meadow to the right, covered with corn lily, meadow goldenrod, aster, and some yarrow.

Note the trail junction to Round Lake (a side trip described below) at 2 miles. For now, bear right and walk 0.1 mile to a flat, noting the fallen, sliced Jeffrey pine next to the path. Go 50 yards farther, then carefully travel up the unsigned, scant trail to the left, which takes you to a stream 20 yards away. Cross this brook, then stroll along the now obvious trail past sage and aspen 0.1 mile to cross a bigger creek. The trail gradually drops, leading you past an enormous Sierra juniper on the left at 2.6 miles. Cross Round Lake's outlet stream at 2.9 miles, then reach the eastern shore of Dardanelles Lake at 3.3 miles.

Highlights of this shallow lake include a 300-foot sheer rock dome on the south shore and two small peninsulas. The surprisingly warm lake also offers comfortable swimming by midsummer. Several campsites lie near the east and north shores. Find the marsh where Indian pond lily flourish on the north side while strolling the shore amid Sierra juniper, western white pine, lodgepole pine, and pinemat manzanita.

Retrace your steps for 1.3 miles, and go right on Round Lake Trail. It stays mostly level through a fir forest, undertaking a brief ascent after 0.3 mile past a maze of big boulders. You reach the aptly named Round Lake 0.7 mile from the trail junction. Plan to take the easy,

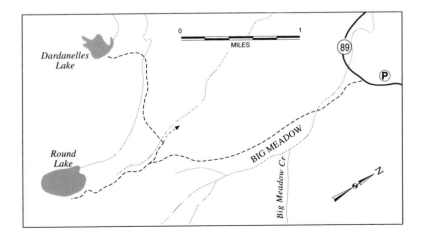

shoreline cross-country stroll past sage, Sierra juniper, and lodgepole and western white pine. Three campsite retreats near the north shore give good views of the sheer rock dome that towers 500 feet above the water on the east side.

97 LAKE MARGARET

Length: 5 miles round trip
Hiking time: 3 hours or overnight
High point: 7,750 feet
Total elevation gain: 550 feet
Difficulty: easy
Season: early July through late October

Water: available from streams and Lake Margaret
Maps: USGS 7.5' Caples Lake, USFS Mokelumne Wilderness
Information: Amador Ranger District, Eldorado National Forest

This hike's gentle trail takes you near the lush green banks of Caples Creek and past huge slabs of granite to Lake Margaret, where you can picnic, swim, and enjoy the mountain scenery. It's a good outing for those wanting a lot of nature for only a little effort.

Take the turnoff on the north side of Highway 88 about 0.2 mile west of the Caples Lake Dam (the trailhead for hike 98, Emigrant Lake) and 0.5 mile east of the turnoff for the Kirkwood Ski Area. Follow the short road 150 yards to its end.

The signed trail begins at the west end of the parking area, just north of the road. Descend through a lodgepole pine and red fir forest at a moderate pitch, then cross a seasonal creek at 0.2 mile. The trail briefly heads east; look straight ahead for glimpses of the high mountain ridge just north of Caples Lake.

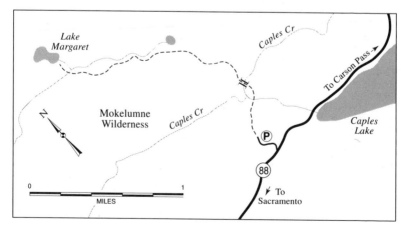

The last stretch of trail before reaching Lake Margaret

The path briefly parallels, then crosses, another seasonal creek. A good campsite lies just to the left of the trail as you near the banks of Caples Creek at 0.6 mile. This also makes a good picnic spot; there's green grass, and the creek's clear waters are deep enough for wading.

The trail quickly reaches the creek itself and then crosses it on a dilapidated wooden bridge. You soon begin a gentle climb through a gully bordered by huge granite hillocks. After the path levels, it skirts a small, lodgepole pine– and willow-ringed pond on the left at 1.2 miles and then crosses some granite.

A much larger pond, surrounded by lodgepole pine and red fir, awaits on the right at 1.6 miles. You soon cross a stream, pass through a large mountain alder thicket, and then note that western white pine have joined the forest cover.

Quaking aspen, with their tremulous green leaves and bright white bark, begin to border the trail at 2.2 miles; they accompany you for 300 yards to the most recently encountered stream, which you cross on a log. You now begin the final ascent to your destination, following rock ducks (cairns) up the gently sloping granite.

After the brief climb, reach the deep waters of Lake Margaret. Numerous granite slabs stretch from high above to far below the lake's surface. You'll find numerous places to swim, either near the shore or out to some of the small granite islands that dot the lake's surface. Campers will find two sites along the eastern shore and two more near the west shore.

EMIGRANT LAKE

Length: 9 miles round trip
Hiking time: 5 hours or overnight
High point: 8,600 feet
Total elevation gain: 950 feet
Difficulty: easy
Season: mid-July through late October

Water: available from Caples Lake and Emigrant Lake
Maps: USGS 7.5' Caples Lake, USFS Mokelumne Wilderness
Information: Amador Ranger District, Eldorado National Forest

This trail offers an easy day hike or overnight trip that's suitable for all. You'll travel through small, flower-filled meadows and a mixed pine/fir forest to deep Emigrant Lake, where tall mountain peaks tower high above.

The trailhead parking area, signed for Caples Lake, is on the south side of Highway 88 by the Caples Lake Dam, which is 4.9 miles west of Carson Pass.

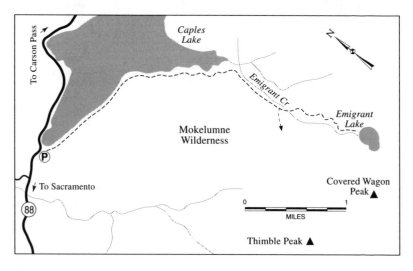

Both steep cliffs and shaded forest border Emigrant Lake.

The signed trail begins near the bathrooms and, after passing a few quaking aspen, contours just above the shore of Caples Lake through a mixed forest of red fir and lodgepole pine. Caples Lake, quite popular for fishing, also offers cool refreshment on hot summer days.

Open views of Round Top's summit (hike 99, Winnemuca Lake and Round Top) appear 1 mile from the trailhead. You'll also see the vast expanse of the high ridge north of Highway 88. At 1.2 miles note the sign for "Emigrant Road"; however, most traces of this historic trail have disappeared.

Continue straight and pass through a small grove of quaking aspen. The trail crosses four seasonal creeks over the next 1.2 miles, each bordered by lush greenery, then angles south along Emigrant Creek and away from Caples Lake.

The path now climbs gently through small meadow patches and past granite boulders and outcrops. Mountain hemlock join the forest as you walk near the willow-lined creek bank and go left at a trail fork at 3.4 miles.

A rock-hop across Emigrant Lake's outlet stream awaits at 4 miles, after which you'll have occasional eastward views through the trees of The Sisters' rocky spires as the climb continues. At 4.3 miles the trail levels and parallels a small meadow near the stream, which is bordered by an abundance of red mountain heather.

Finally, 4.5 miles from the trailhead, you reach the deep, granite-ringed waters of glacier-formed Emigrant Lake. A steep, talus-clad cliff rises from the lake's south shore, and to the southwest lies the broad ridge of 9,565-foot Covered Wagon Peak. Farther west towers 9,805-foot Thimble Peak, a volcanic vent that covered much of this area with lava, volcanic ash, and mudflows from four to twenty million years ago.

Emigrant Lake offers several good swimming sites if you come in late summer. Those who stay overnight will find a campsite just east of the outlet stream, and several others to the west are nestled among lodgepole pine and mountain hemlock.

99 WINNEMUCCA LAKE AND ROUND TOP

Length: 6.3 miles round trip
Hiking time: 5 hours or over-night
High point: 10,381 feet
Total elevation gain: 2,200 feet
Difficulty: strenuous
Season: late July through mid-October

Water: available from streams and lakes
Maps: USGS 7.5' Carson Pass, USGS 7.5' Caples Lake, USFS Mokelumne Wilderness
Information: Amador Ranger District, Eldorado National Forest

This hike takes you past two gorgeous alpine lakes where you can picnic, swim, and camp and then allows you to climb Round Top, where an extensive Sierra Nevada panorama awaits.

Take the Woods Lake campground turnoff, which is on Highway 88's

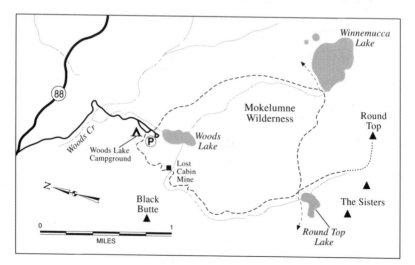

south side 3.2 miles east of the Caples Lake Dam and 1.7 miles west of Carson Pass. Follow the paved road 1.5 miles to the campground, then bear left and park in the day-use picnic area.

The trail, signed for Winnemucca Lake, begins on the east side of the road by a wooden bridge spanning Woods Creek. Cross the bridge, go straight at a three-way junction, and begin a climb through a forest of mountain hemlock, lodgepole pine, and western white pine. At 0.8 mile leave the trees behind and hike across an open hillside covered with sagebrush and a multitude of wildflowers as views of Round Top's summit lure you ever upward.

The sparkling waters of Winnemucca Lake await at 1.5 miles. Here, under Round Top's steep cliffs, you can swim and sunbathe on warm days and also camp at one of the several sites along the south and west shores.

To continue, head right at a trail fork, cross Winnemucca Lake's outlet, then begin climbing westward. As you gain elevation, look north for good views of Desolation Wilderness. At 2.2 miles the trail passes through a small

Round Top rises high above Winnemucca Lake.

saddle populated by whitebark pine before dropping 150 yards to Round Top Lake, which is guarded on the south by the high peaks of The Sisters and Round Top. Those seeking campsites will find two on the lake's northwest side.

If you wish an easy 4.8-mile hike, head downhill to the trailhead at Woods Lake. If you wish to climb Round Top, be sure you have several layers of warm clothing, good boots, sunscreen, sunglasses, a hat, and plenty of food and water. Be aware that there are several steep sections, which can be dangerous when covered with snow, a condition that usually persists well into August.

To begin the ascent, head left at the lake and take a faint trail southwest. It travels along the left side of a gully and climbs 0.5 mile to a saddle between Round Top and the easternmost peak of The Sisters, where you'll have views similar to those from Round Top's summit.

From the saddle scramble 400 yards along Round Top's steep, boulder-shouldered south side to the double-humped summit, elevation 10,381 feet. You can easily surmount the western hump, but avoid the much steeper and more dangerous eastern hump. Fantastic views await in all directions: to the south, you'll see range upon range of high Sierra Peaks, to the southwest lies the bulk of Mokelumne Wilderness, numerous lakes spread out far below on the north side, and the white peaks of Desolation Wilderness beckon to the far north.

When you've imbibed as much of this magnificence as possible, retrace your steps to Round Top Lake and take the 2.5-mile downhill trail signed for Woods Lake. The path initially travels near the lake's outlet stream as Black Butte looms directly ahead and then enters a forest of whitebark pine and mountain hemlock. The trail eventually travels by numerous red fir and western white pine to join a dirt road. Follow the dirt road 0.4 mile to its gated end on the west side of Woods Lake Campground. From here, make your way through the campground to the trailhead.

100 GRANITE LAKE

Length: 4.4 miles round trip
Hiking time: 3 hours or overnight
High point: 8,700 feet
Total elevation gain: 600 feet
Difficulty: easy
Season: mid-July through late October

Water: available from Middle Creek and Granite Lake
Maps: USGS 7.5' Carson Pass, USGS 7.5' Pacific Valley, USFS Mokelumne Wilderness
Information: Amador Ranger District, Eldorado National Forest

This hike offers an easy way in to some of Mokelumne Wilderness' most beautiful territory. The gentle climb to Granite Lake allows good views of high Sierra peaks, and the lake itself offers swimming, picnicking, and relative solitude.

Take Blue Lakes Road, which leaves Highway 88's south side 6.3 miles east of Carson Pass and 2.5 miles west of Highway 89. Ignore a left forking road at 7 miles signed for Wet Meadows, and continue to a paved road junction 11.5 miles from Highway 88. Go right and reach Middle Creek Campground after another 1.5 miles of driving, then continue another 300 yards and park in the lot on the left.

Begin under the shade of mountain hemlock and lodgepole pine, and soon cross Middle Creek on a log bridge. From here, head downstream through a lush area thriving with numerous wildflowers. A trail from the campground comes in from the left at 0.15 mile, after which the main trail begins a gentle southwest climb away from the creek and campground.

First small and then large red fir join the forest cover, eventually followed by western white pine. As you walk past large granite boul-

These hikers were prepared when a summer rainstorm hit Granite Lake.

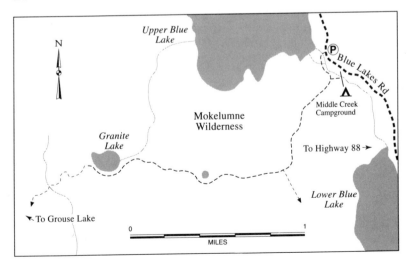

ders, note that the trail tread consists of coarse granite sands, the product of millions of years of erosion.

At 0.7 mile look through tree gaps for views of dozens of high Sierra peaks stretching to the south, west, and north. An unsigned trail takes off on the left near a wilderness boundary sign at 1 mile. Go straight and zigzag up a ridge as you enjoy a northward view of Upper Blue Lake. You'll eventually reach a small granite-encircled pond that sits just to the right of the trail at 1.5 miles.

You then begin a relatively steep ascent, which is made easier by mountain vistas to the southeast. At 1.9 miles the trail crosses a seasonal stream, then passes by large numbers of lupines. The willow-lined banks of Granite Lake's outlet stream at 2.1 miles signal the nearness of the lake itself, which you reach after a final 0.1-mile uphill stretch.

Low ridges of granite surround the deep namesake body of water, where you can wade from the sandy shore into the lake's deep areas on warm days. If you wish to camp, an adequate site awaits on the south shore, with the shade of lodgepole pine, whitebark pine, and mountain hemlock nearby. If you want to do more hiking, continue west on the trail in the direction of Grouse Lake, 4 miles away. You can also easily surmount the surrounding ridges and obtain broad vistas of lakes, valleys, and peaks.

APPENDIX 1: INFORMATION

Almanor Ranger District
Lassen National Forest
P.O. Box 767
Chester, CA 96020
(916) 258-2141

Amador Ranger District
Eldorado National Forest
Star Route 3
Pioneer, CA 95666
(209) 295-4251

Anderson Marsh State Historical
Park
5300 Soda Bay Road
Kelseyville, CA 95451
(707) 994-0688

Beckwourth Ranger District
Plumas National Forest
P.O. Box 7
Mohawk, CA 96013
(916) 836-2575

Big Bar Ranger District
Shasta-Trinity National Forest
Star Route 1, Box 10
Big Bar, CA 96010
(916) 623-6106

Big Basin Redwoods State Park
21600 Big Basin Way
Boulder Creek, CA 95006
(408) 338-6132

Bothe–Napa Valley State Park
3801 Saint Helena Highway
North
Calistoga, CA 94515
(707) 942-4575

Bureau of Land Management,
Arcata Resource Area
1125 16th Street, Room 219
Arcata, CA 95521
(707) 822-7648

Butano State Park
P.O. Box 9
Pescadero, CA 94060
(415) 879-0173

Castle Crags State Park
P.O. Box 80
Castella, CA 96017
(916) 235-2684

Castle Rock State Park
1500 Skyline Boulevard
Los Gatos, CA 95030
(408) 867-2952

City of Chico Parks Division
P.O. Box 3420
Chico, CA 95927
(916) 895-4972

Corning Ranger District
Mendocino National Forest
22000 Corning Road
Corning, CA 96021
(916) 824-5196

D. L. Bliss–Emerald Bay State
Park
P.O. Box 266
Tahoma, CA 95733
(916) 525-7277

East Bay Regional Park District
2950 Peraltal Oaks Court
P.O. Box 5381
Oakland, CA 94605-0381
(510) 635-0135

Eldorado National Forest
Information Center
3070 Camino Heights Drive
Camino, CA 95709
(916) 644-6048

Golden Gate National Recreation Area
Fort Mason, Building 201
San Francisco, CA 94123
(415) 556-0561

Half Moon Bay State Beaches
95 Kelly Avenue
Half Moon Bay, CA 94019
(415) 726-8800

Happy Camp Ranger District
Klamath National Forest
P.O. Box 377
Happy Camp, CA 96039
(916) 493-2243

Hat Creek Ranger District
Lassen National Forest
P.O. Box 220
Fall River Mills, CA 96028
(916) 336-5521

Hayfork Ranger District
Shasta-Trinity National Forest
P.O. Box 159
Hayfork, CA 96041
(916) 628-5227

Henry W. Coe State Park
P.O. Box 846
Morgan Hill, CA 95038
(408) 779-2728

Humboldt Redwoods State Park
P.O. Box 100
Weott, CA 95571
(707) 946-2409

Joseph D. Grant County Park
18405 Mount Hamilton Road
San Jose, CA 95140
(408) 274-6121

Jughandle State Reserve
c/o Mendocino District Headquarters
P.O. Box 440
Mendocino, CA 95460
(707) 937-5804

Lake Tahoe Basin Management Unit
870 Emerald Bay Road, Suite 1
South Lake Tahoe, CA 96150
(916) 573-2600
(Permits and information also available in summer from Lake Tahoe Visitor Center on Highway 89 about 3 miles north of Highway 50. Call [916] 573-2674.)

La Porte Ranger District
Plumas National Forest
P.O. Drawer 369
Challenge, CA 95925
(916) 675-2462

Lassen Volcanic National Park
P.O. Box 100
Mineral, CA 96063-0100
(916) 595-4444

Lava Beds National Monument
Box 867
Tulelake, CA 96134
(916) 667-2282

McArthur–Burney Falls Memorial State Park
Box 1260
Burney, CA 96013
(916) 335-2777

Midpeninsula Regional Open Space District
201 San Antonio Circle, Suite C-135
Mountain View, CA 94040
(415) 691-1200

Mount Diablo State Park
P.O. Box 250
Diablo, CA 94528
(510) 837-2525

Mount Shasta Ranger District
Shasta-Trinity National Forest
204 West Alma
Mount Shasta, CA 96067
(916) 926-4511

Mount Tamalpais State Park
801 Panoramic Highway
Mill Valley, CA 94941
(415) 388-2070

Nevada City Ranger District
Tahoe National Forest
631 Coyote Street
P.O. Box 6003
Nevada City, CA 95959-6003
(916) 265-4531

Point Reyes National Seashore
Point Reyes Station, CA 94956
(415) 663-1092

Prairie Creek Redwoods State
Park
Orick, CA 95555 .
(707) 488-2171

Quincy Ranger District
Plumas National Forest
Box 69
Quincy, CA 95971
(916) 283-0555

Redwood National Park
1111 2nd Street
Crescent City, CA 95531
(707) 464-6101

Richardson Grove State Park
1600 U.S. Highway 101, No. 8
Garberville, CA 95440-0069
(707) 247-3318

Salmon River Ranger District
Klamath National Forest
P.O. Box 280
Etna, CA 96027
(916) 467-5757

Scott River Ranger District
Klamath National Forest
11263 North Highway 3
Fort Jones, CA 96032
(916) 468-5351

Stonyford Ranger District
Mendocino National Forest
5080 Stonyford Ladoga Road
Stonyford, CA 95979
(916) 963-3128

Sugarloaf Ridge State Park
c/o Sonoma District
Headquarters
20 East Spain Street
Sonoma, CA 95476-5729
(707) 938-1519

Truckee Ranger District
Tahoe National Forest
10342 Highway 89 North
Truckee, CA 96161
(916) 587-3558

Van Damme State Park
c/o Mendocino District Headquarters
P.O. Box 440
Mendocino, CA 95460
(707) 937-5804

Warner Mountain Ranger
District
P.O. Box 220
Cedarville, CA 96104
(916) 279-6116

Weaverville Ranger District
Shasta-Trinity National Forest
P.O. Box 1190
Weaverville, CA 96093
(916) 623-2121

Whiskeytown-Shasta-Trinity
National Recreation Area
Whiskeytown Unit
P.O. Box 188
Whiskeytown, CA 96095
(916) 246-1225

Yolla Bolly Ranger District
Shasta-Trinity National Forest
Platina, CA 96076
(916) 352-4211

APPENDIX 2: FURTHER READING

Alt, David D., and Donald W. Hyndman. *Roadside Geology of Northern California.* Missoula: Mountain Press, 1975.

Bakker, Elna. *An Island Called California: An Ecological Introduction.* 2d ed. Berkeley: University of California Press, 1985.

Norris, Robert M., and Robert W. Webb. *Geology of California.* 2d ed. New York: Wiley and Sons, 1990.

San Diego Chapter of the Sierra Club. *Wilderness Basics: The Complete Handbook for Hikers & Backpackers.* 2d ed. Seattle: The Mountaineers, 1993.

Stienstra, Tom. *California Camping.* 1993–1994 ed. San Francisco: Foghorn Press, 1993 (updated yearly).

Storer, Tracy I., and Robert L. Usinger. *Sierra Nevada Natural History.* Berkeley: University of California Press, 1963.

Whitney, Stephen. *A Sierra Club Naturalist's Guide.* San Francisco: Sierra Club Books, 1979.

Audubon Society Field Guides and the Peterson Field Guides give in-depth coverage of plants, animals, and geology.

APPENDIX 3: WHAT TO TAKE

Dayhike Essentials

day pack
first-aid kit
matches
fire starter (for wet wood)
knife (for kindling)
flashlight, extra bulb, batteries
toilet paper
maps
compass
watch
food
water, water purifier
poncho or space blanket
emergency signaling device
wide-brimmed hat
sunglasses, sunblock
wool cap
extra clothing
adequate footwear

Optional Items

insect repellant
camera and film
binoculars
swimsuit

Additional Equipment for Overnights

backpack, waterproof cover
sleeping bag
nylon or plastic ground sheet
air mattress or foam pad
tent
warm jacket or parka
sweater
rain gear
thermal underwear
extra clothing, hiking shorts
gloves
cooking, dishwashing utensils
stove and fuel
small towel
toothbrush
lip protectant
40-foot rope
watch
reading material

INDEX

About the Authors

Both John R. Soares (right) and Marc J. Soares (left) were born in Redding, California. John, the author of *Best Short Hikes in and around the North Sacramento Valley* (The Mountaineers, 1992), has hiked throughout North America and Europe. A resident of Chico, California, he teaches political science at Butte College. Marc, who has walked the trails of Northern California nearly all his life, guides tours at the Redding Arboretum and directs a Sierra Club planting project. He lives in Redding, California, where he works as an independent landscape consultant specializing in native California plants.

THE MOUNTAINEERS, founded in 1906, is a nonprofit outdoor activity and conservation club, whose mission is "to explore, study, preserve, and enjoy the natural beauty of the outdoors...." Based in Seattle, Washington, the club is now the third-largest such organization in the United States, with 14,000 members and four branches throughout Washington State.

The Mountaineers sponsors both classes and year-round outdoor activities in the Pacific Northwest, which include hiking, mountain climbing, ski-touring, snowshoeing, bicycling, camping, kayaking and canoeing, nature study, sailing, and adventure travel. The club's conservation division supports environmental causes through educational activities, sponsoring legislation, and presenting informational programs. All club activities are led by skilled, experienced volunteers, who are dedicated to promoting safe and responsible enjoyment and preservation of the outdoors.

The Mountaineers Books, an active, nonprofit publishing program of the club, produces guidebooks, instructional texts, historical works, natural history guides, and works on environmental conservation. All books produced by The Mountaineers are aimed at fulfilling the club's mission.

If you would like to participate in these organized outdoor activities or in the club's other programs, consider membership in The Mountaineers. For information and an application, write or call The Mountaineers, Club Headquarters, 300 Third Avenue West, Seattle, Washington 98119; (206) 284-6310.

Send or call for our catalog of more than 300 outdoor books:
The Mountaineers Books
1011 SW Klickitat Way, Suite 107, Seattle, WA 98134, 1-800-553-4453

A JOHN HOPE FRANKLIN CENTER BOOK

WORLD-SYSTEMS ANALYSIS   *An Introduction*

Immanuel Wallerstein

DUKE UNIVERSITY PRESS   *Durham and London 2004*

© 2004 Duke University Press
All rights reserved
Printed in the United States of America on acid-free paper ∞
Typeset in Minion by Keystone Typesetting, Inc.
Library of Congress Cataloging-in-Publication Data appear
on the last printed page of this book.

CONTENTS

ACKNOWLEDGMENTS

WHEN I AGREED to write this book, I fortuitously received an invitation from the Universidad Internacional Menéndez Pelayo in Santander, Spain, to give a weeklong summer course on "world-systems analysis." The course consisted of five lectures. The participants were largely graduate students and young faculty members from Spanish universities, who for the most part had relatively little previous exposure to world-systems analysis. There were some forty of them. I thus took advantage of the occasion to give an early version of the five chapters of this book. And I have profited from the feedback they offered me. I thank them.

When I had written a draft of this book, I asked four friends to read it and critique it. These friends were all persons whose judgment as readers and experience as teachers I respect. But they had various degrees of involvement in and attachment to world-systems analysis. I hoped therefore to get a range of reactions, and I did. As with any such exercise, I am grateful to them for saving me from follies and unclarities. They offered me some wise suggestions, which I incorporated. But of course I persisted in my sense of what kind of book I thought most useful to write, and my readers are given the usual exemption for my ignoring some of their advice. Still, the book is better because of the careful readings of Kai Erikson, Walter Goldfrank, Charles Lemert, and Peter Taylor.

TO START *Understanding the World In Which We Live*

THE MEDIA, AND INDEED the social scientists, constantly tell us that two things dominate the world we have been living in since the last decades of the twentieth century: globalization and terrorism. Both are presented to us as substantially new phenomena—the first filled with glorious hope and the second with terrible dangers. The U.S. government seems to be playing a central role in furthering the one and fighting the other. But of course these realities are not merely American but global. What underlies a great deal of the analysis is the slogan of Mrs. Thatcher, who was Great Britain's prime minister from 1979 to 1990: TINA (There Is No Alternative). We are told that there is no alternative to globalization, to whose exigencies all governments must submit. And we are told that there is no alternative, if we wish to survive, to stamping out terrorism ruthlessly in all its guises.

This is not an untrue picture but it is a very partial one. If we look at globalization and terrorism as phenomena that are defined in limited time and scope, we tend to arrive at conclusions that are as ephemeral as the newspapers. By and large, we are not then able to understand the meaning of these phenomena, their origins, their trajectory, and most importantly where they fit in the larger scheme of things. We tend to ignore their history. We are unable to put the pieces together, and we are constantly surprised that our short-term expectations are not met.

How many people expected in the 1980s that the Soviet Union would crumble as fast and as bloodlessly as it did? And how many people expected in 2001 that the leader of a movement few had ever heard of, al-Qaeda, could attack so boldly the Twin Towers in New York and the Pentagon on September 11, and cause so much damage? And yet, seen from a longer perspective, both events form part of a larger scenario whose details we might not have known in advance but whose broad outlines were quite predictable.

Part of the problem is that we have studied these phenomena in separate boxes to which we have given special names—politics, economics, the social structure, culture—without seeing that these boxes are constructs more of our imagination than of reality. The phenomena dealt with in these separate boxes are so closely intermeshed that each presumes the other, each affects the other, each is incomprehensible without taking into account the other boxes. And part of the problem is that we tend to leave out of our analyses of what is and is not "new" the three important turning points of our modern world-system: (1) the long sixteenth century during which our modern world-system came into existence as a capitalist world-economy; (2) the French Revolution of 1789 as a world event which accounts for the subsequent dominance for two centuries of a geoculture for this world-system, one that was dominated by centrist liberalism; and (3) the world revolution of 1968, which presaged the long terminal phase of the modern world-system in which we find ourselves and which undermined the centrist liberal geoculture that was holding the world-system together.

The proponents of world-systems analysis, which this book is about, have been talking about globalization since long before the word was invented—not, however, as something new but as something that has been basic to the modern world-system ever since it began in the sixteenth century. We have been arguing that the separate boxes of analysis—what in the universities are called the disciplines—are an obstacle, not an aid, to understanding the world. We have been arguing that the social reality within which we live and which determines what our options are has not been the multiple national states of which we are citizens but something larger, which we call a world-system. We have been saying that this world-system has had many institutions—states and the interstate system, productive firms, households, classes, identity groups of all sorts—and that these institutions form a matrix which permits the system to operate but at the same time stimulates both the conflicts and the contradictions which permeate the system. We have been arguing that this system is a social creation, with a history, whose origins need to be explained, whose ongoing mechanisms need to be delineated, and whose inevitable terminal crisis needs to be discerned.

In arguing this way, we have not only gone against much of the official wisdom of those in power, but also against much of the conventional knowledge put forth by social scientists for two centuries now. For this reason, we have said that it is important to look anew not only at how the world in which we live works but also at how we have come to think about this world. World-systems analysts see themselves therefore as engaging in a fundamental protest against the ways in which we have thought that we know the world. But we also believe that the emergence of this mode of analysis is a reflection of, an expression of, the real protest about the deep inequalities of the world-system that are so politically central to our current times.

I myself have been engaged in and writing about world-systems analysis for over thirty years. I have used it to describe the history and the mechanisms of the modern world-system. I have used it to delineate the structures of knowledge. I have discussed it as a method and a point of view. But I have never tried to set down in one place the totality of what I mean by world-systems analysis.

Over these thirty years, the kind of work that comes under this rubric has become more common and its practitioners more widespread geographically. Nonetheless, it still represents a minority view, and an oppositional view, within the world of the historical social sciences. I have seen it praised, attacked, and quite often misrepresented and misinterpreted—sometimes by hostile and not very well-informed critics, but sometimes by persons who consider themselves partisans or at least sympathizers. I decided that I would like to explain in one place what I consider its premises and principles, to give a holistic view of a perspective that claims to be a call for a holistic historical social science.

This book is intended for three audiences at once. It is written for the general reader who has no previous specialist knowledge. This person may be a beginning undergraduate in the university system or a member of the general public. Secondly, it is written for the graduate student in the historical social sciences who wants a serious introduction to the issues and perspectives that come under the rubric of world-systems analysis. And finally it is written for the experienced practitioner who wishes to grapple with my particular viewpoint in a young but growing community of scholars.

The book begins by tracing what many readers will think a circuitous path. The first chapter is a discussion of the structures of knowledge of the modern world-system. It is an attempt to explain the historical origins of this mode of analysis. It is only with chapters 2–4 that we discuss the actual mechanisms of the modern world-system. And it is only in chapter 5, the last, that we discuss the possible future we are facing and therefore our contemporary realities. Some readers will prefer to jump to chapter 5 immediately, to make chapter 5 into chapter 1. If I have structured the argument in the order that I have, it is because I believe very strongly that to understand the case for world-systems analysis, the reader (even the young and beginning reader) needs to "unthink" much of what he or she has learned from elementary school on, which is reinforced daily in the mass media. It is only by confronting directly how we have come to think the way we do that we can begin to liberate ourselves to think in ways that I believe permit us to analyze more cogently and more usefully our contemporary dilemmas.

Books are read differently by different people, and I assume that each of the three groups of readers for whom this book is intended will read the book differently. I can only hope that each group, each individual reader, will find it useful. This is an *introduction* to world-systems analysis. It has no pretension of being a summa. The book seeks to cover the whole range of issues, but no doubt some readers will feel that some things are missing, other things overemphasized, and of course some of my arguments simply wrong. The book intends to be an introduction to a way of thinking and therefore is also an invitation to an open debate, in which I hope all three audiences will participate.

WORLD-SYSTEMS ANALYSIS

1 Historical Origins of World-Systems Analysis

From Social Science Disciplines to Historical Social Sciences

WORLD-SYSTEMS ANALYSIS originated in the early 1970s as a new perspective on social reality. Some of its concepts have been in use for a long time and some are new or at least newly named. Concepts can only be understood within the context of their times. This is even more true of whole perspectives, whose concepts have their meaning primarily in terms of each other, of how they make up a set. New perspectives are, in addition, generally best understood if one thinks of them as a protest against older perspectives. It is always the claim of a new perspective that the older, and currently more accepted, one is in some significant way inadequate, or misleading, or tendentious, that the older one therefore represents more a barrier to apprehending social reality than a tool for analyzing it.

Like any other perspective, world-systems analysis has built on earlier arguments and critiques. There is a sense in which almost no perspective can ever be entirely new. Someone has usually said something similar decades or centuries earlier. Therefore, when we speak of a perspective being new, it may only be that the world is ready for the first time to take seriously the ideas it embodies, and perhaps also that the ideas have been repackaged in a way that makes them more plausible and accessible to more people.

The story of the emergence of world-systems analysis is embedded in the history of the modern world-system and the structures of knowledge that grew up as part of that system. It is most useful to trace the beginning of this particular story not to the 1970s but to the mid-eighteenth century. The capitalist world-economy had then been in existence for some two centuries already. The imperative of the endless accumulation of capital had generated a need for constant technological change, a constant expansion of frontiers—geographical, psychological, intellectual, scientific.

There arose in consequence a felt need to know how we know, and to debate how we may know. The millennial claim of religious authorities that they alone had a sure way to know truth had been under challenge in the modern world-system for some time already. Secular (that is, nonreligious) alternatives were increasingly well received. Philosophers lent themselves to this task, insisting that human beings could obtain knowledge by using their minds in some way, as opposed to receiving revealed truth through some religious authority or script. Such philosophers as Descartes and Spinoza—however different they were from each other—were both seeking to relegate theological knowledge to a private corner, separated from the main structures of knowledge.

While philosophers were now challenging the dictates of the theologians, asserting that human beings could discern truth directly by the use of their rational faculties, a growing group of scholars agreed about the role of theologians but argued that so-called philosophical insight was just as arbitrary a source of truth as divine revelation. These scholars insisted on giving priority to *empirical* analyses of reality. When Laplace in the beginning of the nineteenth century wrote a book on the origins of the solar system, Napoleon, to whom he presented the book, noted that Laplace had not mentioned God once in his very thick book. Laplace replied: "I have no need of that hypothesis, Sire." These scholars would now come to be called scientists. Still, we must remember that at least until the late eighteenth century, there was no sharp distinction between science and philosophy in the ways in which knowledge was defined. At that time, Immanuel Kant found it perfectly appropriate to lecture on astronomy and poetry as well as on metaphysics. He also wrote a book on interstate relations. Knowledge was still considered a unitary field.

About this time in the late eighteenth century, there occurred what some now call the "divorce" between philosophy and science. It was those defending empirical "science" who insisted upon this divorce. They said that the *only* route to "truth" was theorizing based on induction from empirical observations, and that these observations had to be done in such a way that others could subsequently replicate and thereby verify the observations. They insisted that metaphysical deduction was speculation and had no "truth"-value. They thus refused to think of themselves as "philosophers."

It was just about this time as well, and indeed in large part as a result of this so-called divorce, that the modern university was born. Built upon the framework of the medieval university, the modern university is really quite a different structure. Unlike the medieval university, it has full-time, paid professors, who are almost never clerics, and who are grouped together not merely in "faculties" but in "departments" or "chairs" within these faculties, each department asserting that it is the locus of a particular "discipline." And the students pursue courses of study which lead to degrees that are defined by the department within which they have studied.

The medieval university had had four faculties: theology, medicine, law, and philosophy. What happened in the nineteenth century was that almost everywhere, the faculty of philosophy was divided into at least two separate faculties: one covering the "sciences"; and one covering other subjects, sometimes called the "humanities," sometimes the "arts" or "letters" (or both), and sometimes retaining the old name of "philosophy." The university was institutionalizing what C. P. Snow would later call the "two cultures." And these two cultures were at war with each other, each insisting that it was the only, or at least the best, way to obtain knowledge. The emphasis of the sciences was on empirical (even experimental) research and hypothesis testing. The emphasis of the humanities was on empathetic insight, what later was called hermeneutic understanding. The only legacy we have today of their erstwhile unity is that all the arts and sciences in the university offer as their highest degree the PhD, doctor of philosophy.

The sciences denied the humanities the ability to discern truth. In the earlier period of unified knowledge, the search for the true, the good, and the beautiful had been closely intertwined, if not identical. But now the scientists insisted that their work had nothing to do with a search for the good or the beautiful, merely the true. They bequeathed the search for the good and the beautiful to the philosophers. And many of the philosophers agreed to this division of labor. So, the division of knowledge into the two cultures came to mean as well creating a high barrier between the search for the true and the search for the good and the beautiful. This then justified the claim of the scientists that they were "value-neutral."

In the nineteenth century, the faculties of science divided themselves into multiple fields called disciplines: physics, chemistry, geology, astronomy, zoology, mathematics, and others. The faculties of humanities divided themselves into such fields as philosophy, classics (that is, Greek and Latin, the writings of Antiquity), art history, musicology, the national language and literature, and languages and literatures of other linguistic zones.

The hardest question was into which faculty one ought to place the study of social reality. The urgency of such a study was brought to the fore by the French Revolution of 1789 and the cultural upheaval it caused in the modern world-system. The French Revolution propagated two quite revolutionary ideas. One was that political change was not exceptional or bizarre but normal and thus constant. The second was that "sovereignty"—the right of the state to make autonomous decisions within its realm—did not reside in (belong to) either a monarch or a legislature but in the "people" who, alone, could legitimate a regime.

Both of these ideas caught on and became widely adopted, despite the political reversals of the French Revolution itself. If political change was now to be considered normal and sovereignty was to reside in the people, it suddenly became imperative for everyone to understand what it was that explained the nature and pace of change, and how the "people" arrived at, could arrive at, the decisions they were said to be making. This is the social origin of what we later came to call the social sciences.

But what were the "social sciences" and how did they situate themselves in the new war between the "two cultures"? These are not easy questions to answer. Indeed, one might argue that these questions have never been satisfactorily answered. Initially what one saw is that the social sciences tended to place themselves in the middle between the "pure sciences" and the "humanities." In the middle, but not comfortably in the middle. For the social scientists did not evolve a separate, third way of knowing; rather they divided themselves between those who leaned toward a "scientific" or "scientistic" view of social science and those who leaned toward a "humanistic" view of social science. The social sciences seemed tied to two horses straining in opposite directions, and pulled apart by them.

The oldest of the social sciences is of course history, an activity and a label that go back thousands of years. In the nineteenth century there occurred a "revolution" in historiography associated with the name of Leopold Ranke, who coined the slogan that history should be written *wie es eigentlich gewesen ist* (as it really did happen). What he was protesting against was the practice of historians to engage in hagiography, telling tales that glorified monarchs or countries, including invented tales. What Ranke was proposing was a more scientific history, one that eschewed speculation and fable.

Ranke was also proposing a specific method by which such history might be written—by searching for documents describing events that were written at the time of the events. Eventually, such documents would come to be stored in what we call archives. It was the assumption of the new historians when they studied the documents in the archives that actors at the time had not been writing for future historians but were revealing what they really thought at the time or at least what they wanted others to believe. Of course, the historians acknowledged that such documents had to be handled carefully, to verify that there was no fraud, but once verified, these documents were considered largely exempt from the intrusive bias of the later historian. To minimize bias further, historians would insist that they could write history only of the "past" and not of the "present," since writing about the present inevitably bore the imprint of the passions of the moment. In any case, archives (which were controlled by the political authorities) were seldom "open" to the historian until a long period had passed (fifty to a hundred years), so they normally did not have access in any case to the important documents about the present. (In the late twentieth century, many governments came under pressure from opposition politicians to open their archives much more quickly. And while this openness has had some effect, it seems also true that governments have found as well new ways of guarding their secrets.)

Nonetheless, despite this more "scientific" bent, the new historians did not choose to be located in the faculty of science, but rather in the faculty of humanities. This might seem strange, since these historians were rejecting the philosophers because of their speculative assertions. In addition they were empiricists, and thus one might have thought they would feel sympathetic vibrations for the natural scientists. But they were empiricists who were by and large suspicious of large-scale generalizations. They were not interested in arriving at scientific laws or even formulating hypotheses, often insisting that each particular "event" had to be analyzed in terms of its own particular history. They argued that human social life was quite unlike the physical phenomena studied by the pure scientists, because of the factor of human will, and this emphasis on what we today call human agency led them to think of themselves as "humanists" rather than "scientists."

But which events were worthy of their regard? Historians had to make decisions about objects of study. That they were relying on written documents from the past already biased what they could possibly study, since the documents in archives were written largely by persons linked to political structures—diplomats, civil servants, political leaders. These documents revealed little about phenomena that were not marked by political or diplomatic occurrences. Furthermore, this approach presumed that the historians were studying a zone in which there existed written documents. In practice, historians in the nineteenth century tended therefore to study first of all their own country, and secondarily other countries which were considered "historical nations," which seemed to mean nations with a history that could be documented in archives.

But in which countries were such historians located? The overwhelming majority (probably 95 percent) were to be found in only five zones: France, Great Britain, the United States, and the various parts of what would later become Germany and Italy. So at first, the history that was written and taught was primarily the history of these five nations. There was in addition a further question to decide: What should be included in the history of a country like France or Germany? What are its boundaries, geographic and temporal? Most historians decided to trace back the story as far as they could, using the territorial boundaries of the present, or even the boundaries as they were claimed at present. The history of France was thus the history of everything that had happened within the boundaries of France as defined in the nineteenth century. This was of course quite arbitrary, but it did serve one purpose—reinforcing contemporary nationalist sentiments—and it was therefore a practice encouraged by the states themselves.

Still, it followed from the historians' practice of restricting themselves to studying the past that they had little to say about the contemporary situations facing their countries. And political leaders felt in need of more information about the present. New disciplines therefore grew up for this purpose. There were mainly three: economics, political science, and sociology. Why, however, would there be *three* disciplines to study the present but only one to study the past? Because the dominant liberal ideology of the nineteenth century insisted that *modernity* was defined by the differentiation of three social spheres: the market, the state, and the civil society. The three spheres operated, it was asserted, according to different logics, and it was good to keep them separated from each other—in social life and therefore in intellectual life. They needed to be studied in different ways, appropriate to each sphere—the market by economists, the state by political scientists, and the civil society by sociologists.

Again the question arose: How can we arrive at "objective" knowledge about these three spheres? Here, the response was different from that given by the historians. In each discipline, the view that came to dominate was that these spheres of life—the market, the state, and the civil society—were governed by laws that could be discerned by empirical analysis and inductive generalization. This was exactly the same view as that which the pure scientists had about their objects of study. So we call these three disciplines nomothetic disciplines (that is, disciplines in search of scientific laws) as opposed to the idiographic discipline which history aspired to be—that is, a discipline that is predicated on the uniqueness of social phenomena.

Again, the question would be posed, where should one focus the study of contemporary phenomena? The nomothetic social scientists were located primarily in the same five countries as the historians, and in the same way studied primarily their own countries (or at most they made comparisons among the five countries). This was to be sure socially rewarded, but in addition the nomothetic social scientists put forward a methodological argument to justify this choice. They said that the best way to avoid bias was to use quantitative data, and that such data were most likely to be located in their own countries in the immediate present. Furthermore, they argued that if we assume the existence of general laws governing social behavior, it would not matter where one studied these phenomena, since what was true in one place and at one time was true in all places at all times. Why not then study phenomena for which one had the most reliable data—that is, the most quantified and replicable data?

Social scientists did have one further problem. The four disciplines together (history, economics, sociology, and political science) studied in effect only a small portion of the world. But in the nineteenth century, the five countries were imposing colonial rule on many other parts of the world, and were engaged in commerce and sometimes in warfare with still other parts of the world. It seemed important to study the rest of the world as well. Still, the rest of the world seemed somehow different, and it seemed inappropriate to use four West-oriented disciplines to study parts of the world that were not considered "modern." As a result, two additional disciplines arose.

One of these disciplines was called anthropology. The early anthropologists studied peoples who were under actual or virtual colonial rule. They worked on the premise that the groups they were studying did not enjoy modern technology, did not have writing systems of their own, and did not have religions that extended beyond their own group. They were generically called "tribes": relatively small groups (in terms of population and the area they inhabited), with a common set of customs, a common language, and in some cases a common political structure. In nineteenth-century language, they were considered "primitive" peoples.

One of the essential conditions for studying these peoples was that they fell under the political jurisdiction of a modern state, which guaranteed order and the safe access of the anthropologist. Since these peoples were culturally so different from those who studied them, the principal mode of investigation was what was called "participant observation," in which the investigator lives among the people for some time, seeking to learn the language and discern the whole range of their customary ways. He or she often made use of local intermediaries as interpreters (both linguistically and culturally). This exercise was called writing an ethnography, and it was based on "fieldwork" (as opposed to library work or archival work).

It was assumed that the peoples had no "history," except one following the imposition of rule by modern outsiders which had resulted in "culture contact" and therefore some cultural change. This change meant that the ethnographer normally tried to reconstruct the customs as they existed before the culture contact (which usually was relatively recent), and these customs were then assumed to have existed from time immemorial up to the imposition of colonial rule. Ethnographers served in many ways as the primary interpreters of their peoples to the modern outsiders who governed them. They recast in language understandable to these outsiders the rationale behind the customary ways. They were thus useful to the colonial rulers by offering information that could make the governors more cognizant of what they could and could not do (or should not do) in their administration.

The world was however made up of more than just the "modern" states and these so-called primitive peoples. There were large regions outside the pan-European zone which had what was called in the nineteenth century a "high civilization"—for example, China, India, Persia, the Arab world. All these zones had certain common characteristics: writing; a dominant language which was used in the writing; and a single dominant "world" religion which however was not Christianity. The reason for these common features was of course very simple. All these zones had been in the past, and sometimes continued to be even in the present, the location of bureaucratic "world-empires" that had embraced large areas, and therefore developed a common language, a common religion, and many common customs. This is what was meant when they were called "high civilizations."

These regions all shared another feature in the nineteenth century. They were no longer as strong militarily or technologically as the pan-European world. So the pan-European world considered that they were not "modern." Still, their inhabitants clearly did not meet the description of "primitive" peoples, even by pan-European standards. The question then was how they might be studied and what had to be studied about them. Since they were culturally so different from Europeans, and since they had texts written in languages that were so different from those of their European investigators, and since their religions were so different from Christianity, it seemed that those who were to study them required long, patient training in esoteric skills if they were to understand very much about them. Philological skills were particularly useful in deciphering ancient religious texts. The people who acquired such skills began to call themselves Orientalists, a name derived from the classic West-East distinction which had existed for a long time within European intellectual traditions.

And what did the Orientalists study? In one sense, it might be said that they also did ethnographies; that is, they sought to describe the range of customs they discovered. But these were not for the most part ethnographies based on fieldwork, but rather derived from reading the texts. The persistent question that was in the back of their minds was how to explain that these "high civilizations" were not "modern" like the pan-European world. The answer the Orientalists seemed to put forth was that there was something in the composite culture of these civilizations which had "frozen" their history, and had made it impossible for them to move forward, as had the Western

Christian world, to "modernity." It followed that these countries thus required assistance from the pan-European world if they were to move forward to modernity.

The anthropologists-ethnographers studying primitive peoples and the Orientalists studying high civilizations had one epistemological commonality. They were both emphasizing the particularity of the group they were studying as opposed to analyzing generic human characteristics. Therefore they tended to feel more comfortable on the idiographic rather than the nomothetic side of the controversy. For the most part, they thought of themselves as being in the humanistic, hermeneutic camp of the two-culture split rather than the science camp.

The nineteenth century saw the spread and replication, more or less, of the departmental structures and emphases outlined here—in university after university, country after country. The structures of knowledge were taking form and the universities offered them a home. In addition, the scholars in each discipline began to create extra-university organizational structures to consolidate their turf. They created journals for their discipline. They founded national and international associations for their discipline. They even created library categories to group together the books presumably belonging to their discipline. By 1914 the labels had become rather standard. They continued to spread and largely prevail until at least 1945, in many ways right into the 1960s.

In 1945, however, the world changed in very important ways, and as a result this configuration of the social science disciplines came under significant challenge. Three things occurred at that time. First, the United States became the unquestioned hegemonic power of the world-system, and thus its university system became the most influential one. Secondly, the countries of what was now being called the Third World were the locus of political turbulence and geopolitical self-assertion. Thirdly, the combination of an economically expanding world-economy and a strong increase in democratizing tendencies led to an incredible expansion of the world university system (in terms of faculty, students, and number of universities). These three changes in tandem wreaked havoc on the neat structures of knowledge that had evolved and been consolidated in the previous 100 to 150 years.

Consider first of all the impact of U.S. hegemony and Third World self-assertion. Their joint occurrence meant that the division of labor within the social sciences—history, economics, sociology, political science to study the West; anthropology and Orientalism to study the rest—was worse than useless to policymakers in the United States. The United States needed scholars who could analyze the rise of the Chinese Communist Party more than it needed scholars who could decipher Taoist scriptures, scholars who could interpret the force of African nationalist movements or the growth of an urban labor force more than scholars who could elaborate the kinship patterns of Bantu peoples. And neither Orientalists nor ethnographers could help very much in this regard.

There was a solution: train historians, economists, sociologists, and political scientists to study what was going on in these other parts of the world. This was the origin of a U.S. invention—"area studies"—which had an enormous impact on the university system in the United States (and then the world). But how could one reconcile what seemed to be relatively "idiographic" in nature—the study of a geographic or cultural "area"—and the "nomothetic" pretensions of economists, sociologists, political scientists, and by now even some historians? There emerged an ingenious intellectual solution to this dilemma: the concept of "development."

Development, as the term came to be used after 1945, was based on a familiar explanatory mechanism, a theory of stages. Those who used this concept were assuming that the separate units—"national societies"—all developed in the same fundamental way (thus satisfying the nomothetic demand) but at distinct paces (thus acknowledging how different the states seemed to be at the present time). Presto! One would then be able to introduce specific concepts to study the "others" at the present time while arguing that eventually, all states would turn out more or less the same. This sleight of hand had a practical side as well. It meant that the "most developed" state could offer itself as a model for the "less developed" states, urging the latter to engage in a sort of mimicry, and promising a higher standard of living and a more liberal governmental structure ("political development") at the end of the rainbow.

This obviously was a useful intellectual tool for the United States, and its government and foundations did all they could to encourage the expansion of area studies in the major (and even the minor) universities. Of course, at that time there was a cold war between the United States and the Soviet Union. The Soviet Union knew a good thing when it saw one. It too adopted the concept of stages of development. To be sure, Soviet scholars changed the terminology for rhetorical purposes, but the basic model was the same. They did however make one significant change: the Soviet Union, not the United States, was used as the model state in the Soviet version.

Now let us see what happens when we put together the impact of area studies with the expansion of the university system. Expansion meant more persons seeking the PhD degree. This seemed a good thing, but remember the requirement that a doctoral dissertation be an "original" contribution to knowledge. Every additional person doing research meant a more and more difficult search for originality. This difficulty encouraged academic poaching, since originality was defined as being located within the disciplines. Persons in each discipline began to carve out subspecialties in subjects that previously had belonged to other disciplines. This led to considerable overlapping and erosion of the firm boundaries between disciplines. There were now *political* sociologists and *social* historians and every other combination of which one could think.

The changes in the real world affected the self-definition of the scholars. The disciplines that formerly specialized in the non-Western world found themselves looked upon with political suspicion in the countries they had traditionally studied. As a result, the term "Orientalism" gradually disappeared, its former practitioners often becoming historians. Anthropology was forced to redefine its focus rather radically, since both the concept of the "primitive" and the reality it was supposed to reflect were disappearing. In some ways, anthropologists "came home," beginning to study as well the countries from which the majority of them originated. As for the four other disciplines, they now for the first time had faculty members specializing in parts of the world with which their curricula had not previously been concerned. The whole distinction between modern and non-modern zones was disintegrating.

All this on the one hand led to increasing uncertainty about traditional truths (what was sometimes called the "confusion" within disciplines) and on the other hand opened the way for the heretical calling into question of some of these truths, especially by the growing number of scholars who came from the non-Western world or who were part of the cadre of newly trained Western scholars bred by area studies. In the social sciences, four debates in the period 1945–70 set the scene for the emergence of world-systems analysis: the concept of core-periphery developed by the United Nations Economic Commission for Latin America (ECLA) and the subsequent elaboration of "dependency theory"; the utility of Marx's concept of the "Asiatic mode of production," a debate that took place among communist scholars; the discussion among historians of western Europe about the "transition from feudalism to capitalism"; the debate about "total history" and the triumph of the *Annales* school of historiography in France and then in many other parts of the world. None of these debates were entirely new, but each became salient in this period, and the result was a major challenge to the social sciences as they had developed up to 1945.

Core-periphery was an essential contribution of Third World scholars. True, there had been some German geographers in the 1920s who had suggested something similar, as had Romanian sociologists in the 1930s (but then Romania had a social structure similar to that of the Third World). But it was only when Raúl Prebisch and his Latin American "young Turks" at the

ECLA got to work in the 1950s that the theme became a significant focus of social science scholarship. The basic idea was very simple. International trade was not, they said, a trade between equals. Some countries were stronger economically than others (the core) and were therefore able to trade on terms that allowed surplus-value to flow from the weaker countries (the periphery) to the core. Some would later label this process "unequal exchange." This analysis implied a remedy for the inequality: actions by the states in the periphery to institute mechanisms that would equalize the exchange over the middle run.

Of course, this simple idea left out an immense amount of detail. And it therefore led to vigorous debates. There were debates between its advocates and those who held to a more traditional view of international trade notably propounded by David Ricardo in the nineteenth century: that if all follow their "comparative advantage," all will receive maximal benefits. But there were also debates among the advocates of a core-periphery model themselves. How did it work? Who really benefited from the unequal exchange? What measures would be effective to counteract it? And to what degree did these measures require political action more than economic regulation?

It was on this latter theme that "dependency" theorists developed their amended versions of core-periphery analysis. Many insisted that political revolution would be a prerequisite for any real equalizing action. Dependency theory, as it developed in Latin America, seemed on the surface to be primarily a critique of the economic policies practiced and preached by the Western powers (especially the United States). Andre Gunder Frank coined the phrase "the development of underdevelopment" to describe the results of the policies of large corporations, major states in the core zones, and interstate agencies which promoted "free trade" in the world-economy. Underdevelopment was seen not as an original state, the responsibility for which lay with the countries that were underdeveloped, but as the consequence of historical capitalism.

But the dependency theories were making as well, even perhaps to a greater extent, a critique of Latin American communist parties. These parties had espoused a theory of stages of development, arguing that Latin American countries were still feudal or "semi-feudal" and therefore had not yet undergone a "bourgeois revolution," which they said had to precede a "proletarian revolution." They deduced that Latin American radicals needed to cooperate with so-called progressive bourgeois to bring about the bourgeois revolution, in order that subsequently the country might proceed to socialism. The *dependistas*, inspired as many were by the Cuban revolution, said that the official communist line was a mere variant of the official U.S. government line (build liberal bourgeois states and a middle class first). The dependistas countered this line of the communist parties *theoretically*, by arguing that Latin American states were already part and parcel of the capitalist system and that therefore what was needed was socialist revolutions now.

Meanwhile, in the Soviet Union, in the east European communist states, and within the French and Italian communist parties, a debate was commencing about the "Asiatic mode of production." When Marx had, quite briefly, outlined the set of stages of economic structures through which humanity had evolved, he added a category which he found difficult to place in the linear progression he was describing. He called it the "Asiatic mode of production," using this term to describe the large, bureaucratic, and autocratic empires that had grown up historically in China and India at least. These were exactly the "high civilizations" of the Orientalists, whose writings Marx had been reading.

In the 1930s Stalin decided that he did not like this concept. He apparently thought it could be used as a description both of Russia historically and of the regime over which he then presided. He undertook to revise Marx by simply eliminating the concept from legitimate discussion. This omission created a lot of difficulties for Soviet (and other communist) scholars. They had to stretch arguments to make various moments of Russian and various Asian histories fit the categories of "slavery" and "feudalism," which remained legitimate. But one didn't argue with Joseph Stalin.

When Stalin died in 1953, many scholars seized the occasion to reopen the question and to suggest that maybe there was something in Marx's original idea. But doing that reopened the question of inevitable stages of development and therefore of developmentalism as an analytic framework and policy directive. It forced these scholars to reengage with non-Marxist social science in the rest of the world. Basically, this debate was the scholarly equivalent of the speech in 1956 by Khrushchev, then general secretary of the Communist Party of the Soviet Union (CPSU), at the XXth Party Congress in which he denounced the "personality cult" of Stalin and acknowledged "errors" in what had previously been unquestioned policy. Like Khrushchev's speech, the debate about the Asiatic mode of production led to doubts, and cracked the rigid conceptual inheritances of so-called orthodox Marxism. It made possible a fresh look at the analytic categories of the nineteenth century, eventually even those of Marx himself.

Simultaneously, a debate was going on among Western economic historians about the origins of modern capitalism. Most of the participants thought of themselves as Marxists, but they were not bound by party constraints. The debate had its origins in the publication in 1946 of Maurice Dobb's *Studies in the Development of Capitalism*. Dobb was an English

Marxist economic historian. Paul Sweezy, an American Marxist economist, wrote an article challenging Dobb's explanation of what both of them called "the transition from feudalism to capitalism." After that, many others entered the fray.

For those on Dobb's side of this debate, the issue was posed as endogenous versus exogenous explanations. Dobb found the roots of the transition from feudalism to capitalism in elements *internal* to the states, specifically in England. Sweezy was accused by Dobb and his supporters with crediting *external* factors, particularly trade flows, and ignoring the fundamental role of changes in the structure of production, and therefore of class relations. Sweezy and others responded by suggesting that England was in fact part of a large European-Mediterranean zone, whose transformations accounted for what was occurring in England. Sweezy used empirical data from the work of Henri Pirenne (non-Marxist Belgian historian and a forefather of the Annales school of historiography, who had famously argued that the rise of Islam led to a breakdown of trade routes with western Europe and to its economic stagnation). Those who supported Dobb said that Sweezy was overemphasizing the importance of trade (a so-called external variable) and neglecting the crucial role of the relations of production (a so-called internal variable).

The debate was important for several reasons. First of all, it seemed to have political implications (like the arguments of the dependistas). Conclusions about the mechanisms of the transition from feudalism to capitalism might have implications about a putative transition from capitalism to socialism (as indeed some of the participants explicitly pointed out). Secondly, the whole debate pushed many persons who were economists by training into looking more closely at historical data, which would open them up to some of the arguments that were being put forth by the Annales group in France. Thirdly, the debate was essentially about the unit of analysis, although this language was never used. The Sweezy side was raising questions about the meaningfulness of using a country, projected backward in time, as the unit within which social action should be analyzed, rather than some larger unit within which there was a division of labor (such as the European-Mediterranean zone). Fourthly, just like the debate about the Asiatic mode of production, this debate had the consequence of breaking the crust of a version of Marxism (analyzing relations of production only, and only within a state's borders) that had become more an ideology than a scholarly argument open to debate.

Those involved in this debate were almost all Anglophone scholars. The Annales group, by contrast, originated in France and for a long time had resonance only in those areas of the scholarly world where French cultural influence was great: Italy, Iberia, Latin America, Turkey, and certain parts of eastern Europe. The Annales group had emerged in the 1920s as a protest, led by Lucien Febvre and Marc Bloch, against the highly idiographic, highly empiricist bent of dominant French historiography, which was furthermore almost exclusively devoted to political history. The Annales group argued several counterdoctrines: Historiography should be "total"—that is, it should look at the integrated picture of historical development in all social arenas. Indeed, the economic and social underpinnings of this development were thought to be more important than the political surface, and furthermore it was possible to study them systematically, not always in the archives. And long-term generalizations about historical phenomena were in fact both possible and desirable.

In the interwar years, the influence of Annales was quite minimal. Suddenly, after 1945 it blossomed, and under the direction of the second-generation leader Fernand Braudel, it came to dominate the historiographical scene in France and then in many other parts of the world. It began for the first time to penetrate the Anglophone world. Institutionally, the Annales group presided over a new university institution in Paris, an institution built on the premise that historians had to learn from and integrate the findings of the other, traditionally more nomothetic social science disciplines, and that these in turn had to become more "historical" in their work. The Braudelian era represented both an intellectual and an institutional attack on the traditional isolation of the social science disciplines from each other.

Braudel put forward a language about social times that came to inflect further work. He criticized "event-dominated" or episodic history (*histoire événementielle*), by which he meant traditional idiographic, empiricist, political historiography, as "dust." It was dust in a double sense: that it spoke about ephemeral phenomena; and that it got into our eyes, preventing us from seeing the real underlying structures. But Braudel also criticized the search for timeless, eternal truths, considering the purely nomothetic work of many social scientists as mythical. In between these two extremes, he insisted on two other social times that the two cultures had neglected: structural time (or long-lasting, but not eternal, basic structures that underlay historical systems), and the cyclical processes within the structures (or medium-run trends, such as the expansions and contractions of the world-economy). Braudel also emphasized the issue of the unit of analysis. In his first major work, he insisted that the sixteenth-century Mediterranean, which he was studying, constituted a "world-economy" (*économie-monde*), and he made the history of this world-economy the object of his study.

All four of these debates occurred essentially in the 1950s and 1960s. They largely occurred separately, without reference one to the other, and often unbeknown one to the other. Yet collectively, they represented a major critique of the existing structures of knowledge. This intellectual upheaval was followed by the cultural shock of the revolutions of 1968. And those events brought the pieces together. The world revolution of 1968 of course primarily concerned a series of major political issues: the hegemony of the United States and its world policies, which had led it into the Vietnam war; the relatively passive attitude of the Soviet Union, which the 1968 revolutionaries saw as "collusion" with the United States; the inefficacy of the traditional Old Left movements in opposing the status quo. We shall discuss these issues later.

In the process of the upheaval, however, the revolutionaries of 1968, who had their strongest base in the world's universities, also began to raise a number of issues about the structures of knowledge. At first, they raised questions about direct political involvement of university scholars in work that supported the world status quo—such as physical scientists who did war-related research and social scientists who provided material for counterinsurgency efforts. Then they raised questions about neglected areas of work. In the social sciences, this meant the neglected histories of many oppressed groups: women, "minority" groups, indigenous populations, groups with alternative sexual dispositions or practices. But eventually, they began to raise questions about underlying epistemologies of the structures of knowledge.

It is at this point, in the early 1970s, that people began to speak explicitly about world-systems analysis as a perspective. World-systems analysis was an attempt to combine coherently concern with the unit of analysis, concern with social temporalities, and concern with the barriers that had been erected between different social science disciplines.

World-systems analysis meant first of all the substitution of a unit of analysis called the "world-system" for the standard unit of analysis, which was the national state. On the whole, historians had been analyzing national histories, economists national economies, political scientists national political structures, and sociologists national societies. World-systems analysts raised a skeptical eyebrow, questioning whether any of these objects of study really existed, and in any case whether they were the most useful loci of analysis. Instead of national states as the object of study, they substituted "historical systems" which, it was argued, had existed up to now in only three variants: minisystems; and "world-systems" of two kinds—world-economies and world-empires.

Note the hyphen in world-system and its two subcategories, world-economies and world-empires. Putting in the hyphen was intended to underline that we are talking not about systems, economies, empires *of the* (whole) world, but about systems, economies, empires *that are* a world (but quite possibly, and indeed usually, not encompassing the entire globe). This is a key initial concept to grasp. It says that in "world-systems" we are dealing with a spatial/temporal zone which cuts across many political and cultural units, one that represents an integrated zone of activity and institutions which obey certain systemic rules.

Actually, of course, the concept was initially applied primarily to the "modern world-system" which, it is argued, takes the form of a "world-economy." This concept adapted Braudel's usage in his book on the Mediterranean, and combined it with the core-periphery analysis of ECLA. The case was made that the modern world-economy was a capitalist world-economy—not the first world-economy ever but the first world-economy to survive as such for a long period and thrive, and it did this precisely by becoming fully capitalist. If the zone that was capitalist was not thought to be a state but rather a world-economy, then Dobb's so-called internal explanation of the transition from feudalism to capitalism made little sense, since it implied that the transition occurred multiple times, state by state, within the same world-system.

There was in this way of formulating the unit of analysis a further link to older ideas. Karl Polanyi, the Hungarian (later British) economic historian, had insisted on the distinction between three forms of economic organization which he called reciprocal (a sort of direct give and take), redistributive (in which goods went from the bottom of the social ladder to the top to be then returned in part to the bottom), and market (in which exchange occurred in monetary forms in a public arena). The categories of types of historical systems—minisystems, world-empires, and world-economies— seemed to be another way of expressing Polanyi's three forms of economic organization. Mini-systems utilized reciprocity, world-empires redistribution, and world-economies market exchanges.

The Prebisch categories were incorporated as well. A capitalist world-economy was said to be marked by an axial division of labor between core-like production processes and peripheral production processes, which resulted in an unequal exchange favoring those involved in core-like production processes. Since such processes tended to group together in particular countries, one could use a shorthand language by talking of core and peripheral zones (or even core and peripheral states), as long as one remembered that it was the production processes and not the states that were core-like and peripheral. In world-systems analysis, core-periphery is a *relational* concept, not a pair of terms that are reified, that is, have separate essential meanings.

What then makes a production process core-like or peripheral? It came to be seen that the answer lay in the degree to which particular processes were relatively monopolized or relatively free market. The processes that were relatively monopolized were far more profitable than those that were free market. This made the countries in which more core-like processes located wealthier. And given the unequal power of monopolized products vis-à-vis products with many producers in the market, the ultimate result of exchange between core and peripheral products was a flow of surplus-value (meaning here a large part of the real profits from multiple local productions) to those states that had a large number of core-like processes.

Braudel's influence was crucial in two regards. First, in his later work on capitalism and civilization, Braudel would insist on a sharp distinction between the sphere of the free market and the sphere of monopolies. He called only the latter capitalism and, far from being the same thing as the free market, he said that capitalism was the "anti-market." This concept marked a direct assault, both substantively and terminologically, on the conflation by classical economists (including Marx) of the market and capitalism. And secondly, Braudel's insistence on the multiplicity of social times and his emphasis on structural time—what he called the *longue durée*—became central to world-systems analysis. For world-systems analysts, the *longue durée* was the duration of a particular historical system. Generalizations about the functioning of such a system thus avoided the trap of seeming to assert timeless, eternal truths. If such systems were not eternal, then it followed that they had beginnings, lives during which they "developed," and terminal transitions.

On the one hand, this view strongly reinforced the insistence that social science had to be historical, looking at phenomena over long periods as well as over large spaces. But it also opened, or reopened, the whole question of "transitions." Dobb and Sweezy had put forward quite different explanations of the transition from feudalism to capitalism, but they shared the sense that whatever explained the transition, it was an inevitable occurrence. This conviction reflected the Enlightenment theory of progress, which had informed both classical liberal thought and classical Marxist thought. World-systems analysts began to be skeptical about the inevitability of progress. They saw progress as a possibility rather than a certainty. They wondered whether one could even describe the construction of a capitalist world-economy as progress. Their skeptical eye allowed them to incorporate within an account of human history the realities of those systems that had been grouped under the label "Asiatic mode of production." One didn't need to worry any longer whether these structures were located at some particular point on a linear historical curve. And one could now ask why the transition from feudalism to capitalism occurred at all (as though the possibility that it might not have occurred were a real alternative), and not assume its inevitability and look merely at what were the immediate causes of the transition.

The third element in world-systems analysis was its lack of deference to the traditional boundaries of the social sciences. World-systems analysts analyzed total social systems over the *longue durée*. Thus they felt free to analyze materials that had once been considered the exclusive concern of historians or economists or political scientists or sociologists, and to analyze them within a single analytical frame. The resulting world-systems analysis was not multidisciplinary, since the analysts were not recognizing the intellectual legitimacy of these disciplines. They were being unidisciplinary.

Of course, the triple set of critiques—world-systems rather than states as units of analysis, insistence on the *longue durée*, and a unidisciplinary approach—represented an attack on many sacred cows. It was quite expectable that there would be a counterattack. It came, immediately and vigorously, from four camps: nomothetic positivists, orthodox Marxists, state autonomists, and cultural particularists. The main criticism of each has been that its basic premises have not been accepted by world-systems analysis. This is of course correct but hardly an intellectually devastating argument.

Nomothetic positivists have argued that world-systems analysis is essentially narrative, its theorizing based on hypotheses that have not been rigorously tested. Indeed, they have often argued that many of the propositions of world-systems analysis are not disprovable, and therefore inherently invalid. In part, this is a critique of insufficient (or nonexistent) quantification of the research. In part, this is a critique of insufficient (or nonexistent) reduction of complex situations to clearly defined and simple variables. In part, this is a suggestion of the intrusion of value-laden premises into the analytic work.

Of course, this is in effect the reverse of the critique by world-systems analysis of nomothetic positivism. World-systems analysts insist that rather than reduce complex situations to simpler variables, the effort should be to complexify and contextualize all so-called simpler variables in order to understand real social situations. World-systems analysts are not against quantification per se (they would quantify what can usefully be quantified), but (as the old joke about the drunk teaches us) they feel that one should not look for the lost key only under the street lamp just because the light is better (where there are more quantifiable data). One searches for the most appropriate data in function of the intellectual problem; one doesn't choose the problem because hard, quantitative data are available. This debate can be what the French call a dialogue of the deaf. In the end, the issue is not an abstract issue about correct methodology but is about whether world-systems analysts or rather nomothetic positivists can offer more plausible explanations of historical reality and therefore throw more light on long-term, large-scale social change.

If nomothetic positivists sometimes give the impression of insisting on a cramped and humorless set of intellectual constraints, so-called orthodox Marxists can give them a run for their money. Orthodox Marxism is mired in the imagery of nineteenth-century social science, which it shares with classical liberalism: capitalism is inevitable progress over feudalism; the factory system is the quintessential capitalist production process; social processes are linear; the economic base controls the less fundamental political and cultural superstructure. The critique by Robert Brenner, an orthodox Marxist economic historian, of world-systems analysis is a good example of this point of view.

The Marxist criticism of world-systems analysis is therefore that in discussing a core-peripheral axis of the division of labor, it is being circulationist and neglecting the productionist base of surplus-value and the class struggle between the bourgeoisie and the proletariat as the central explanatory variable of social change. World-systems analysis is charged with failing to treat non-wage-labor as anachronistic and en route to extinction. Once again, the critics are inverting criticisms leveled at them. World-systems analysts have insisted that wage-labor is only one of the many forms of labor control within a capitalist system, and not at all the most profitable one from the point of view of capital. They have insisted that the class struggle and all other forms of social struggle can be understood and evaluated only within the world-system taken as a whole. And they have insisted that states in the capitalist world-economy do not have the autonomy or isolation which makes it possible to label them as having a particular mode of production.

The state-autonomist critique is a bit the obverse of the orthodox Marxist critique. Whereas the orthodox Marxists argue that world-systems analysis ignores the determining centrality of the mode of production, the state-autonomists argue that world-systems analysis makes the political sphere into a zone whose realities are derived from, determined by, the economic base. The critiques of the sociologist Theda Skocpol and the political scientist Aristide Zolberg argue this case, inspired by the earlier work of the German historian Otto Hintze. This group insists that one cannot explain what goes on at the state level or the interstate level simply by thinking of these arenas as part of a capitalist world-economy. The motivations that govern action in these arenas, they say, are autonomous and respond to pressures other than behavior in the market.

Finally, with the rise of the various "post"-concepts linked to cultural studies, world-systems analysis has been attacked with arguments analogous to those used by the state-autonomists. World-systems analysis is said to derive the superstructure (in this case, the cultural sphere) from its economic base and to disregard the central and autonomous reality of the cultural sphere (see for example the critique of the cultural sociologist Stanley Aronowitz). World-systems analysts are accused of having the faults both of nomothetic positivism and of orthodox Marxism, although world-systems analysts see themselves as critics of both these schools of thought. World-systems analysis is charged with being just one more version of "grand narrative." Despite the claim that world-systems analysis is devoted to "total history," it is taxed with economism, that is, with giving priority to the economic sphere over other spheres of human activity. Despite its early and strong attack against Eurocentrism, it is accused of being Eurocentric by not accepting the irreducible autonomy of different cultural identities. In short, it neglects the centrality of "culture."

Of course, world-systems analysis is indeed a grand narrative. World-systems analysts argue that all forms of knowledge activity necessarily involve grand narratives, but that some grand narratives reflect reality more closely than others. In their insistence on total history and unidisciplinarity, world-systems analysts refuse to substitute a so-called cultural base for an economic base. Rather, as we have said, they seek to abolish the lines between economic, political, and sociocultural modes of analysis. Above all, world-systems analysts do not wish to throw the baby out with the bath. To be against scientism is not to be against science. To be against the concept of timeless structures does not mean that (time-bound) structures do not exist. To feel that the current organization of the disciplines is an obstacle to overcome does not mean that there does not exist collectively arrived-at knowledge (however provisional or heuristic). To be against particularism disguised as universalism does not mean that all views are equally valid and that the search for a pluralistic universalism is futile.

What these four critiques have in common is the sense that world-systems analysis lacks a central actor in its recounting of history. For nomothetic positivism, the actor is the individual, *homo rationalis*. For orthodox Marxism, the actor is the industrial proletariat. For the state-autonomists, it is political man. For cultural particularists, each of us (different from all the others) is an actor engaged in autonomous discourse with everyone else. For world-systems analysis, these actors, just like the long list of structures that one can enumerate, are the products of a process. They are not primordial atomic elements, but part of a systemic mix out of which they emerged and upon which they act. They act freely, but their freedom is constrained by their biographies and the social prisons of which they are a part. Analyzing their prisons liberates them to the maximum degree that they can be liberated. To the extent that we each analyze our social prisons, we liberate ourselves from their constraints to the extent that we can be liberated.

Lastly, it must be emphasized that for world-systems analysts, time and space—or rather that linked compound TimeSpace—are not unchanging external realities which are somehow just there, and within whose frames social reality exists. TimeSpaces are constantly evolving constructed realities whose construction is part and parcel of the social reality we are analyzing. The historical systems within which we live are indeed systemic, but they are historical as well. They remain the same over time yet are never the same from one minute to the next. This is a paradox, but not a contradiction. The ability to deal with this paradox, which we cannot circumvent, is the principal task of the historical social sciences. This is not a conundrum, but a challenge.

2   The Modern World-System as a Capitalist World-Economy

Production, Surplus Value, and Polarization

THE WORLD IN WHICH we are now living, the modern world-system, had its origins in the sixteenth century. This world-system was then located in only a part of the globe, primarily in parts of Europe and the Americas. It expanded over time to cover the whole globe. It is and has always been a *world-economy*. It is and has always been a *capitalist* world-economy. We should begin by explaining what these two terms, world-economy and capitalism, denote. It will then be easier to appreciate the historical contours of the modern world-system—its origins, its geography, its temporal development, and its contemporary structural crisis.

What we mean by a world-economy (Braudel's *économie-monde*) is a large geographic zone within which there is a division of labor and hence significant internal exchange of basic or essential goods as well as flows of capital and labor. A defining feature of a world-economy is that it is *not* bounded by a unitary political structure. Rather, there are many political units inside the world-economy, loosely tied together in our modern world-system in an interstate system. And a world-economy contains many cultures and groups—practicing many religions, speaking many languages, differing in their everyday patterns. This does not mean that they do not evolve some common cultural patterns, what we shall be calling a geoculture. It does mean that neither political nor cultural homogeneity is to be expected or found in a world-economy. What unifies the structure most is the division of labor which is constituted within it.

Capitalism is not the mere existence of persons or firms producing for sale on the market with the intention of obtaining a profit. Such persons or firms have existed for thousands of years all across the world. Nor is the existence of persons working for wages sufficient as a definition. Wage-labor has also been known for thousands of years. We are in a capitalist system only when the system gives priority to the *endless* accumulation of capital. Using such a definition, only the modern world-system has been a capitalist system. Endless accumulation is a quite simple concept: it means that people and firms are accumulating capital in order to accumulate still more capital, a process that is continual and endless. If we say that a system "gives priority" to such endless accumulation, it means that there exist structural mechanisms by which those who act with other motivations are penalized in some way, and are eventually eliminated from the social scene, whereas those who act with the appropriate motivations are rewarded and, if successful, enriched.

A world-economy and a capitalist system go together. Since world-economies lack the unifying cement of an overall political structure or a homogeneous culture, what holds them together is the efficacy of the division of labor. And this efficacy is a function of the constantly expanding wealth that a capitalist system provides. Until modern times, the world-economies that had been constructed either fell apart or were transformed *manu militari* into world-empires. Historically, the only world-economy to have survived for a long time has been the modern world-system, and that is because the capitalist system took root and became consolidated as its defining feature.

Conversely, a capitalist system cannot exist within any framework except that of a world-economy. We shall see that a capitalist system requires a very special relationship between economic producers and the holders of political power. If the latter are too strong, as in a world-empire, their interests will override those of the economic producers, and the endless accumulation of capital will cease to be a priority. Capitalists need a large market (hence minisystems are too narrow for them) but they also need a multiplicity of states, so that they can gain the advantages of working with states but also can circumvent states hostile to their interests in favor of states friendly to their interests. Only the existence of a multiplicity of states within the overall division of labor assures this possibility.

A capitalist world-economy is a collection of many institutions, the combination of which accounts for its processes, and all of which are intertwined with each other. The basic institutions are the market, or rather the markets; the firms that compete in the markets; the multiple states, within an interstate system; the households; the classes; and the status-groups (to use Weber's term, which some people in recent years have renamed the "identities"). They are all institutions that have been created within the framework of the capitalist world-economy. Of course, such institutions have some similarities to institutions that existed in prior historical systems to which we have given the same or similar names. But using the same name to describe institutions located in different historical systems quite often confuses rather than clarifies analysis. It is better to think of the set of institutions of the modern world-system as contextually specific to it.

Let us start with markets, since these are normally considered the essential feature of a capitalist system. A market is both a concrete local structure in which individuals or firms sell and buy goods, and a virtual institution across space where the same kind of exchange occurs. How large and wide-spread any virtual market is depends on the realistic alternatives that sellers and buyers have at a given time. In principle, in a capitalist world-economy the virtual market exists in the world-economy as a whole. But as we shall see, there are often interferences with these boundaries, creating narrower and more "protected" markets. There are of course separate virtual markets for all commodities as well as for capital and different kinds of labor. But over time, there can also be said to exist a single virtual world market for all the factors of production combined, despite all the barriers that exist to its free functioning. One can think of this complete virtual market as a magnet for all producers and buyers, whose pull is a constant political factor in the decision-making of everyone—the states, the firms, the households, the classes, and the status-groups (or identities). This complete virtual world market is a reality in that it influences all decision making, but it never functions fully and freely (that is, without interference). The totally free market functions as an ideology, a myth, and a constraining influence, but never as a day-to-day reality.

One of the reasons it is not a day-to-day reality is that a totally free market, were it ever to exist, would make impossible the endless accumulation of capital. This may seem a paradox because it is surely true that capitalism cannot function without markets, and it is also true that capitalists regularly say that they favor free markets. But capitalists in fact need not totally free markets but rather markets that are only partially free. The reason is clear. Suppose there really existed a world market in which all the factors of production were totally free, as our textbooks in economics usually define this—that is, one in which the factors flowed without restriction, in which there were a very large number of buyers and a very large number of sellers, and in which there was perfect information (meaning that all sellers and all buyers knew the exact state of all costs of production). In such a perfect market, it would always be possible for the buyers to bargain down the sellers to an absolutely minuscule level of profit (let us think of it as a penny), and this low level of profit would make the capitalist game entirely uninteresting to producers, removing the basic social underpinnings of such a system.

What sellers always prefer is a monopoly, for then they can create a relatively wide margin between the costs of production and the sales price, and thus realize high rates of profit. Of course, perfect monopolies are extremely difficult to create, and rare, but quasi-monopolies are not. What one needs most of all is the support of the machinery of a relatively strong state, one which can enforce a quasi-monopoly. There are many ways of doing this. One of the most fundamental is the system of patents which reserves rights in an "invention" for a specified number of years. This is what basically makes "new" products the most expensive for consumers and the most profitable for their producers. Of course, patents are often violated and in any case they eventually expire, but by and large they protect a quasi-monopoly for a time. Even so, production protected by patents usually remains only a quasi-monopoly, since there may be other similar products on the market that are not covered by the patent. This is why the normal situation for so-called leading products (that is, products that are both new and have an important share of the overall world market for commodities) is an oligopoly rather than an absolute monopoly. Oligopolies are however good enough to realize the desired high rate of profits, especially since the various firms often collude to minimize price competition.

Patents are not the only way in which states can create quasi-monopolies. State restrictions on imports and exports (so-called protectionist measures) are another. State subsidies and tax benefits are a third. The ability of strong states to use their muscle to prevent weaker states from creating counter-protectionist measures is still another. The role of the states as large-scale buyers of certain products willing to pay excessive prices is still another. Finally, regulations which impose a burden on producers may be relatively easy to absorb by large producers but crippling to smaller producers, an asymmetry which results in the elimination of the smaller producers from the market and thus increases the degree of oligopoly. The modalities by which states interfere with the virtual market are so extensive that they constitute a fundamental factor in determining prices and profits. Without such interferences, the capitalist system could not thrive and therefore could not survive.

Nonetheless, there are two inbuilt anti-monopolistic features in a capitalist world-economy. First of all, one producer's monopolistic advantage is another producer's loss. The losers will of course struggle politically to remove the advantages of the winners. They can do this by political struggle within the states where the monopolistic producers are located, appealing to doctrines of a free market and offering support to political leaders inclined to end a particular monopolistic advantage. Or they do this by persuading other states to defy the world market monopoly by using their state power to sustain competitive producers. Both methods are used. Therefore, over time, every quasi-monopoly is undone by the entry of further producers into the market.

Quasi-monopolies are thus self-liquidating. But they last long enough (say thirty years) to ensure considerable accumulation of capital by those who control the quasi-monopolies. When a quasi-monopoly does cease to exist, the large accumulators of capital simply move their capital to new leading products or whole new leading industries. The result is a cycle of leading products. Leading products have moderately short lives, but they are constantly succeeded by other leading industries. Thus the game continues. As for the once-leading industries past their prime, they become more and more "competitive," that is, less and less profitable. We see this pattern in action all the time.

Firms are the main actors in the market. Firms are normally the competitors of other firms operating in the same virtual market. They are also in conflict with those firms from whom they purchase inputs and those firms to which they sell their products. Fierce intercapitalist rivalry is the name of the game. And only the strongest and the most agile survive. One must remember that bankruptcy, or absorption by a more powerful firm, is the daily bread of capitalist enterprises. Not all capitalist entrepreneurs succeed in accumulating capital. Far from it. If they all succeeded, each would be likely to obtain very little capital. So, the repeated "failures" of firms not only weed out the weak competitors but are a condition sine qua non of the endless accumulation of capital. That is what explains the constant process of the concentration of capital.

To be sure, there is a downside to the growth of firms, either horizontally (in the same product), vertically (in the different steps in the chain of production), or what might be thought of as orthogonally (into other products not closely related). Size brings down costs through so-called economies of scale. But size adds costs of administration and coordination, and multiplies the risks of managerial inefficiencies. As a result of this contradiction, there has been a repeated zigzag process of firms getting larger and then getting smaller. But it has not at all been a simple up-and-down cycle. Rather, worldwide there has been a secular increase in the size of firms, the whole historical process taking the form of a ratchet, two steps up then one step back, continuously. The size of firms also has direct political implications. Large size gives firms more political clout but also makes them more vulnerable to political assault—by their competitors, their employees, and their consumers. But here too the bottom line is an upward ratchet, toward more political influence over time.

The axial division of labor of a capitalist world-economy divides production into core-like products and peripheral products. Core-periphery is a relational concept. What we mean by core-periphery is the degree of profitability of the production processes. Since profitability is directly related to the degree of monopolization, what we essentially mean by core-like production processes is those that are controlled by quasi-monopolies. Peripheral processes are then those that are truly competitive. When exchange occurs, competitive products are in a weak position and quasi-monopolized products are in a strong position. As a result, there is a constant flow of surplus-value from the producers of peripheral products to the producers of core-like products. This has been called unequal exchange.

To be sure, unequal exchange is not the only way of moving accumulated capital from politically weak regions to politically strong regions. There is also plunder, often used extensively during the early days of incorporating new regions into the world-economy (consider, for example, the conquistadores and gold in the Americas). But plunder is self-liquidating. It is a case of killing the goose that lays the golden eggs. Still, since the consequences are middle-term and the advantages short-term, there still exists much plunder in the modern world-system, although we are often "scandalized" when we learn of it. When Enron goes bankrupt, after procedures that have moved enormous sums into the hands of a few managers, that is in fact plunder. When "privatizations" of erstwhile state property lead to its being garnered by mafia-like businessmen who quickly leave the country with destroyed enterprises in their wake, that is plunder. Self-liquidating, yes, but only after much damage has been done to the world's productive system, and indeed to the health of the capitalist world-economy.

Since quasi-monopolies depend on the patronage of strong states, they are largely located—juridically, physically, and in terms of ownership—within such states. There is therefore a geographical consequence of the core-peripheral relationship. Core-like processes tend to group themselves in a few states and to constitute the bulk of the production activity in such states. Peripheral processes tend to be scattered among a large number of states and to constitute the bulk of the production activity in these states. Thus, for shorthand purposes we can talk of core states and peripheral states, so long as we remember that we are really talking of a relationship between production processes. Some states have a near even mix of core-like and peripheral products. We may call them semiperipheral states. They have, as we shall see, special political properties. It is however not meaning-ful to speak of semiperipheral production processes.

Since, as we have seen, quasi-monopolies exhaust themselves, what is a core-like process today will become a peripheral process tomorrow. The economic history of the modern world-system is replete with the shift, or downgrading, of products, first to semiperipheral countries, and then to peripheral ones. If circa 1800 the production of textiles was possibly the preeminent core-like production process, by 2000 it was manifestly one of the least profitable peripheral production processes. In 1800 these textiles were produced primarily in a very few countries (notably England and some other countries of northwestern Europe); in 2000 textiles were produced in virtually every part of the world-system, especially cheap textiles. The pro-cess has been repeated with many other products. Think of steel, or auto-mobiles, or even computers. This kind of shift has no effect on the structure of the system itself. In 2000 there were other core-like processes (e.g. aircraft production or genetic engineering) which were concentrated in a few coun-tries. There have always been new core-like processes to replace those which become more competitive and then move out of the states in which they were originally located.

The role of each state is very different vis-à-vis productive processes de-pending on the mix of core-peripheral processes within it. The strong states, which contain a disproportionate share of core-like processes, tend to em-phasize their role of protecting the quasi-monopolies of the core-like pro-cesses. The very weak states, which contain a disproportionate share of peripheral production processes, are usually unable to do very much to affect the axial division of labor, and in effect are largely forced to accept the lot that has been given them.

The semiperipheral states which have a relatively even mix of production processes find themselves in the most difficult situation. Under pressure from core states and putting pressure on peripheral states, their major con-cern is to keep themselves from slipping into the periphery and to do what they can to advance themselves toward the core. Neither is easy, and both require considerable state interference with the world market. These semi-peripheral states are the ones that put forward most aggressively and most publicly so-called protectionist policies. They hope thereby to "protect" their production processes from the competition of stronger firms outside, while trying to improve the efficiency of the firms inside so as to compete better in the world market. They are eager recipients of the relocation of erstwhile leading products, which they define these days as achieving "economic de-velopment." In this effort, their competition comes not from the core states but from other semiperipheral states, equally eager to be the recipients of relocation which cannot go to all the eager aspirants simultaneously and to the same degree. In the beginning of the twenty-first century, some obvious countries to be labeled semiperipheral are South Korea, Brazil, and India—countries with strong enterprises that export products (for example steel, automobiles, pharmaceuticals) to peripheral zones, but that also regularly relate to core zones as importers of more "advanced" products.

The normal evolution of the leading industries—the slow dissolution of the quasi-monopolies—is what accounts for the cyclical rhythms of the world-economy. A major leading industry will be a major stimulus to the expansion of the world-economy and will result in considerable accumulation of capital. But it also normally leads to more extensive employment in the world-economy, higher wage-levels, and a general sense of relative prosperity. As more and more firms enter the market of the erstwhile quasi-monopoly, there will be "overproduction" (that is, too much production for the real effective demand at a given time) and consequently increased price competition (because of the demand squeeze), thus lowering the rates of profit. At some point, a buildup of unsold products results, and consequently a slowdown in further production.

When this happens, we tend to see a reversal of the cyclical curve of the world-economy. We talk of stagnation or recession in the world-economy. Rates of unemployment rise worldwide. Producers seek to reduce costs in order to maintain their share of the world market. One of the mechanisms is relocation of the production processes to zones that have historically lower wages, that is, to semiperipheral countries. This shift puts pressure on the wage levels in the processes still remaining in core zones, and wages there tend to become lower as well. Effective demand which was at first lacking because of overproduction now becomes lacking because of a reduction in earnings of the consumers. In such a situation, not all producers necessarily lose out. There is obviously acutely increased competition among the diluted oligopoly that is now engaged in these production processes. They fight each other furiously, usually with the aid of their state machineries. Some states and some producers succeed in "exporting unemployment" from one core state to the others. Systemically, there is contraction, but certain core states and especially certain semiperipheral states may seem to be doing quite well.

The process we have been describing—expansion of the world-economy when there are quasi-monopolistic leading industries and contraction in the world-economy when there is a lowering of the intensity of quasi-monopoly—can be drawn as an up-and-down curve of so-called A- (expansion) and B- (stagnation) phases. A cycle consisting of an A-phase followed by a B-phase is sometimes referred to as a Kondratieff cycle, after the econo-mist who described this phenomenon with clarity in the beginning of the twentieth century. Kondratieff cycles have up to now been more or less fifty to sixty years in length. Their exact length depends on the political measures taken by the states to avert a B-phase, and especially the measures to achieve recuperation from a B-phase on the basis of new leading industries that can stimulate a new A-phase.

A Kondratieff cycle, when it ends, never returns the situation to where it was at the beginning of the cycle. That is because what is done in the B-phase in order to get out of it and return to an A-phase changes in some important way the parameters of the world-system. The changes that solve the immediate (or short-run) problem of inadequate expansion of the world-economy (an essential element in maintaining the possibility of the endless accumulation of capital) restore a middle-run equilibrium but begin to create problems for the structure in the long run. The result is what we may call a secular trend. A secular trend should be thought of as a curve whose abscissa (or x-axis) records time and whose ordinate (or y-axis) measures a phenomenon by recording the proportion of some group that has a certain characteristic. If over time the percentage is moving upward in an overall linear fashion, it means by definition (since the ordinate is in percentages) that at some point it cannot continue to do so. We call this reaching the asymptote, or 100 percent point. No characteristic can be as-cribed to more than 100 percent of any group. This means that as we solve the middle-run problems by moving up on the curve, we will eventually run into the long-run problem of approaching the asymptote.

Let us suggest one example of how this works in a capitalist world-economy. One of the problems we noted in the Kondratieff cycles is that at a certain point major production processes become less profitable, and these processes begin to relocate in order to reduce costs. Meanwhile, there is increasing unemployment in core zones, and this affects global effective demand. Individual firms reduce their costs, but the collectivity of firms finds it more difficult to find sufficient customers. One way to restore a sufficient level of world effective demand is to increase the pay levels of ordinary workers in core zones, something which has frequently occurred at the latter end of Kondratieff B-periods. This thereby creates the kind of effective demand that is necessary to provide sufficient customers for new leading products. But of course higher pay levels may mean lesser profits for the entrepreneurs. At a world level this can be compensated for by expand-ing the pool of wage workers elsewhere in the world, who are willing to work at a lower level of wages. This can be done by drawing new persons into the wage-labor pool, for whom the lower wage represents in fact an increase in real income. But of course every time one draws "new" persons into the wage-labor pool, one reduces the number of persons remaining outside the wage-labor pool. There will come a time when the pool is diminished to the point where it no longer exists effectively. We are reaching the asymptote. We shall return to this issue in the last chapter when we discuss the structural crisis of the twenty-first century.

Obviously, a capitalist system requires that there be workers who provide the labor for the productive processes. It is often said that these laborers are proletarians, that is, wage-workers who have no alternative means of support (because they are landless and without monetary or property reserves). This is not quite accurate. For one thing, it is unrealistic to think of workers as isolated individuals. Almost all workers are linked to other persons in household structures that normally group together persons of both sexes and of different age-levels. Many, perhaps most, of these household structures can be called families, but family ties are not necessarily the only mode by which households can be held together. Households often have common residences, but in fact less frequently than one thinks.

A typical household consists of three to ten persons who, over a long period (say thirty years or so), pool multiple sources of income in order to survive collectively. Households are not usually egalitarian structures internally nor are they unchanging structures (persons are born and die, enter or leave households, and in any case grow older and thus tend to alter their economic role). What distinguishes a household structure is some form of obligation to provide income for the group and to share in the consumption resulting from this income. Households are quite different from clans or tribes or other quite large and extended entities, which often share obligations of mutual security and identity but do not regularly share income. Or if there exist such large entities which are income-pooling, they are dysfunctional for the capitalist system.

We first must look at what the term "income" covers. There are in fact generically five kinds of income in the modern world-system. And almost all households seek and obtain all five kinds, although in different proportions (which turns out to be very important). One obvious form is wage-income, by which is meant payment (usually in money form) by persons outside the household for work of a member of the household that is performed outside the household in some production process. Wage-income may be occasional or regular. It may be payment by time employed or by work accomplished (piecework). Wage-income has the advantage to the employer that it is "flexible" (that is, continued work is a function of the employer's need), although the trade union, other forms of syndical action by workers, and state legislation have often limited employers' flexibility in many ways. Still, employers are almost never obligated to provide lifetime support to particular workers. Conversely, this system has the disadvantage to the employer that when more workers are needed, they may not be readily available for employment, especially if the economy is expanding. That is, in a system of wage-labor, the employer is trading not being required to pay workers in periods when they are not needed for the guarantee that the workers are available when they are needed.

A second obvious source of household income is subsistence activity. We usually define this type of work too narrowly, taking it to mean only the efforts of rural persons to grow food and produce necessities for their own consumption without passing through a market. This is indeed a form of subsistence production, and this kind of work has of course been on a sharp decline in the modern world-system, which is why we often say that subsistence production is disappearing. By using such a narrow definition, we are however neglecting the numerous ways in which subsistence activity is actually increasing in the modern world. When someone cooks a meal or washes dishes at home, this is subsistence production. When a homeowner assembles furniture bought from a store, this is subsistence production. And when a professional uses a computer to send an e-mail which, in an earlier day, a (paid) secretary would have typed, he or she is engaged in subsistence production. Subsistence production is a large part of household income today in the most economically wealthy zones of the capitalist world-economy.

A third kind of household income we might generically call petty commodity production. A petty commodity is defined as a product produced within the confines of the household but sold for cash on a wider market. Obviously, this sort of production continues to be very widespread in the poorer zones of the world-economy but is not totally absent anywhere. In richer zones we often call it free-lancing. This kind of activity involves not only the marketing of produced goods (including of course intellectual goods) but also petty marketing. When a small boy sells on the street cigarettes or matches one by one to consumers who cannot afford to buy them in the normal quantity that is packaged, this boy is engaged in petty-commodity production, the production activity being simply the disassembly of the larger package and its transport to the street market.

A fourth kind of income is what we can generically call rent. Rent can be drawn from some major capital investment (offering urban apartments for rent, or rooms within apartments) or from locational advantage (collecting a toll on a private bridge) or from capital ownership (clipping coupons on bonds, earning interest on a savings account). What makes it rent is that it is ownership and not work of any kind that makes possible the income.

Finally, there is a fifth kind of income, which in the modern world we call transfer payments. These may be defined as income that comes to an individual by virtue of a defined obligation of someone else to provide this income. The transfer payments may come from persons close to the household, as when gifts or loans are given from one generation to the other at the time of birth, marriage, or death. Such transfer payments between households may be made on the basis of reciprocity (which in theory ensures no extra income over a lifetime but tends to smooth out liquidity needs). Or transfer payments may occur through the efforts of the state (in which case one's own money may simply be returning at a different moment in time), or through an insurance scheme (in which one may in the end benefit or lose), or through redistribution from one economic class to another.

As soon as we think about it, we all are familiar with the income-pooling that goes on in households. Picture a middle-class American family, in which the adult male has a job (and perhaps moonlights at a second), the adult female is a caterer operating out of her home, the teenage son has a paper route, and the twelve-year-old daughter babysits. Add in perhaps the grandmother who draws a widow's pension and who also occasionally babysits for a small child, and the room above the garage that is rented out. Or picture the working-class Mexican household in which the adult male has migrated to the United States illegally and is sending home money, the adult female is cultivating a plot at home, the teenage girl is working as a domestic (paid in money and in kind) in a wealthy Mexican's home, and the subteen boy is peddling small items in the town market after school (or instead of school). Each of us can elaborate many more such combinations.

In actual practice, few households are without all five kinds of income. But one should notice right away that the persons within the household who tend to provide the income may correlate with sex or age categories. That is to say, many of these tasks are gender- and age-defined. Wage-labor was for a long time largely considered the province of males between the ages of fourteen or eighteen to sixty or sixty-five. Subsistence and petty-commodity production have been for the most part defined as the province of adult women and of children and the aged. State transfer income has been largely linked to wage earning, except for certain transfers relating to child rearing. Much political activity of the last hundred years has been aimed at overcoming the gender specificity of these definitions.

As we have already noted, the relative importance of the various forms of income in particular households has varied widely. Let us distinguish two major varieties: the household where wage-income accounts for 50 percent or more of the total lifetime income, and the household where it accounts for less. Let us call the former a "proletarian household" (because it seems to be heavily dependent on wage-income, which is what the term proletarian is supposed to invoke); and let us then call the latter a "semiproletarian household" (because there is doubtless at least some wage-income for most members of it). If we do this, we can see that an employer has an advantage in employing those wage-laborers who are in a semiproletarian household. Whenever wage-labor constitutes a substantial component of household income, there is necessarily a floor for how much the wage-earner can be paid. It must be an amount that represents at least a proportionate share of the reproduction costs of the household. This is what we can think of as an *absolute* minimum wage. If, however, the wage-earner is ensconced in a household that is only semiproletarian, the wage-earner can be paid a wage *below* the absolute minimum wage, without necessarily endangering the survival of the household. The difference can be made up by additional income provided from other sources and usually by other members of the household. What we see happening in such cases is that the other producers of income in the household are in effect transferring surplus-value to the employer of the wage-earner over and above whatever surplus-value the wage-earner himself is transferring, by permitting the employer to pay less than the absolute minimum wage.

It follows that in a capitalist system employers would in general prefer to employ wage-workers coming from semiproletarian households. There are however two pressures working in the other direction. One is the pressure of the wage-workers themselves who seek to be "proletarianized," because that in effect means being better paid. And one is the contradictory pressure on the employers themselves. Against their individual need to lower wages, there is their collective longer-term need to have a large enough effective demand in the world-economy to sustain the market for their products. So over time, as a result of these two very different pressures, there is a slow increase in the number of households that are proletarianized. Nonetheless, this description of the long-term trend is contrary to the traditional social science picture that capitalism as a system requires primarily proletarians as workers. If this were so, it would be difficult to explain why, after four to five hundred years, the proportion of proletarian workers is not much higher than it is. Rather than think of proletarianization as a capitalist necessity, it would be more useful to think of it as a locus of struggle, whose outcome has been a slow if steady increase, a secular trend moving toward its asymptote.

There are classes in a capitalist system, since there are clearly persons who are differently located in the economic system with different levels of income who have differing interests. For example, it is obviously in the interest of workers to seek an increase in their wages, and it is equally obviously in the interest of employers to resist these increases, at least in general. But, as we have just seen, wage-workers are ensconced in households. It makes no sense to think of the workers belonging to one class and other members of their household to another. It is obviously households, not individuals, that are located within classes. Individuals who wish to be class-mobile often find that they must withdraw from the households in which they are located and locate themselves in other households, in order to achieve such an objective. This is not easy but it is by no means impossible.

Classes however are not the only groups within which households locate themselves. They are also members of status-groups or identities. (If one calls them status-groups, one is emphasizing how they are perceived by others, a sort of objective criterion. If one calls them identities, one is emphasizing how they perceive themselves, a sort of subjective criterion. But under one name or the other, they are an institutional reality of the modern world-system.) Status-groups or identities are ascribed labels, since we are born into them, or at least we usually think we are born into them. It is on the whole rather difficult to join such groups voluntarily, although not impossible. These status-groups or identities are the numerous "peoples" of which all of us are members—nations, races, ethnic groups, religious communities, but also genders and categories of sexual preferences. Most of these categories are often alleged to be anachronistic leftovers of pre-modern times. This is quite wrong as a premise. Membership in status-groups or identities is very much a part of modernity. Far from dying out, they are actually growing in importance as the logic of a capitalist system unfolds further and consumes us more and more intensively.

If we argue that households locate themselves in a class, and all their members share this location, is this equally true of status-groups or identities? There does exist an enormous pressure within households to maintain a common identity, to be part of a single status-group or identity. This pressure is felt first of all by persons who are marrying and who are required, or at least pressured, to look within the status-group or identity for a partner. But obviously, the constant movement of individuals within the modern world-system plus the normative pressures to ignore status-group or identity membership in favor of meritocratic criteria have led to a considerable mixing of original identities within the framework of households. Nonetheless, what tends to happen in each household is an evolution toward a single identity, the emergence of new, often barely articulated status-group identities that precisely reify what began as a mixture, and thereby reunify the household in terms of status-group identities. One element in the demand to legitimate gay marriages is this felt pressure to reunify the identity of the household.

Why is it so important for households to maintain singular class and status-group identities, or at least pretend to maintain them? Such a homogenization of course aids in maintaining the unity of a household as an income-pooling unit and in overcoming any centrifugal tendencies that might arise because of internal inequalities in the distribution of consumption and decision making. It would however be a mistake to see this tendency as primarily an internal group defense mechanism. There are important benefits to the overall world-system from the homogenizing trends within household structures.

Households serve as the primary socializing agencies of the world-system. They seek to teach us, and particularly the young, knowledge of and respect for the social rules by which we are supposed to abide. They are of course seconded by state agencies such as schools and armies as well as by religious institutions and the media. But none of these come close to the households in actual impact. What however determines how the households will socialize their members? Largely how the secondary institutions frame the issues for the households, and their ability to do so effectively depends on the relative homogeneity of the households—that is, they have and see themselves as having a defined role in the historical social system. A household that is certain of its status-group identity—its nationality, its race, its religion, its ethnicity, its code of sexuality—knows exactly how to socialize its members. One whose identity is less certain but that tries to create a homogenized, even if novel, identity can do almost as well. A household that would openly avow a permanently split identity would find the socialization function almost impossible to do, and might find it difficult to survive as a group.

Of course, the powers that be in a social system always hope that socialization results in the acceptance of the very real hierarchies that are the product of the system. They also hope that socialization results in the internalization of the myths, the rhetoric, and the theorizing of the system. This does happen in part but never in full. Households also socialize members into rebellion, withdrawal, and deviance. To be sure, up to a point even such antisystemic socialization can be useful to the system by offering an outlet for restless spirits, provided that the overall system is in relative equilibrium. In that case, one can anticipate that the negative socializations may have at most a limited impact on the functioning of the system. But when the historical system comes into structural crisis, suddenly such antisystemic socializations can play a profoundly unsettling role for the system.

Thus far, we have merely cited class identification and status-group identification as the two alternative modes of collective expression for households. But obviously there are multiple kinds of status-groups, not always totally consonant one with the other. Furthermore, as historical time has moved on, the number of kinds of status-groups has grown, not diminished. In the late twentieth century, people often began to claim identities in terms of sexual preferences which were not a basis for household construction in previous centuries. Since we are all involved in a multiplicity of status-groups or identities, the question arises whether there is a priority order of identities. In case of conflicts, which should prevail? Which does prevail? Can a household be homogeneous in terms of one identity but not in terms of another? The answer obviously is yes, but what are the consequences?

We must look at the pressures on households coming from outside. Most of the status-groups have some kind of trans-household institutional expression. And these institutions place direct pressure on the households not merely to conform to their norms and their collective strategies but to give them priority. Of the trans-household institutions, the states are the most successful in influencing the households because they have the most immediate weapons of pressure (the law, substantial benefits to distribute, the capacity to mobilize media). But wherever the state is less strong, the religious structures, the ethnic organizations, and similar groups may become the strongest voices insisting on the priorities of the households. Even when status-groups or identities describe themselves as antisystemic, they may still be in rivalry with other antisystemic status-groups or identities, demanding priority in allegiance. It is this complicated turmoil of household identities that underlies the roller coaster of political struggle within the modern world-system.

The complex relationships of the world-economy, the firms, the states, the households, and the trans-household institutions that link members of classes and status-groups are beset by two opposite—but symbiotic—ideological themes: universalism on the one hand and racism and sexism on the other.

Universalism is a theme prominently associated with the modern world-system. It is in many ways one of its boasts. Universalism means in general the priority to general rules applying equally to all persons, and therefore the rejection of particularistic preferences in most spheres. The only rules that are considered permissible within the framework of universalism are those which can be shown to apply directly to the narrowly defined proper functioning of the world-system.

The expressions of universalism are manifold. If we translate universalism to the level of the firm or the school, it means for example the assigning of persons to positions on the basis of their training and capacities (a practice otherwise known as meritocracy). If we translate it to the level of the household, it implies among other things that marriage should be contracted for reasons of "love" but not those of wealth or ethnicity or any other general particularism. If we translate it to the level of the state, it means such rules as universal suffrage and equality before the law. We are all familiar with the mantras, since they are repeated with some regularity in public discourse. They are supposed to be the central focus of our socialization. Of course, we know that these mantras are unevenly advocated in various locales of the world-system (and we shall want to discuss why this is so), and we know that they are far from fully observed in practice. But they have become the official gospel of modernity.

Universalism is a positive norm, which means that most people assert their belief in it, and almost everyone claims that it is a virtue. Racism and sexism are just the opposite. They too are norms, but they are negative norms, in that most people deny their belief in them. Almost everyone declares that they are vices, yet nonetheless they are norms. What is more, the degree to which the negative norms of racism and sexism are observed is at least as high as, in fact for the most part much higher than, the virtuous norm of universalism. This may seem to be an anomaly. But it is not.

Let us look at what we mean by racism and sexism. Actually these are terms that came into widespread use only in the second half of the twentieth century. Racism and sexism are instances of a far wider phenomenon that has no convenient name, but that might be thought of as anti-universalism, or the active institutional discrimination against all the persons in a given status-group or identity. For each kind of identity, there is a social ranking. It can be a crude ranking, with two categories, or elaborate, with a whole ladder. But there is always a group on top in the ranking, and one or several groups at the bottom. These rankings are both worldwide and more local, and both kinds of ranking have enormous consequences in the lives of people and in the operation of the capitalist world-economy.

We are all quite familiar with the worldwide rankings within the modern world-system: men over women, Whites over Blacks (or non-Whites), adults over children (or the aged), educated over less educated, heterosexuals over gays and lesbians, the bourgeois and professionals over workers, urbanites over rural dwellers. Ethnic rankings are more local, but in every country, there is a dominant ethnicity and then the others. Religious rankings vary across the world, but in any particular zone everyone is aware of what they are. Nationalism often takes the form of constructing links between one side of each of the antinomies into fused categories, so that, for example, one might create the norm that adult White heterosexual males of particular ethnicities and religions are the only ones who would be considered "true" nationals.

There are several questions which this description brings to our attention. What is the point of professing universalism and practicing anti-universalism simultaneously? Why should there be so many varieties of anti-universalism?

Is this contradictory antinomy a necessary part of the modern world-system? Universalism and anti-universalism are in fact both operative day to day, but they operate in different arenas. Universalism tends to be the operative principle most strongly for what we could call the cadres of the world-system—neither those who are at the very top in terms of power and wealth, nor those who provide the large majority of the world's workers and ordinary people in all fields of work and all across the world, but rather an in-between group of people who have leadership or supervisory roles in various institutions. It is a norm that spells out the optimal recruitment mode for such technical, professional, and scientific personnel. This in-between group may be larger or smaller according to a country's location in the world-system and the local political situation. The stronger the country's economic position, the larger the group. Whenever universalism loses its hold even among the cadres in particular parts of the world-system, however, observers tend to see dysfunction, and quite immediately there emerge political pressures (both from within the country and from the rest of the world) to restore some degree of universalistic criteria.

There are two quite different reasons for this. On the one hand, universalism is believed to ensure relatively competent performance and thus make for a more efficient world-economy, which in turn improves the ability to accumulate capital. Hence, normally those who control production processes push for such universalistic criteria. Of course, universalistic criteria arouse resentment when they come into operation only after some particularistic criterion has been invoked. If the civil service is only open to persons of some particular religion or ethnicity, then the choice of persons within this category may be universalistic but the overall choice is not. If universalistic criteria are invoked only at the time of choice while ignoring the particularistic criteria by which individuals have access to the necessary prior training, again there is resentment. When, however, the choice is truly universalistic, resentment may still occur because choice involves exclusion, and we may get "populist" pressure for untested and unranked access to position. Under these multiple circumstances, universalistic criteria play a major social-psychological role in legitimating meritocratic allocation. They make those who have attained the status of cadre feel justified in their advantage and ignore the ways in which the so-called universalistic criteria that permitted their access were not in fact fully universalistic, or ignore the claims of all the others to material benefits given primarily to cadres. The norm of universalism is an enormous comfort to those who are benefiting from the system. It makes them feel they deserve what they have.

On the other hand, racism, sexism, and other anti-universalistic norms perform equally important tasks in allocating work, power, and privilege within the modern world-system. They seem to imply exclusions from the social arena. Actually they are really modes of inclusion, but of inclusion at inferior ranks. These norms exist to justify the lower ranking, to enforce the lower ranking, and perversely even to make it somewhat palatable to those who have the lower ranking. Anti-universalistic norms are presented as codifications of natural, eternal verities not subject to social modification. They are presented not merely as cultural verities but, implicitly or even explicitly, as biologically rooted necessities of the functioning of the human animal.

They become norms for the state, the workplace, the social arena. But they also become norms into which households are pushed to socialize their members, an effort that has been quite successful on the whole. They justify the polarization of the world-system. Since polarization has been increasing over time, racism, sexism, and other forms of anti-universalism have become ever more important, even though the political struggle against such forms of anti-universalism has also become more central to the functioning of the world-system.

The bottom line is that the modern world-system has made as a central, basic feature of its structure the simultaneous existence, propagation, and practice of both universalism and anti-universalism. This antinomic duo is as fundamental to the system as is the core-peripheral axial division of labor.

3   The Rise of the States-System

Sovereign Nation-States, Colonies, and the Interstate System

THE MODERN STATE is a sovereign state. Sovereignty is a concept that was invented in the modern world-system. Its prima facie meaning is totally autonomous state power. But modern states in fact exist within a larger circle of states, what we have come to call the interstate system. So we shall have to investigate the degree and the content of this presumed autonomy. The historians talk of the emergence of the "new monarchies" in England, France, and Spain at the end of the fifteenth century, at just the moment of onset of the modern world-system. As for the interstate system, its ancestry is usually attributed to the development of Renaissance diplomacy on the Italian peninsula, and its institutionalization is usually thought to be the Peace of Westphalia in 1648. Westphalia, signed by most of the states of Europe, codified certain rules of interstate relations that set limits to as well as guarantees of relative autonomy. These rules were elaborated and expanded later under the rubric of international law.

The new monarchies were centralizing structures. That is, they sought to ensure that regional power structures were effectively subordinated to the overall authority of the monarch. And they sought to ensure this by strengthening (really by creating) a civil and military bureaucracy. Most crucially, they sought to give themselves strength by securing some significant taxing powers with enough personnel actually to collect the taxes.

In the seventeenth century, the rulers of these new monarchies declared themselves "absolute" monarchs. This seems to suggest that they had unlimited power. In actual fact they lacked not only unlimited power but very much power at all. Absolute monarchs merely claimed the right to have unlimited power. The term "absolute" comes from the Latin *absolutus*, which meant not that the monarch is all-powerful but that the monarch is not subject to (is absolved from) the laws and therefore cannot be legitimately constrained by any human from doing what the ruler thinks best. This allowed for arbitrary power, but it didn't mean that the monarch had effective power, which as we have said was relatively low. To be sure, the states sought through the centuries to overcome this lack of real power, and they had a certain amount of success in achieving this. Consequently, one of the secular trends of the modern world-system from its beginning (at least until about the 1970s, as we shall see) was a slow, steady increase in real state power. If we compare the real power (ability to get decisions actually carried out) of Louis XIV of France (who reigned 1661–1715), usually taken as the arch-symbol of absolute power, with say the prime minister of Sweden in the year 2000, we will see that the latter had more real power in Sweden in 2000 than Louis in France in 1715.

The major tool that the monarchs used to increase their effective power was the construction of bureaucracies. And since they at first did not have the tax revenues with which to pay for bureaucracies, they found a solution in the sale of offices, which gave the monarchs an increase in both bureaucrats and revenue—and therefore some additional power, albeit less than if they had been able to recruit bureaucrats directly, as they would at later times. Once the rulers had a minimal bureaucracy in place, they sought to use it to give the states control over all sorts of political functions: tax collection, the courts, legislation, and enforcement agencies (police and army). At the same time, they sought to eliminate or at least limit the autonomous authority of local notables in all these fields. They also sought to create an informational network to make sure that their intentions were respected. The French elaborated the institution of prefects—persons who represented the central state and were resident in the various parts of the country—and this institution was emulated in various ways by almost all modern states.

Sovereignty was a claim of authority not only internally but externally—that is, vis-à-vis other states. It was first of all a claim of fixed boundaries, within which a given state was sovereign, and therefore within which no other state had the right to assert any kind of authority—executive, legislative, judicial, or military. To be sure, these claims of the states that other states should not "interfere" in their domestic affairs have always been more honored in the breach than sedulously observed. But the mere claim has nonetheless served to constrain the degree of interference. Nor have borders been unchanging. Border claims between states have been constant and recurrent. Nonetheless, at any given moment there almost always exist de facto realities about the borders within which sovereignty is exercised.

There is one further fundamental feature of sovereignty. It is a claim, and claims have little meaning unless they are recognized by others. Others may not *respect* the claims, but that is in many ways less important than that they *recognize* them formally. Sovereignty is more than anything else a matter of legitimacy. And in the modern world-system, the legitimacy of sovereignty requires reciprocal recognition. Sovereignty is a hypothetical trade, in which two potentially (or really) conflicting sides, respecting de facto realities of power, exchange such recognitions as their least costly strategy.

Reciprocal recognition is a fundament of the interstate system. There have often been entities that have proclaimed their existence as sovereign states but failed to receive the recognition of most other states. But without such recognition, the proclamation is relatively worthless, even if the entity retains de facto control of a given territory. Such an entity is in a perilous condition. However, at any given time most states are recognized by all other states. There are usually nonetheless a few putative states which are recognized by no one, or sometimes by only one or two other states (which in effect are protector states). The most difficult situation is that in which a state is recognized by a significant number of other states but is also not recognized by a significant number. This situation may occur in the wake of secessions or revolutionary changes in regimes. Such a split in the recognition process creates a dilemma and a tension in the interstate system which the states concerned eventually will try to resolve, in one direction or the other.

We can easily find three examples of the variety of possible situations in the world-system in the first decade of the twenty-first century. The United States and Cuba, although politically hostile to each other, did not contest each other's sovereignty, nor did other countries. In a second case, in China, the proclamation of the People's Republic in 1949—with the new government gaining de facto control of the mainland and the previous government effectively retreating to Taiwan while still claiming nonetheless to be the sovereign authority of the Republic of China as a whole—created one of those middle situations in which part of the world recognized one government and part the other as the sovereign authority of all of China. This situation was largely resolved in the 1970s, when the United Nations recognized the credentials of the People's Republic of China for China's seat in the General Assembly and Security Council and withdrew the credentials of the Republic of China (which controlled de facto only Taiwan). This step occurred at about the same time as the United States and then many other countries recognized the legitimacy of the People's Republic as the sole government of "one China," while not disturbing de facto control of Taiwan by the erstwhile government of China. After that, there remained only a few (mostly small) countries which continued to recognize the Republic of China as the legitimate government of the whole of China, but the overwhelming balance was on the side of the People's Republic. The third situation was that of the Turkish Republic of Northern Cyprus. It claimed to be a sovereign state and had de facto authority on the northern half of the island. But it was recognized as sovereign only by Turkey. It therefore had no international legitimacy, the rest of the world still acknowledging the theoretical sovereignty of Cyprus over the land area occupied by the Turkish Republic of Northern Cyprus. Were it not for the strong (ultimately military) support of Turkey, the Turkish Republic of Northern Cyprus would have soon ceased to exist. We see in these three instances the crucial role of reciprocal recognition.

We might look at one hypothetical, but plausible, situation. Suppose, when the Parti Québécois first came to power in Quebec in 1976, it had immediately declared Quebec to be a sovereign state (which was after all the principal program of the party), and suppose that the Canadian government had vigorously opposed this, politically and perhaps militarily. Suppose then that France had recognized Quebec, Great Britain had refused to do so, and the United States had tried to remain neutral. What might have happened, and would Quebec have been a sovereign state?

Reciprocity also operates internally, although we conventionally use a different language to describe it. Local authorities must "recognize" the sovereign authority of the central state, and in a sense the central authority must recognize the legitimate authority and define the sphere of the local authorities. In many countries, this mutual recognition is enshrined in a constitution or in specific legislation that specifies the division of power between center and localities. This agreement can and often does break down. If the breakdown is serious, we have what is called a civil war. Such a war may be won by the center. But it may also be won by the local authority or authorities, and in this case, there may be either a revision of the rules governing the division of powers in the existing state boundaries or the creation of one or more new sovereign states through secession, which then poses the issue for the newly created states of obtaining recognition in the interstate arena. The breakup of Yugoslavia is a good example of this, a breakup which left somewhat unresolved several questions of boundaries and autonomies, such that a decade after the breakup there existed de facto boundaries which were still being contested.

Sovereignty thus is a legal claim with major political consequences. It is because of these consequences that issues involving sovereignty are central to political struggle, both internally within states and internationally between states. From the point of view of entrepreneurs operating in the capitalist world-economy, the sovereign states assert authority in at least seven principal arenas of direct interest to them: (1) States set the rules on whether and under what conditions commodities, capital, and labor may cross their borders. (2) They create the rules concerning property rights within their states. (3) They set rules concerning employment and the compensation of employees. (4) They decide which costs firms must internalize. (5) They decide what kinds of economic processes may be monopolized, and to what degree. (6) They tax. (7) Finally, when firms based within their boundaries may be affected, they can use their power externally to affect the decisions of other states. This is a long list, and just looking at it makes one realize that from the point of view of firms, state policies are crucial.

The relationship of states to firms is a key to understanding the functioning of the capitalist world-economy. The official ideology of most capitalists is laissez-faire, the doctrine that governments should not interfere with the working of entrepreneurs in the market. It is important to understand that as a general rule, entrepreneurs assert this ideology loudly but do not really want it to be implemented, or at least not fully, and certainly do not usually act as though they believed it was sound doctrine.

Let us start with boundaries. A sovereign state has in theory the right to decide what may cross its boundaries, and under what conditions. The stronger the state, the larger its bureaucratic machinery and therefore the greater its ability to enforce decisions concerning trans-boundary transactions. There are three principal kinds of trans-boundary transactions: the movement of goods, of capital, and of persons. Sellers wish for their goods to traverse boundaries without interference and without taxation. On the other hand, competing sellers within the boundaries being entered may very much want the state to interfere by imposing quotas or tariffs, or by giving subsidies to their own products. Any decision that the state takes favors one entrepreneur or the other. There does not exist a neutral position. The same is true of capital flows.

The trans-boundary movement of persons has always been the most closely controlled, and of course concerns firms in that it concerns workers. In general, the influx of workers from one country to another is a market plus for entrepreneurs in the receiving country and a market minus for those already resident in the receiving country, if one uses a simple short-run supply and demand model. This leaves out of the picture two elements that may very much be central to the debate: the impact on the internal social structure of any given country of immigration; and the long-run economic impact of immigration (which might be quite positive even if the short-run impact is quite negative, at least for some persons). Once again, there exists no neutral position.

Property rights are of course the centerpiece of the capitalist system. There is no way to accumulate capital endlessly unless one can hold on to the capital that one has accumulated. Property rights are all those laws which limit the ways in which the state can confiscate the money, extended kin can lay claim to a share in the money, and others can steal the money. In addition, the capitalist system operates on the basis of a minimum level of reciprocal trust in the honesty of transactions, and thus preventing fraud is a major social requirement. This is all so obvious that it seems scarcely worth saying. But of course the key actor in this protection of property rights is the state, which alone has the legitimate right to set the rules. Obviously, none of these rights are without some limits. And of course there are many actions whose description as protected property rights is a matter of debate. Differences lead to conflicts which must then be adjudicated—by the courts of the states. But without some state-guaranteed protections, the capitalist system cannot function at all.

Entrepreneurs have long acted, and still often do act, as if the arena in which they are most anxious that the state abstain from setting rules is the workplace. They are particularly concerned about all matters governing their relation to those they employ—levels of recompense, conditions of work, length of the work week, assurances of safety, and modes of hiring and firing. Workers, on the contrary, have long demanded that the state interfere in precisely these questions to help them achieve what they consider reasonable work situations. Obviously such state interference tends to strengthen workers in the short run in their conflicts with employers, so their approbation is usually a given. But many entrepreneurs have also seen that in the long run, state interference may be of use to them as well. Ensuring long-term labor supply, creating effective demand, and minimizing social disorder may all be in part consequences of such state interference in the workplace. Consequently a certain amount of interference may be very welcome to employers—at least to those which are larger and are operating according to longer-run perspectives.

One of the less noticed corners in which the state's role is crucial to firms is in deciding what proportion of the costs of production is actually paid by the firm. Economists speak quite often of costs being externalized. What this means is that a certain part of the costs of production are shifted from the balance sheet of the firm to that amorphous external entity, society. The possibility of externalizing costs may seem to run counter to a basic premise of capitalist activity. Presumably a firm produces for profit, the profit consisting of the difference between sales receipts and costs of production. The profit is then a reward for efficient production. The tacit assumption—and the moral justification of the profits—is that the producer is paying all the costs.

In practice, however, it does not work that way. The profit is a reward not merely for efficiency but for greater access to the assistance of the state. Few producers pay all the costs of their production. There are three different costs that are normally externalized in significant measure: costs of toxicity; costs of exhaustion of materials; costs of transport. Almost all production processes involve some kind of toxicity, that is, some kind of residual damage to the environment, whether it is disposal of material or chemical waste, or simply long-term transformation of the ecology. The least expensive way for a producer to deal with waste is to cast it aside, outside its property. The least expensive way to deal with transformation of the ecology is to pretend it isn't happening. Both ways reduce the immediate costs of production. But these costs are then externalized, in the sense that either immediately or, more usually, much later, someone must pay for the negative consequences, by means of either a proper cleanup or restitution of the ecology. This someone is everyone else—the taxpayers in general, through their instrumentality the state.

The second mode of externalizing costs is to ignore the exhaustion of materials. In the end, all production processes use some primary materials, organic or inorganic, which are part of the transformation processes that result in a "final" good sold on the market. Primary materials are exhaustible, some quite speedily, some extremely slowly, most at some intermediate pace. Once again, replacement costs are almost never part of the internalized costs of production. Thus eventually, the world has either to renounce the use of such materials or seek to replace them in some way. In part, it does so by innovation, and one can make an argument that in this case the economic cost of non-replacement is small or nil. But in many other cases this is not possible, and then the state must step in once again to engage in the process of restoring or re-creating the materials, and this is of course paid for by someone other than those who pocketed the profits. A good example of materials that have not been adequately replaced is the world wood supply. The forests of Ireland were cut down in the seventeenth century. And throughout the history of the modern world-system, we have been cutting down forests of all kinds without replacing them. Today we discuss the consequences of not protecting what is considered the *last* major rain forest in the entire world, the Amazon area in Brazil.

Finally, there is the cost of transport. While it is true that firms generally pay fees for transporting goods coming to them or from them, they seldom pay the full costs. Creating the necessary infrastructure of transportation—

bridges, canals, railway networks, airports—represents a very large cost, and this cost is normally borne, in large part, not by the firms which make use of the infrastructure but by the collectivity. The justification is that the costs are so massive, and the reward for an individual firm so small, that the infrastructure would never come into existence without a large input of costs from the state. This may well be true, if perhaps exaggerated, but it is further evidence of the critical role of state involvement in the process of the endless accumulation of capital.

We have already discussed how central the creation of monopolies or rather quasi-monopolies are to the accumulation of capital. We need only remember that every decision to make possible a quasi-monopoly of any kind, whatever the mechanism, represents an advantage to some but a disadvantage to others. Here as elsewhere, there exist no neutral positions for the state in enabling capital accumulation. For capital accumulation is always capital accumulation by particular persons, firms, or entities. And competition between capitalists is unavoidable in a capitalist system.

In discussions of state "interference" with firms, it is most often noted that states tax. Of course they do. They could not exist without taxation. And we have noticed how the most crucial element in the establishment of the state structures was acquiring not the authority but the effective ability to tax. No one, it is said, likes taxes. In fact the opposite is true, although few avow it. Everyone—firms and workers alike—wants the things that states can offer them with the money that the states have obtained through taxation. There are basically two problems that people have with taxes. One is the feeling or suspicion that the states are using the taxes not to help the honest taxpayers we all assume ourselves to be, but to help others (the politicians, the bureaucrats, rival firms, the poor and undeserving, even foreigners). To this extent we wish taxes to be lower, and these undesirable uses of the taxes to cease. The second complaint about taxes is of course true: the money that is taxed is money that otherwise would have been available to each person to spend at his or her own discretion. So basically, one is yielding control over this money to some collective body, which is deciding how to spend it.

In point of fact, most people and most firms are willing to be taxed in order to provide the minimum services that each person and each firm thinks will serve its interests. But no one is willing, or ready, to be taxed more than that. The question is always the location of the line which separates legitimate from illegitimate levels of taxation. Since persons and firms have different interests, they draw the line differently. And since, in addition to the amount of taxes, the state can and does choose among a vast array of modes of taxation, persons and firms prefer those modes which affect them least and others most. It is no wonder then that taxes are certain and that tax struggles are endemic to politics in the modern world. The state cannot be neutral, but it can certainly affect seriously the benefits that firms and persons will derive from its tax policies.

Finally, we have been discussing the role of the state in relation to firms as though this were a matter internal to the state's boundaries. But of course firms are affected by the decisions not only of their own state but of many other states, insofar as their goods, capital, or personnel cross or have crossed state boundaries, a process that is constant and massive. Few firms can afford to be indifferent to the policies of states which are not their own, in terms of domiciliation. The question is how the firms can deal with these other states. And the answer is in two ways—directly and indirectly. The direct way is to behave as though they were domiciled in the other state, and to use all the mechanisms and arguments they would use with their own—bribery, political pressure, exchange of advantages. This may suffice, but often the "foreign" firm is at a considerable disadvantage in the local political arena. If the "foreign" firm is domiciled in a "strong" state, it can appeal to its own state to use state power to put pressure on the other state to get it to accede to the needs and demands of the strong state's entrepreneurs. And of course, this process is central to the life of the interstate system. In the last third of the twentieth century, U.S. manufacturers of automobiles and steel,and airlines, were not shy about asking the U.S. government to pressure Japan and western Europe to change their policies in ways that would improve the position of U.S. manufacturers and the access that U.S. air carriers had to transoceanic traffic rights.

The large majority of the population in any state is accounted for by the households of those who work for the firms and other organizations. The capitalist system provides for a certain mode of dividing up the surplus-value that is produced, and obviously at any given moment this is a zero-sum game. The larger the portion allocated to the accumulation of capital, the smaller the one that can be allocated as compensation for those who work for the production units creating this surplus-value. One of the basic realities is that this division of the surplus-value has some limits (it cannot be 100 percent one way and 0 percent the other), but the gamut of possibilities in between is very large, certainly in the short run, and even in the longer run up to a point.

It follows logically that there will be a constant struggle over this allocation of the surplus-value. This is what has been called the class struggle. Whatever one feels about the politics of the class struggle, it is an unavoidable analytic category, which can be verbally disguised but never ignored. And it is quite clear that in this ongoing class struggle (which is no doubt a very complex phenomenon, with no simple binary distribution of loyalties), the state is a central actor in shifting the allocation in one direction or the other. Hence, both sides organize politically to put pressure on the state as an executive and legislative structure. If one takes a long view of the internal politics of the multiple states throughout the history of the capitalist world-economy, one can see that it took quite a while, several centuries, before the working strata were able to organize themselves sufficiently to play the political game with any minimal degree of efficacy.

The historic turning-point was undoubtedly the French Revolution. For the French Revolution brought about the two fundamental changes in the geoculture of the modern world-system that we have already noted: it made change, political change, into a "normal" phenomenon, something inherent in the nature of things and in fact desirable. This was the political expression of the theory of progress that was so central to Enlightenment ideas. And secondly, the French Revolution reoriented the concept of sovereignty, from the monarch or the legislature to the people. When the genie of the people as sovereign escaped from the bottle, it would never be put back inside. It became the common wisdom of the entire world-system.

One of the central consequences of the idea that the people were sovereign is that the people were now defined as "citizens." Today, the concept is so elementary that we find it hard to understand how radical was the shift from "subjects" to "citizens." To be a citizen meant to have the right to participate, on an equal level with all other citizens, in the basic decisions of the state. To be a citizen meant that there were no persons with statuses higher than that of citizen (such as aristocrats). To be a citizen meant that everyone was being accepted as a rational person, capable of political decision. The logical consequence of the concept of citizen was universal suffrage. And as we know, the political history of the following 150 years was one of steady expansion of the suffrage in country after country.

Today, virtually every country claims that its citizens are all equal, and exercise their sovereignty through a system of universal suffrage. Except we know that in reality this is not really so. Only part of the population exercises the full rights of citizenship in most countries. For if the people are sovereign, we must then decide who falls within the category of the people, and many, it turns out, are excluded. There are some exclusions which seemed "obvious" to most people: those who are merely visitors to the country (aliens); those who are too young to have judgment; those who are insane. But what about women? And persons from minority ethnic groups? And those without property? And those who are imprisoned as felons? Once one starts on the path of enumerating the exceptions to the term "people," the list can get very long. The "people," which began as a concept of inclusion, turned rather quickly into a concept of exclusion.

As a consequence, the politics of inclusion and exclusion became a center-piece of national politics throughout the following two centuries. Those who were excluded sought to be included, and those who were already included were most often inclined to keep eligibility for citizens' rights defined narrowly, maintaining the exclusions. This meant that those who were seeking inclusion had to organize outside the parliamentary channels in order for their cause to be heard. That is, quite simply, they had to engage in demonstrative, rebellious, sometimes revolutionary activity.

This led to a great strategic debate among the powerful in the early nineteenth century. On the one hand, there were those whose fears led them to feel that these movements had to be suppressed (and indeed the very idea of popular sovereignty rejected). They called themselves conservatives and extolled "traditional" institutions—the monarchy, the church, the notables, the family—as bulwarks against change. But opposed to them was another group which thought that this strategy was doomed to failure, and that only by accepting the inevitability of *some* change could they limit the degree and the speed of the change. This group called themselves liberals, and they extolled the educated individual as the model citizen and the specialist as the only person who could wisely determine the details of social and political decisions. They argued that all others should slowly be admitted to full citizens' rights when their education had become sufficient to enable them to make balanced choices. By embracing progress, the liberals sought to frame its definition in such a way that the "dangerous classes" would become less dangerous and those with "merit" would play the key roles in political, economic, and social institutions. There was of course a third group, the radicals, who would associate themselves with the antisystemic movements, indeed lead them for the most part.

In this trinity of ideologies that emerged in the wake of the French Revolution—conservatism, liberalism, and radicalism—it was the centrist liberals who succeeded in dominating the scene in the world-system, at least for a very long time. Their program of modulated change would be enacted everywhere, and they would persuade both the conservatives and the radicals to modulate their positions such that both conservatives and radicals came in practice to be virtual avatars of centrist liberalism.

The politics of all these movements were affected by the strength of the states in which they were located. As we know, some states are stronger than other states. But what does it mean to be a strong state internally? Strength certainly is not indicated by the degree of arbitrariness or ruthlessness of the central authority, although this is a frequent criterion that many observers use. Dictatorial behavior by state authorities is more often a sign of weakness than of strength. Strength of states is most usefully defined as the ability to get legal decisions actually carried out. (Remember our earlier example of Louis XIV versus a contemporary prime minister of Sweden.) One simple measure that one might use is the percentage of taxes levied that are actually collected and reach the taxing authority. Tax evasion is of course pandemic. But the difference between what strong states can collect (somewhere near 80 percent) and what weak states can collect (more like 20 percent) is enormous. The lower figure is explained by a weaker bureaucracy, and the inability to collect taxes in turn deprives the state of the funds with which to strengthen the bureaucracy.

The weaker the state, the less wealth can be accumulated through economically productive activities. This consequently makes the state machinery itself a prime locus, perhaps the prime locus, of wealth accumulation—through larceny and bribery, at high and low levels. It is not that this does not occur in strong states—it does—but that in weak states it becomes the preferred means of capital accumulation, which in turn weakens the ability of the state to perform its other tasks. When the state machinery becomes the main mode of capital accumulation, all sense of regular transfer of office to successors becomes remote, which leads to wildly falsified elections (if any are held at all) and rambunctious transfers of power, which in turn necessarily expands the political role of the military. States are, in theory, the only legitimate users of violence and should possess the monopoly of its use. The police and military are the prime vehicle of this monopoly, and in theory are merely instruments of state authorities. In practice, this monopoly is diluted, and the weaker the state, the more it is diluted. As a result it is very difficult for political leaders to maintain effective control of the country, and this in turn increases the temptation for the military to take control of the executive directly whenever a regime seems unable to guarantee internal security. What is crucial to note is that these phenomena are not the result of wrong policies but of the endemic weakness of state structures in zones where the large majority of production processes are peripheral and are therefore weak sources of capital accumulation. In states that have raw materials which are very lucrative on the world market (such as oil), the income available to the states is essentially rent, and here too the actual control of the machinery guarantees that much of the rent can be siphoned off into private hands. It is no accident then that such states fall frequently into situations in which the military assumes direct rule.

Finally, we should underline the degree to which weakness means the relative strength of local notables (barons, warlords) who are able to enforce their control over non-state regions by control of some local military forces, combined often with some local legitimation (of ethnicity or traditional family or aristocratic dominance). In the twentieth century, some of this local authority came to be acquired by movements that began as national antisystemic movements and, in the course of struggle, transmuted themselves into local fiefdoms. Such local baronies tend to bring out the mafioso side of capitalist entrepreneurial activity. Mafias are basically predators that feed on the production process. When there are non-monopolized products, which are not highly profitable for the individual firm, one of the few ways in which one can accumulate large sums of capital is to establish a monopolistic funnel through which production passes, and to do so by the use of non-state force. Mafias are notorious for their involvement in illegal products (such as drugs) but are often involved in quite legal forms of production activity as well. And mafia-style capitalist activity is of course dangerous and inherently life-threatening to the mafias themselves. Hence historically mafiosi, once successful in accumulating capital, seek (often in the very next generation) to launder their money and transform themselves into legal entrepreneurs. But of course wherever tight state control breaks down or is limited, there are always new mafias that emerge.

One of the ways in which states try to reinforce their authority and to become stronger and diminish the role of mafias is to transform their population into a "nation." Nations are to be sure myths in the sense that they are all social creations, and the states have a central role in their construction. The process of creating a nation involves establishing (to a large degree inventing) a history, a long chronology, and a presumed set of defining characteristics (even if large segments of the group included do not in fact share those characteristics).

We should think of the concept "nation-state" as an asymptote toward which all states aspire. Some states claim that they do not, that they are "multinational," but in fact even such states seek to create a pan-state identity. A good example is the Soviet Union which, when it existed, claimed that it was multinational, but also promoted the idea of a "Soviet" people. The same is true of Switzerland or Canada. Nationalism is a status-group identity, perhaps the one most crucial to maintaining the modern world-system, based as it is on a structure of sovereign states located within an interstate system. Nationalism serves as the minimal cement of state structures. If one looks closely, nationalism is not a phenomenon merely of weak states. It is in fact extremely strong in the wealthiest states, even if it is publicly invoked less frequently than in states of middling strength. Once again, the public pursuit of nationalist themes on the part of state leaders should be analyzed as an attempt to strengthen the state, not evidence that the state is already strong. Historically, the states have had three main modes of creating nationalism: the state school system, service in the armed forces, and public ceremonies. All three are in constant use.

States, as we have emphasized, exist within the framework of an interstate system, and their relative strength is not merely the degree to which they can effectively exercise authority internally but the degree to which they can hold their heads high in the competitive environment of the world-system. All states are theoretically sovereign, but strong states find it far easier to "intervene" in the internal affairs of weaker states than vice versa, and everyone is aware of that.

Strong states relate to weak states by pressuring them to keep their frontiers open to those flows of factors of production that are useful and profitable to firms located in the strong states, while resisting any demands for reciprocity in this regard. In the debates on world trade, the United States and the European Union are constantly demanding that states in the rest of the world open their frontiers to flows of manufactures and services from them. They however quite strongly resist opening fully their own frontiers to flows of agricultural products or textiles that compete with their own products from states in peripheral zones. Strong states relate to weak states by pressuring them to install and keep in power persons whom the strong states find acceptable, and to join the strong states in placing pressures on other weak states to get them to conform to the policy needs of the strong states. Strong states relate to weak states by pressuring them to accept cultural practices—linguistic policy; educational policy, including where university students may study; media distribution—that will reinforce the long-term linkage between them. Strong states relate to weak states by pressuring them to follow their lead in international arenas (treaties, international organizations). And while strong states may buy off the individual leaders of weak states, weak states as states buy the protection of strong states by arranging appropriate flows of capital.

Of course, the weakest states are those we call colonies, by which we mean administrative units that are defined as non-sovereign and fall under the jurisdiction of another state, normally distant from it. The origin of modern colonies is in the economic expansion of the world-system. In this expansion, strong states at the core tried to incorporate new zones into the processes of the modern world-system. Sometimes they encountered bureaucratic units which were strong enough to become defined as sovereign states even if not strong enough to stay out of the expanding world-system. But often the militarily strong states (mostly located in western Europe, but the United States, Russia, and Japan must be added to the list) encountered areas where the political structures were quite weak. To ensure the incorporation of such areas into the world-system in a satisfactory manner, these areas were conquered and colonial regimes installed.

The colonies performed internally the same kinds of functions that sovereign states performed: they guaranteed property rights; they made decisions about traversal of boundaries; they arranged modes of political participation (almost always extremely limited); they enforced decisions about the workplaces and often decided on what kinds of production were to be pursued or favored in the colony. But of course the personnel who made these decisions were overwhelmingly persons sent out by the colonizing power and not persons of the local population. The colonial powers justified their assumption of authority and the distribution of roles to persons from the "metropolitan" country by a combination of arguments: racist arguments about the cultural inferiority and inadequacy of the local populations; and self-justifying arguments about the "civilizing" role the colonial administration was performing.

The basic reality was that the colonial state was simply the weakest kind of state in the interstate system, with the lowest degree of real autonomy, and therefore maximally subject to exploitation by firms and persons from a different country, the so-called metropolitan country. Of course, one of the objectives of the colonizing power was not merely to ensure its control of the production processes in the colony but also to make sure that no other relatively strong state in the world-system could have access to the resources or the markets of the colony, or at most minimal access. It was therefore inevitable that at some point, there should come to be political mobilization of the populations of the colonies in the form of movements of national liberation, whose object would be defined as obtaining independence (that is, the status of a sovereign state) as the first step on the path to improving the relative position of the country and its populations in the world-economy.

However, paying attention only to the relationship of strong states to weak states can lead us to neglect the very crucial relation of strong states to strong states. Such states are by definition rivals, bearing responsibility to different sets of rival firms. But as in the competition between large firms, the competition between strong states is tempered by a contradiction. While each is against the other in a sort of putative zero-sum game, they have a common interest in holding together the interstate system, and the modern world-system as a whole. So the actors are pushed simultaneously in opposite directions: toward an anarchic interstate system and toward a coherent and orderly interstate system. The result, as might be expected, is structures that are normally in between the two types.

In this contradictory struggle, we should not neglect the special role of the semiperipheral states. These states, of intermediate strength, spend their energy running very fast in order at the very least to stay in their intermediate place, but hoping as well that they may rise on the ladder. They use state power in the internal and interstate arena quite consciously to raise the status of their state as a producer, as an accumulator of capital, and as a military force. Their choice is ultimately quite simple: either they will succeed in moving up the hierarchical ladder (or at least staying put) or they will be pushed down.

They must choose their alliances and their economic opportunities carefully and swiftly. For semiperipheral states are primarily in competition with each other. If, for example, during a Kondratieff B-phase there is significant relocation of an erstwhile leading industry, it will usually go to semiperipheral countries. But not, however, to all of them; perhaps only to one or two of them. There is not enough space in the production structure of the whole system to permit this kind of relocation (called "development") simultaneously in too many countries. Which one of perhaps fifteen countries will be the locus of such relocation is not easy to determine in advance or even to explain in retrospect. What is easy to grasp is that not every country can be so favored, or profits would plummet downward too rapidly and too steeply.

The competition between strong states and the efforts of semiperipheral states to increase their status and their power result in an ongoing interstate rivalry which normally takes the form of a so-called balance of power, by which one means a situation in which no single state can automatically get its way in the interstate arena. This does not mean that the stronger states do not attempt to achieve precisely this degree of power. There are however two quite different ways in which states might realize dominance. One is to transform the world-economy into a world-empire. The second is to obtain what may be called hegemony in the world-system. It is important to distinguish the two modalities, and to understand why no state has been able to transform the modern world-system into a world-empire but several states have, at different times, achieved hegemony.

By a world-empire we mean a structure in which there is a single political authority for the whole world-system. There have been several serious attempts to create such a world-empire in the last five hundred years. The first was that of Charles V in the sixteenth century (continued in weakened form by his heirs). The second was that of Napoleon at the beginning of the nineteenth century. The third was that of Hitler in the mid-twentieth century. All were formidable; all were ultimately defeated and unable to consummate their goals.

On the other hand, three powers achieved hegemony, albeit for only relatively brief periods. The first was the United Provinces (today called the Netherlands) in the mid-seventeenth century. The second was the United Kingdom in the mid-nineteenth century. And the third was the United States in the mid-twentieth century. What allows us to call them hegemonic

4 The Creation of a Geoculture

Ideologies, Social Movements, Social Science

THE FRENCH REVOLUTION, as we have noted, was a turning-point in the cultural history of the modern world-system, having brought about two fundamental changes that may be said to constitute the basis of what became the geoculture of the modern world-system: the normality of political change and the refashioning of the concept of sovereignty, now vested in the people who were "citizens." And this concept, as we have said, although meant to include, in practice excluded very many.

The political history of the modern world-system in the nineteenth and twentieth centuries became the history of a debate about the line that divides the included from the excluded, but this debate was occurring *within the framework of a geoculture that proclaimed the inclusion of all as the definition of the good society*. This political dilemma was fought out in three different arenas—the ideologies, the antisystemic movements, and the social sciences. These arenas seemed to be separate. They claimed they were separate. But in fact, they were intimately linked the one with the others. Let us discuss each in turn.

An ideology is more than a set of ideas or theories. It is more than a moral commitment or a worldview. It is a coherent strategy in the social arena from which one can draw quite specific political conclusions. In this sense, one did not need ideologies in previous world-systems, or indeed even in the modern world-system before the concept of the normality of change, and that of the citizen who was ultimately responsible for such change, were adopted as basic structural principles of political institutions. For ideologies presume that there exist competing groups with competing long-term strategies of how to deal with change and who best should take the lead in dealing with it. The ideologies were born in the wake of the French Revolution.

The first to be born was the ideology of conservatism. This was the ideology of those who thought that the French Revolution and its principles were a social disaster. Almost immediately, some basic texts were written, one by Edmund Burke in England in 1790 and then a series by Joseph de Maistre in France. Both authors had previously been moderate reformers in their views. Both would now enunciate an arch-conservative ideology in reaction to what seemed to them a dangerous attempt of radical intervention in the basic structure of social order.

What particularly upset them was the argument that the social order was infinitely malleable, infinitely improvable, and that human political intervention could and should accelerate the changes. Conservatives considered such intervention hybris, and very dangerous hybris at that. Their views were rooted in a pessimistic view of man's moral capacities; they found false and intolerable the fundamental optimism of the French revolutionaries. They felt that whatever shortcomings existed in the social order in which we live ultimately caused less human evil than the institutions that would be created out of such hybris. After 1793 and the Reign of Terror, in which French revolutionaries sent other French revolutionaries to the guillotine for not being revolutionary enough, conservative ideologues tended to formulate their views by saying that revolution as a process led, almost inevitably, to such a reign of terror.

Conservatives were therefore counter-revolutionaries. They were "reactionaries" in the sense that they were reacting to the drastic changes of the revolution and wished to "restore" what now began to be called the *ancien régime*. Conservatives were not necessarily totally opposed to any evolution of customs and rules. They simply preached acute caution, and insisted that the only ones to decide on any such changes had to be the responsible people in the traditional social institutions. They were especially suspicious of the idea that everyone could be a citizen—with equal rights and duties—since most people, in their view, did not have, would never have, the judgment necessary to make important sociopolitical decisions. They put their faith instead in hierarchical political and religious structures—in the large ones of course, but in a sense even more in the *local* structures: the best families, the "community," whatever came under the heading of notables. And they put their faith in the family, that is, the hierarchical, patriarchal family structure. Faith in hierarchy (as both inevitable and desirable) is the hallmark of conservatism.

The political strategy was clear—restore and maintain the authority of these traditional institutions, and submit to their wisdom. If the result was very slow political change, or even no political change at all, so be it. And if these institutions decided to implement a process of slow evolution, so be it also. Respect for hierarchy was, conservatives believed, the sole guarantor of order. Conservatives thus abhorred democracy, which for them signaled the end of respect for hierarchy. They were furthermore suspicious of widespread access to education, which for them ought to be reserved for the training of élite cadres. Conservatives believed that the gulf between the capacities of the upper and lower classes was not only insuperable but part of basic human character and hence mandated by heaven.

The French Revolution, narrowly defined, did not last very long. It transmuted into the regime of Napoleon Bonaparte, who transposed its universalistic self-assurance and missionary zeal into French imperial expansion justified by revolutionary heritage. Politically, conservative ideology was on the rise everywhere after 1794, and presumably ensconced in power after Napoleon's defeat in 1815 in a Europe dominated by the Holy Alliance. Those who thought that any return to the ancien régime was both undesirable and impossible had to regroup and develop a counter-ideology. This counter-ideology came to be called liberalism.

The liberals wished to shed the albatross of association with the reign of terror and yet salvage what they thought was the underlying spirit that emerged from the French Revolution. They insisted that change was not only normal but inevitable, because we live in a world of eternal progress toward the good society. They acknowledged that overhasty change could be, indeed was, counterproductive, but they insisted that *traditional* hierarchies were untenable and basically illegitimate. The slogan of the French Revolution that appealed to them most was "careers open to talents" (*la carrière ouverte aux talents*), an idea today more familiar in the phrases "equality of opportunity" and "meritocracy." It was around such slogans that liberals would build their ideology. Liberals made a distinction between different kinds of hierarchies. They were not against what they thought of as *natural* hierarchies; they were against *inherited* hierarchies. Natural hierarchies, they argued, were not only natural but acceptable to the mass of the population and therefore a legitimate and legitimated basis of authority, whereas inherited hierarchies made social mobility impossible.

Against conservatives who were the "Party of Order," liberals presented themselves as the "Party of Movement." Changing situations required constant *reform* of the institutions. But the consequent social change should occur at a natural pace—that is, neither too slowly nor too rapidly. The question that liberals broached was who should take the lead in such necessary reforms. They put no trust in traditional hierarchies, national or local, clerical or secular. But they were also very suspicious of the mass of the population, the mob, who they thought were essentially uneducated and consequently irrational.

This meant, the liberals concluded, that there was only one group that should take the lead and the responsibility for deciding on what changes were necessary—the specialists. Specialists, by definition, understood the realities of whatever they had studied and therefore could best formulate the reforms that were necessary and desirable. Specialists, by their training, were inclined to be prudent and insightful. They appreciated both the possibilities and the pitfalls of change. Since every *educated* person was a specialist in something, it followed that those who would be allowed to exercise the role of citizen were those who were educated and were therefore specialists. Others might eventually be admitted to this role, when they had received the proper education to permit them to join the society of rational, educated men.

But what kind of education? The liberals argued that education had now to shift from the "traditional" forms of knowledge, what we today call the humanities, toward the only theoretical basis of practical knowledge, science. Science (replacing not only theology but philosophy as well) offered the path for material and technological progress, and hence for moral progress. Of all the kinds of specialists, the scientists represented the acme of intellectual work, the *summum bonum*. Only political leaders who based their immediate programs on scientific knowledge were reliable guides to future welfare. As can be readily seen, liberalism was a quite moderate ideology in terms of social change. Indeed, it has always emphasized its moderation, its "centrism" in the political arena. In the 1950s a leading American liberal, Arthur Schlesinger Jr., wrote a book about liberalism, which he entitled *The Vital Center*.

In the first half of the nineteenth century, the ideological scene was basically a conflict between conservatives and liberals. There really was no strong group espousing a more radical ideology. Those who were inclined to be radical often attached themselves to liberal movements as a small appendage, or sought to create small loci of dissenting views. They called themselves democrats, or radicals, or sometimes socialists. They of course had no sympathy for conservative ideology. But they found that the liberals, even while accepting the normality of change and supporting (at least in theory) the concept of citizenship, were extremely timid and actually quite afraid of fundamental change.

It was the "world revolution" of 1848 that transformed the ideological panorama from one with two ideological contenders (conservatives versus liberals) into one with three—conservatives on the right, liberals in the center, and radicals on the left. What happened in 1848? Essentially two things. On the one hand, there occurred the first true "social revolution" of the modern era. For a very brief period, a movement supported by urban workers seemed to acquire some power in France, and this movement had resonances in other countries. The political prominence of this group wouldn't last long. But it was frightening to those who had power and privilege. At the same time, there was another revolution, or series of revolutions, which the historians have called "the springtime of the nations." In a number of countries, there were national or nationalist uprisings. They were equally unsuccessful, and equally frightening to those with power. The combination marked the beginning of a pattern that would engage the world-system for the next century and more: antisystemic movements as key political players.

The world revolution of 1848 was a sudden flame that was doused, and acute repression followed for many years. But the revolution raised major questions about strategies, that is, ideologies. The conservatives drew a clear lesson from these events. They saw that the blindly reactionary tactics of Prince Metternich, who served for forty years as the minister of state (in effect, foreign minister) of Austria-Hungary and had been the moving spirit behind the Holy Alliance designed to stifle all revolutionary movements in Europe, and all who stood with him, were counterproductive. Their tactics did not in the long run work to conserve traditions nor to guarantee order. Instead they provoked angers, resentments, and subversive organization, and therefore undermined order. Conservatives noticed that the only country to avoid a revolution in 1848 was England, even though it had had the most significant radical movement in Europe in the preceding decade. The secret seemed to be the mode of conservatism preached and practiced there between 1820 and 1850 by Sir Robert Peel, which consisted of timely (but limited) concessions aimed at undercutting the long-term appeal of radical action. Over the next two decades, Europe saw Peelite tactics take root in what came to be called "enlightened conservatism," which thrived not only in England but in France and Germany as well.

Meanwhile, the radicals also drew strategic lessons from their failures in the revolutions of 1848. They no longer wished to play the role of appendage of the liberals. But spontaneity, which had been a major resource of pre-1848 radicals, had demonstrated its acute limitations. Spontaneous violence had the effect of throwing paper on a fire. The fire flamed up but just as quickly went out. Such violence was not a very durable fuel. Some radicals before 1848 had preached an alternative, that of creating utopian communities which withdrew from involvement with the larger social arena. But this project seemed to have little attraction for most people, and had even less impact on the overall historical system than spontaneous rebellion. Radicals searched for a more effective alternative strategy, and they would find one in organization—systematic, long-term organization that would prepare the ground politically for fundamental social change.

Finally, liberals also drew a lesson from the revolutions of 1848. They came to realize that it was insufficient to preach the virtues of relying upon specialists to effectuate reasonable and timely social change. They had to operate actively in the political arena so that matters would in fact be turned over to the specialists. And for them this meant dealing with both their ancient conservative rivals and their newly emerging radical rivals. If liberals wished to present themselves as the political center, they had to work at it with a program that was "centrist" in its demands, and a set of tactics that would locate them somewhere halfway between conservative resistance to any change and radical insistence on extremely rapid change.

The period between 1848 and the First World War saw the delineation of a clear liberal program for the core countries of the modern world-system. These countries sought to establish themselves as "liberal states"—that is, states based on the concept of citizenship, a range of guarantees against arbitrary authority, and a certain openness in public life. The program that the liberals developed had three main elements: gradual extension of the suffrage and, concomitant with this and essential to it, the expansion of access to education; expanding the role of the state in protecting citizens against harm in the workplace, expanding health facilities and access to them, and ironing out fluctuations in income in the life cycle; forging citizens of a state into a "nation." If one looks closely, these three elements turn out to be a way of translating the slogan of "liberty, equality, and fraternity" into public policy.

There are two main things to be noticed about this liberal program. The first is that it was implemented in large part by the time of the First World War, at least in the pan-European world. The second is that the liberal parties were not always those who in fact did the most to implement the program. Somewhat curiously, the liberal program was implemented to a significant degree by non-liberals—a consequence of the revisions in strategies of the three ideologies that occurred after the revolutions of 1848. The liberals retreated somewhat, becoming timid in prosecuting their own program. They feared bringing on the turmoil of 1848 a second time. The conservatives, on the other hand, decided that the liberal program was modest and essentially sensible. They began to legislate it—Disraeli's extension of the suffrage, Napoleon III's legalization of the trade unions, Bismarck's invention of the welfare state. And the radicals began to settle for these limited reforms, indeed argue for them, while building their organizational base for a future accession to governmental power.

The combination of these three tactical shifts by the three ideological groups meant that the liberal program became in effect the common defining feature of the geoculture, the conservatives and the radicals having transformed themselves into mere variants or avatars of the liberals, with whom their differences became marginal rather than fundamental. It is especially in the third pillar of "fraternity" that we can see a steady coming-together of the three ideological positions. How does one create a nation? By underlining how citizenship excludes the others out there. One creates a nation by preaching nationalism. Nationalism was taught in the nineteenth century through three main institutions: the primary schools, the army, and the national celebrations.

The primary schools were the lodestar of the liberals, applauded by the radicals, and acceded to by the conservatives. They turned workers and peasants into citizens who possessed the minimum capacities needed to perform national duties: the famous trio of reading, writing, and arithmetic. The schools taught civic virtues, overriding the particularisms and prejudices of the family structures. And above all, they taught the national language. At the beginning of the nineteenth century, few European countries had in practice a single national language. By the end, most of them did.

Nationalism is secured by hostility to enemies. Most states in the core sought to instill this hostility toward some neighbor, on some ground or other. But there was another, ultimately more important, form of this hostility, that of the pan-European world facing the rest of the world, a hostility institutionalized as racism. This was located in the diffusion of the concept of "civilization"—in the singular, as opposed to the plural. The pan-European world, dominating the world-system economically and politically, defined itself as the heart, the culmination, of a civilizational process which it traced back to Europe's presumed roots in Antiquity. Given the state of its civilization and its technology in the nineteenth century, the pan-European world claimed the duty to impose itself, culturally as well as politically, on everyone else—Kipling's "White man's burden," the "manifest destiny" of the United States, France's *mission civilisatrice*.

The nineteenth century became the century of renewed direct imperialism, with this added nuance. Imperial conquest was no longer merely the action of the state, or even of the state encouraged by the churches. It had become the passion of the nation, the duty of the citizens. And this last part of the liberal program was taken up with a vengeance by the conservatives, who saw in it a sure way of muting class divisions and thereby guaranteeing internal order. When virtually all European socialist parties opted in 1914 to support their national side in the war, it was clear that the conservative belief about the effect of nationalism on the erstwhile dangerous classes had been correct.

The triumph of liberalism in defining the geoculture of the modern world-system in the nineteenth century and most of the twentieth was made possible institutionally by the development of the legal underpinnings of the liberal state. But it was also made possible by the rise and steadily increasing importance of the antisystemic movements. This may seem paradoxical, since antisystemic movements presumably exist to undermine the system, not to sustain it. Nonetheless, the activities of these movements served on the whole to reinforce the system considerably. Dissecting this seeming paradox is crucial to understanding the way in which the capitalist world-economy—constantly growing in size and wealth and simultaneously in the polarization of its benefits—has been held together.

Inside the states, attempts by groups to achieve inclusion as citizens became a central focus of the antisystemic movements, that is, organizations which sought to bring about fundamental changes in social organization. They were in a sense seeking to implement the slogan of liberty, equality, and fraternity in a way different from that of the liberals. The excluded group that was the earliest to create serious organizations was the urban industrial working class, what was called the proletariat. This group was concentrated in a few urban localities and its members found it easy to communicate with one another. When they began to organize, their conditions of work and level of recompense were obviously poor. And they played a crucial role in the major productive activities that generated surplus-value.

By the middle of the nineteenth century, workplace organizations (trade unions) and public arena organizations (workers' and socialist parties) began to emerge, first in the strongest centers of industrial production (western Europe and North America) and then elsewhere. For most of the nineteenth century and a good part of the twentieth century, the state machineries were hostile to these organizations, as were the firms. It followed that the class struggle was a lopsided field of contention, in which the "social movement" was fighting a difficult, uphill battle for successive, relatively small concessions.

In this pattern of muted political struggle, there was a further element which returns us to our discussion of households and status-group identities. The social movement defined its struggle as that of the workers versus the capitalists. But who were the "workers"? In practice, they tended to be defined as adult males of the dominant ethnic group in a given country. They were for the most part skilled or semiskilled workers, with some education, and they constituted the bulk of the industrial labor force worldwide in the nineteenth century. Those who were "excluded" from this category found that since they seemed to have little place in the socialist/workers' organizations, they had to organize themselves in status-group categories (women on the one hand and racial, religious, linguistic, and ethnic groups on the other). These groups were often quite as antisystemic as the labor and socialist movements, but they defined their immediate grievances quite differently.

However, in organizing themselves along these lines, they entered into competition with and often opposition to the class-based organizations of the workers. From circa 1830 to 1970, the history of the relations between these two kinds of antisystemic movements was one of great tension, even hostility, with at most occasional interludes of sympathy and cooperation. What is more, during this period the multiple status-group identity organizations found it no easier to cooperate with each other than any of them did with the labor and socialist organizations.

However these status-group identity organizations defined their long-run objectives (and many of them were silent about this), their middle-run objectives were all grouped around the theme of extending citizenship rights to them as excluded groups. They all faced at least reluctance, more often active hostility, to their proposals to include them within the framework of full citizens in the liberal state. They faced two fundamental issues of strategy. The first was what kind of middle-run strategy would be most efficacious. The second was what kinds of alliances each variety of antisystemic movement should establish with the other variants. Neither question was easily or rapidly solved.

Excluded groups had some obvious, immediate difficulties in political organization. The law often restricted their right to organize in many ways. The potential members were for the most part individually weak in terms of quotidian power. They did not have collectively (or for the most part individually) significant access to money. The major institutions of the various states tended to be hostile to their efforts. The groups were thus easily oppressed. In short, the process of organizing was long and slow, and they spent the most part of this period merely keeping their organizational head above water.

One basic debate involved whether it was more important for the oppressed groups to change themselves or to change the institutions that were oppressing them. This was sometimes phrased as the difference between a cultural strategy and a political strategy. For example, for a nationalist group, is it more important to revive a dying national language or to elect persons from the group to the legislature? For a workers' movement, is it more important to refuse the legitimacy of all states (anarchism) or to transform the existing states? The quarrels inside the movements over strategy were fierce, unyielding, very divisive, and strongly felt by the participants.

To be sure, the two emphases were not necessarily exclusive of each other, but many felt that they led in quite different strategic directions. The case for the cultural option, if we may call it that, was always that political changes were in the end superficial and co-optative and vitiated the radical, or antisystemic, underlying objectives. There was also a sociopsychological argument—that the system held ordinary people captive by organizing their psyches, and that undoing the socialization of these psyches was an indispensable prerequisite for social change. The case for the political option was that the proponents of the cultural option were naïve victims of delusions, because they assumed that the powers that be would permit them to make the kind of serious cultural changes they envisaged. Those arguing for the political option always emphasized the realities of power, and insisted that transforming the relations of power, not changing the psyches of the oppressed, was the prerequisite to any real change.

What happened historically is that after thirty to fifty years of both friendly and unfriendly debate, the proponents of the political option won the internal battles in all the antisystemic movements. The constant suppression of the activities of movements of either emphasis by the powers that be made the cultural options in their various forms seem unviable for the antisystemic movements. More and more persons turned to being "militant," and more and more militants turned to being "well organized," and the combination could only be efficiently realized by groups that had chosen the political option. By the beginning of the twentieth century, one could say not only that the political option had won out in this debate over strategy but that the antisystemic movements had agreed—each variety separately, but in parallel ways—on a two-step agenda of action: first obtain power in the state; then transform the world/the state/the society.

Of course there remained a great deal of ambiguity in this two-step strategy. The main question was what it meant to obtain power in the state, and how one could do it in any case. (The question of how to transform the world/the state/the society was less often debated, perhaps because it was seen as a question of the future rather than of the present.) For example, was power in the state achieved by extending the suffrage? By participating in elections and then in governments? Did it involve sharing power or taking power from others? Did it involve changing state structures or simply controlling the existing ones? None of these questions was ever fully answered, and most organizations survived best by allowing partisans of different, often contradictory, answers to remain within their fold.

Even once the two-step political strategy was made the central focus of organizational action, the internal debates did not cease. For the question then became: How could one take over the state machinery? The classic debate was that between the Second and Third Internationals, a debate that had begun earlier within the framework of the social democratic parties. It was often framed, a bit misleadingly, as the debate between reformism and revolutionary activity. When Eduard Bernstein urged upon the German Social-Democratic Party his "revisionism," what was it he was arguing? Essentially the core of the argument involved a series of successive premises: The majority of the population were "workers," by which he meant industrial workers and their families. Universal (male) suffrage would make all these workers full citizens. The workers would vote according to their interests, which meant to support the Social-Democratic Party. Ergo, once there was universal male suffrage, the workers would vote the Social-Democrats into power. Once in power, the Social-Democrats would pass the necessary legislation to transform the country into a socialist society. Each of these successive premises seemed to be logical. Each turned out to be false.

The revolutionary position was different. As formulated classically by Lenin, it was that in many countries proletarians were not the majority of the population. In many countries, there was no free electoral process; and if there were, the bourgeoisie would not really respect the results if the proletariat tried to vote itself into power. The bourgeoisie simply would not permit it. The revolutionaries suggested a series of counterpremises: The urban proletariat was the only progressive historical actor. Even the urban proletarians, not to speak of other parts of the population (rural workers, for example), were not always aware of their own interests. Militants of workers' parties were able to define the interests of the urban proletariat more clearly than the average proletarian, and could induce the workers to understand their interests. These militants could organize in a clandestine fashion and could achieve power by an insurrection which would gain the support of the urban proletariat. They could then impose a "dictatorship of the proletariat" and transform the country into a socialist society. Each of these successive premises seemed to be logical. Each turned out to be false.

One of the biggest problems of the antisystemic movements in the late nineteenth century and most of the twentieth was their incapacity to find much common ground. The dominant attitude in each variety of antisystemic movement was that the grievances which its adherents articulated were the fundamental ones and that the grievances of other varieties of movements were secondary and distracting. Each variety insisted that its grievances be dealt with first. Each argued that dealing successfully with its grievances would create a situation in which the other grievances could be solved subsequently and consequently.

We see this first of all in the difficult relations between the worker/socialist movements and the women's movements. The attitude of the trade unions to women's movements was basically that the employment of women was a mechanism used by employers to obtain cheaper labor and that it therefore represented a threat to the interests of the working classes. Most urban workers during the nineteenth century and for a good part of the twentieth century believed in a social model in which married women should be housewives who stayed out of the labor market. In place of the entry of women into the labor market, trade unions struggled to obtain what was called a "family wage," by which was meant a wage sufficient for the male industrial worker to support himself, his wife, and his non-adult children.

Socialist parties were, if anything, even more dubious about the role of women's organizations. Except for the women's groups which defined themselves as sections of socialist parties and whose objective was to organize the wives and daughters of the party members for educational tasks, women's organizations were considered bourgeois organizations, since their leadership most often came from the ranks of bourgeois women, and their objectives were therefore seen as being of at most secondary interest to the working class. As for women's suffrage, while in theory socialist parties were in favor of it, in practice they were highly skeptical. They believed that working-class women were less likely than working-class men to vote for socialist parties because of the influence on them of religious organizations that were hostile to the socialist parties.

The women's organizations returned the favor. They saw the worker and socialist movements as perpetuators of the patriarchal attitudes and policies against which they were struggling. Middle-class women in suffragist organizations often made the argument that they were more educated than working-class men, and that by liberal logic, it followed that they should be granted full citizenship rights first, which historically was not the case in most countries. The legal rights to inherit, to handle money, to sign contracts, and in general to be independent persons in the eyes of the law were generally of much greater relevance to those families that had property. And women's campaigns against social problems (alcoholism, mistreatment of women and children) and for control of their own bodies were often directed more immediately against working-class men than against middle-class men.

The relationship of worker/social movements to ethnic/nationalist movements exhibited parallel difficulties. Within countries, the workers' movements saw ethnic movements of any kind as mechanisms through which to divide the working classes. Demands by oppressed ethnic and racial groups for inclusion in the job market met the same response as demands by women. They were seen essentially as something serving the interests of the employers, making it possible for them to obtain cheaper labor. Many trade unions sought to exclude such "minorities" from the job market, not of course entirely but from the somewhat higher-paid segment of the job market that had been traditionally reserved for workers from the dominant ethnic group. The drive to exclude minorities also strengthened opposition to permitting immigration from zones which would give rise to or strengthen the ranks of such minorities. It even strengthened opposition to (or at least reluctance about) moves to end various forms of coerced labor, as these would make it possible for workers who would thereby be liberated to compete in the free labor market.

Once again, the antagonism was even stronger when it was a question for the worker/social movement of relating to a full-fledged nationalist movement, seeking secession from the state within which the workers movement was formed. This was so whether that movement was in a region of the country itself or in a colonial territory "overseas" controlled by this state. Basically, the worker/social movements charged such nationalist movements (as they did women's movements) with being essentially bourgeois organizations pursuing the interests of a bourgeoisie (if a different one from the one against which the nationalist movement was fighting). The worker/social movements argued that national "independence" would not bring any necessary advantage to the working classes of the country that seceded. It might even set them back if the old "imperial" power had a legislature or power structure less hostile to the interests of the workers than the putative "independent" power. In any case, socialist parties tended to insist that all bourgeois states were alike and that the only important question was whether the working class would be able to come to power in one state or the other. Hence, nationalism was a delusion and a diversion.

Here too the nationalist movements responded in kind. They argued that national oppression was real, immediate, and overwhelming. They argued that any attempt to pursue a workers' agenda meant that the "people" would be divided and thus weakened in their attempt to secure their national rights. They argued that if there were special problems concerning the working classes, they could best be handled within the framework of an independent state. And indeed the cultural demands they were making (for example, regarding language) coincided with the direct interests of the working classes of the country the nationalist movement was trying to establish, which were far more likely to utilize the proposed national language than the official language of the political structure against which the nationalists were rebelling.

Finally, the relations of women's organizations to ethnic/nationalist organizations were no better. The same arguments were used on both sides. On the one hand, the women's organizations argued that they got no gain from the increased citizenship rights of minorities or from the achievement of national independence. But they also often put forward the claim that educated middle-class women were denied the vote while virtually illiterate minority or immigrant men were being given the vote. In the case of national independence, they argued that they were no more likely to be granted citizenship rights in the new state than in the previous state. Once again, the antagonism was returned. The ethnic/nationalist movements saw the women's movements as representing the interests of the oppressing group—the dominant ethnic group within a country, the imperial power in colonial territories. They saw the problem of women's rights as secondary and one that could best be handled after their own grievances were resolved.

It is not that there was a lack of persons (and even groups) who tried to overcome these antagonisms, and to argue the fundamental synergy of the various movements. These persons sought to unify the struggles, and in particular situations they made some progress in this regard. But the overall picture from 1848 to at least 1945 was that such unifiers had little impact on the worldwide pattern of the antisystemic movements. The three major variants of these movements, which are (1) worker/social, (2) ethnic/nationalist, and (3) women's, remained essentially in their separate corners, each fighting the battle for its own proposals and ignoring or even fighting the others. On the other hand, to a striking degree, despite this lack of coordination (not to speak of cooperation), the strategies of the various kinds of movements turned out to be parallel. The long-term history of these movements is that by the late twentieth century, they had all achieved their ostensible primary objective—formal integration into citizenship—and none had achieved their subsequent objective, using their control of the states to transform societies. This is a story to which we shall return.

With the ideologies elaborated and constrained, with the antisystemic movements channeling the energies of discontent, all that remained to ensure the efficacy of a geoculture was its theoretical apparatus. This was the task of the social sciences. We have already told the story of the rise of the two cultures in chapter 1. Let us retell this story briefly as a phenomenon of the emerging geoculture.

Social science is a term invented in the nineteenth century. The terms "science" and "social" each need explanation. Why science? In the nineteenth century, science was the code word for achieving progress, the great accepted common goal of the world-system. Today, this seems to us unremarkable. But at the time, it represented, as we have seen, a basic change in the value-systems dominating the world of knowledge: from Christian redemption to Enlightenment ideas of human progress. The ensuing so-called divorce between philosophy and science, what we would later call the "two cultures," led to the epistemological debate about how we know what we know.

In the nineteenth century, in the structures of knowledge (especially in the newly revived university system) and in the general world of culture, the scientists began to gain preeminence over the philosophers or humanists. The scientists said that they and they alone could achieve truth. They said they were totally uninterested as scientists in the good or the beautiful, since one could not empirically verify such concepts. They gave over the search for the good and the beautiful to the humanists, who by and large were ready to take refuge there, adopting in many ways Keats's lines of poetry: "Beauty is truth; truth, beauty; that is all / Ye know on earth and all ye need to know." In a sense, the humanists ceded control over the search for truth to the scientists. And in any case, what the concept of the two cultures had achieved was the radical separation, for the first time in the history of humanity, in the world of knowledge between the true, the good, and the beautiful.

As the scientists concentrated on the study of material phenomena and the humanists on the study of creative works, it became clear that there was an important arena whose location in this division was not clear. This was the arena of social action. But the French Revolution had made knowledge about the social arena a central concern of public authorities. If political change was normal and the people were sovereign, it mattered very much to understand what the rules were by which the social arena was constituted and how it operated. The search for such knowledge came to be called social science. Social science was born in the nineteenth century and was immediately and inherently an arena both of political confrontation and of a struggle between the scientists and the humanists to appropriate this arena for their mode of knowing. For those in the public arena (the states and capitalist enterprises), controlling social science meant in a sense the ability to control the future. And for those located in the structures of knowledge, both the scientists and the humanists regarded this terrain as an important annex in their not-so-fraternal struggle for control of power and for intellectual supremacy in the university systems.

In the second half of the nineteenth century and the first half of the twentieth, as we have argued, six names had been widely accepted as those treating social reality—history, economics, political science, sociology, anthropology, and Oriental studies. The underlying logic of the six names, and therefore the division of labor in the study of social reality, derived from the world social situation of the nineteenth century. There were three lines of cleavage. The first was between the study of the Western "civilized" world and the study of the non-modern world. The second distinction was that made within the Western world between the study of the past and the study of the present. And the third was that made within the Western present between what liberal ideology had designated as the three separate arenas of modern, civilized social life: the market, the state, and the civil society. In terms of epistemology, the social sciences collectively placed themselves in between the natural sciences and the humanities, and therefore were torn apart by the epistemological struggle between the two cultures. What happened in fact was that the three studies of the Western present (economics, political science, and sociology) largely moved into the scientistic camp and deemed themselves nomothetic disciplines. The other three disciplines—history, anthropology, and Oriental studies—resisted this siren call and tended to consider themselves humanistic or idiographic disciplines.

This neat division of labor was premised on a certain structure of the world-system: a world dominated by the West, in which the "rest" were either colonies or semicolonies. When this assumption ceased to be true, essentially after 1945, the boundary-lines began to seem less obvious and less helpful than they had previously been, and the division of labor began to come unstuck. The story of what happened to the social sciences, along with what happened to the ideologies and to the antisystemic movements, is the story of the impact of the world revolution of 1968 on the world-system, to which we come.

In terms of the geoculture that had been constructed in the mirror of the three ideologies, and sustained paradoxically by the very antisystemic movements created to struggle against it, the role of the social sciences was to supply the intellectual underpinnings of the moral justifications that were being used to reinforce the mechanisms of operation of the modern world-system. In this task, they were largely successful, at least up until the world revolution of 1968.

The Modern World-System in Crisis

Bifurcation, Chaos, and Choices

W E H A V E S A I D that historical systems have lives. They come into existence at some point in time and space, for reasons and in ways that we can analyze. If they survive their birth pangs, they pursue their historical life within the framework and constraints of the structures that constitute them, following their cyclical rhythms and trapped in their secular trends. These secular trends inevitably approach asymptotes that aggravate considerably the internal contradictions of the system: that is, the system encounters problems it can no longer resolve, and this causes what we may call systemic crisis. Most often, people use the word crisis loosely, simply to mean a difficult period in the life of any system. But whenever the difficulty can be resolved in some way, then there is not a true crisis but simply a difficulty built into the system. True crises are those difficulties that *cannot* be resolved within the framework of the system, but instead can be overcome only by going outside of and beyond the historical system of which the difficulties are a part. To use the technical language of natural science, what happens is that the system bifurcates, that is, finds that its basic equations can be solved in two quite different ways. We can translate this into everyday language by saying that the system is faced with two alternative solutions for its crisis, both of which are intrinsically possible. In effect, the members of the system collectively are called upon to make a historical choice about which of the alternative paths will be followed, that is, what kind of new system will be constructed.

Since the existing system can no longer function adequately within its defined parameters, making a choice about the way out, about the future system (or systems) which are to be constructed, is inevitable. But which choice the participants collectively will make is inherently unpredictable. The process of bifurcating is chaotic, which means that every small action during this period is likely to have significant consequences. We observe that under these conditions, the system tends to oscillate wildly. But eventually it leans in one direction. It normally takes quite some time before the definitive choice is made. We can call this a period of transition, one whose outcome is quite uncertain. At some point, however, there is a clear outcome and then we find ourselves ensconced in a different historical system.

The modern world-system in which we are living, which is that of a capitalist world-economy, is currently in precisely such a crisis, and has been for a while now. This crisis may go on another twenty-five to fifty years. Since one central feature of such a transitional period is that we face wild oscillations of all those structures and processes we have come to know as an inherent part of the existing world-system, we find that our short-term expectations are necessarily quite unstable. This instability can lead to considerable anxiety and therefore violence as people try to preserve acquired privileges and hierarchical rank in a very unstable situation. In general, this process can lead to social conflicts that take a quite unpleasant form.

When did this crisis start? Geneses of phenomena are always the most debatable topic in scientific discourse. For one can always find forerunners and forebodings of almost anything in the near past, but also of course in the very far past. One plausible moment at which to start the story of this contemporary systemic crisis is the world revolution of 1968, which unsettled the structures of the world-system considerably. This world revolution marked the end of a long period of liberal supremacy, thereby dislocating the geoculture that had kept the political institutions of the world-system intact. And dislocating this geoculture unhinged the underpinnings of the capitalist world-economy and exposed it to the full force of political and cultural shocks to which it had always been subject, but from which it had previously been somewhat sheltered.

The shock of 1968 to which we shall return is not, however, enough to explain a crisis in the system. There have to have been long-existing structural trends which were beginning to reach their asymptotes, and therefore made it no longer possible to overcome the repeated difficulties into which any system gets itself because of its cyclical rhythms. Only when we have perceived what these trends are and why the recurrent difficulties can no longer be easily resolved can we then understand why and how the shock of 1968 precipitated an unraveling of the geoculture which had been binding the system together.

In the ceaseless quest for accumulation, capitalists are constantly seeking ways of increasing the sales prices of their products and reducing the costs of production. Producers cannot however arbitrarily raise sales prices to just any level. They are constrained by two considerations. The first is the existence of competitive sellers. This is why the creation of oligopolies is so important, because they reduce the number of alternative sellers. The second is the level of effective demand—how much money buyers have in total—and the choices that consumers make because their buying-power is limited.

The level of effective demand is affected primarily by the world distribution of income. Obviously, the more money each buyer has, the more he or she can buy. This simple fact creates an inherent and continuing dilemma for capitalists. On the one hand, they want as much profit as possible, and therefore wish to minimize the amount of surplus that goes to anyone else, for example their employees. On the other hand, at least some capitalists must allow for some redistribution of the surplus-value created, or there would normally be too few buyers overall for the products. So, intermittently at least some producers in fact favor increased remuneration for employees to create a higher effective demand.

Given the level of effective demand at any given time, the choices that consumers make are decided by what economists call the elasticity of demand. This refers to the value that each buyer places on alternate uses of his or her money. Purchases vary in the eyes of the buyer from the indispensable to the totally optional. These valuations are the result of an interplay between individual psychologies, cultural pressures, and physiological requirements. The sellers can only have a limited impact on the elasticity of demand, although marketing (in the broadest sense) is designed precisely to affect consumer choice.

The net consequence for the seller is that the seller can never raise the price to a level where (a) competitors can sell more cheaply, (b) buyers do not have the money to purchase the product, or (c) buyers are not ready to allocate that much of their money to the purchase. Given the inbuilt ceiling to sales price levels, producers usually spend most of their energy in the effort to accumulate capital in finding ways to reduce the costs of production, something which is often termed efficiency of production. To understand what is happening in the contemporary world-system, we have to look at the reasons why the costs of production have been rising worldwide over time despite all the efforts of producers, thereby reducing the margin between the costs of production and the possible sales prices. In other words, we need to understand why there has been a growing squeeze on the average worldwide rate of profits.

There are three main costs of production for any producer. The producer must remunerate the personnel who work in the enterprise. The producer must purchase the inputs of the production process. And the producer must pay the taxes that are levied by any and all governmental structures which have the authority to levy them on the particular production process. We need to examine each of these three costs in turn, and in particular to see why each has been steadily rising over the *longue durée* of the capitalist world-economy.

How does an employer decide how much to remunerate an employee? There may be laws, which set minimum levels. There are certainly customary wages at any given time and place, although these are subject to constant revision. Basically, the employer would almost always like to offer a figure lower than the employee would like to receive. Producer and worker negotiate about this; they struggle over this question, constantly and repeatedly. The outcome of any such negotiation or struggle depends on the strengths of each side—economic, political, and cultural.

Employees may grow stronger in the bargaining because their skills are rare. There is always a supply-and-demand element in determining levels of remuneration. Or the employees may grow stronger because they organize with each other and engage in syndical action. This applies not only to the production workers (both skilled technicians and unskilled workers) but also to managerial personnel (both senior managers and middle-level cadres). This is the part of the question of economic strength internal to each productive enterprise. There is also an external part. The overall state of the economy, locally and worldwide, determines the level of unemployment and therefore how desperate each side of each production unit is to come to a remuneration arrangement.

The political strengths derive from a combination of the political machinery and arrangements in the state-structure, the strength of syndical organization by the workers, and the degree to which employers need to secure the support of managers and middle-level cadres to hold off the demands of ordinary workers. And what we mean by cultural strength—the mores of the local and national community—is usually the result of prior political strengths.

In general, in any production area the syndical power of workers will tend to increase over time, by dint of organization and education. Repressive measures may be used to limit the effects of such organization, but then there are costs attached to this too—perhaps higher taxes, perhaps higher remuneration to cadres, perhaps the need to employ and pay for repressive personnel. If one looks at the most profitable loci of production—oligopolistic firms in leading sectors—there is a further factor at play, in that highly profitable firms do not wish to lose production time because of workers' discontent. As a result, remuneration costs in such firms tend to rise as time goes on, but sooner or later these same production units come to face increased competition and therefore may need to restrain price increases, resulting in lower rates of profit.

There is only one significant counter to the consequent creeping rise in remuneration costs—runaway factories. By moving production to places where the current costs of production are much lower, the employer not only gets lower costs of remuneration but gains political strength in the zone out of which the enterprise is partially moving, in that existing employees may be willing to accept lower rates of remuneration to prevent further "flight" of jobs. Of course, there is a negative in this for the employer. If there weren't, the production site would have moved much earlier. There are the costs of moving. And in these other zones, the transaction costs are normally higher—because of the increased distance from eventual customers, poorer infrastructure, and higher costs of "corruption"—that is, unavowed remuneration to non-employees.

The trade-off between remuneration costs and transactions costs plays itself out in a cyclical manner. Transactions costs tend to be the primary consideration in times of economic expansion (Kondratieff A-phases) while remuneration costs are the primary consideration in times of economic stagnation (B-phases). Still, one has to ask why there exist zones of lower remuneration at all. The reason has to do with the size of the non-urban population in a given country or region. Wherever the non-urban population is large, there are large pockets of persons who are partially, even largely, outside the wage-economy. Or changes in land use in the rural areas are forcing some persons to leave. For such persons, the opportunity of wage-employment in urban areas usually represents a significant increase in the overall income of the household of which they are a part, even if the wages are significantly below the worldwide norm of remuneration. So, at least at first, the entry of such persons into a local wage-force is a win-win arrangement—lower costs of remuneration for the employer, higher income for the employees. Wages are lower there not only for unskilled workers but for cadres as well. Peripheral zones usually are lower-price, lower-amenity zones and the wages of cadres are accordingly below the norm of core zones.

The problem is that the political strengths of employer and employee are not fixed in stone. They evolve. If at first the newly urbanized employees have difficulty adjusting to urban life and are unaware of their potential political strengths, this state of ignorance does not last forever. Certainly, within twenty-five years the employees or their descendants become adjusted to the realities of the new situation and become aware of the low level of their remuneration in terms of world norms. The reaction is to begin to engage in syndical action. The employer then rediscovers the conditions from which the enterprise had sought to escape by moving its production operation in the first place. Eventually, in a future period of economic downturn, the producer may again try the "runaway factory" tactic.

Over time, however, the number of zones in which this particular solution to rising remuneration costs can be effectuated in the capitalist world-economy has become ever fewer. The world has been deruralizing, in large part precisely because of this mode of restraining remuneration costs by relocating production processes. In the last half of the twentieth century, there was a radical reduction in the share of the world population that lives in rural areas. And the first half of the twenty-first century threatens to eliminate the remaining pockets of serious rural concentration. When there are no zones into which the factories can run away, there will be no way to reduce seriously the levels of remuneration for employees worldwide.

The steadily rising level of remuneration is not the only problem which producers are facing. The second is the cost of inputs. By inputs, I include both machinery and materials of production (whether these are so-called raw materials or semi-finished and finished products). The producer of course buys these on the market and pays what must be paid for them. But there are three hidden costs for which producers do not necessarily pay. They are the costs of disposal of waste (especially toxic materials), the costs of renewing raw materials, and what are generically called infrastructural costs. The ways of evading these costs are manifold, and not paying for these costs has been a major element in keeping down the cost of inputs.

The primary mode of minimizing the costs of disposal is dumping, that is, placing waste in some public area with minimal or no treatment. When these are toxic materials, the result, in addition to clutter, is noxious consequences for the ecosphere. At some point, the consequences of clutter and noxious effects become perceived as a social problem, and the collectivity is forced to address it. But clutter and noxious effects behave a bit like the absence of rural zones nearby. A producer can always move on to a new area, thereby eliminating the problem, until these "unspoiled" areas are exhausted. Worldwide, this is what has been happening in the capitalist world-economy. It is only really in the second half of the twentieth century that the potential exhaustion of dumping grounds has come to be perceived as a social problem.

The problem of renewal of raw materials is a parallel problem. The purchaser of raw materials is normally uninterested in their long-run availability. And sellers are notoriously ready to subordinate long-run viability to short-run gains. Over five hundred years, this has led to successive exhaustions and increases in the costs of obtaining such resources. These trends have only partially been counteracted by technological advances in creating alternative resources.

The two exhaustions—of dumping space and natural resources—have become the subject of a major social movement of environmentalists and Greens in recent decades, who have sought governmental intervention to meet collective needs. To meet these needs however requires money, a great deal of money. Who will pay? There are only two real possibilities—the collectivity, through taxation, and the producers who use the raw materials. To the extent that the producers are being required to pay for them—economists call this internalization of costs—the costs of production are rising for individual producers.

Finally, there is the issue of infrastructure, a term which refers to all those physical institutions outside the production unit which form a necessary part of the production and distribution process—roads, transport services, communications networks, security systems, water supply. These are costly, and ever more costly. Once again, who is footing the bill? Either the collectivity, which means taxation, or the individual firms, which means increased costs. It should be noted that to the degree the infrastructure is privatized, the bill is paid by the individual firms (even if other firms are making profits out of operating the infrastructure, and even if individual persons are paying increased costs for their own consumption).

The pressure to internalize costs represents for productive firms a significant increase in the costs of production which, over time, has more than overcome the cost advantages that improvements in technology have made possible. And this internalization of costs omits the growing problem that these firms are having as a result of penalties imposed by the courts and legislatures for damages caused by past negligence.

The third cost that has been rising over time is that of taxation. Taxes are a basic element in social organization. There have always been and always will be taxes of one sort or another. But who pays, and how much, is the subject of endless political struggle. In the modern world-system, there have been two basic reasons for taxation. One is to provide the state structures with the means to offer security services (armies and police forces), build infrastructure, and employ a bureaucracy with which to provide public services as well as collect taxes. These costs are inescapable, although obviously there can be strong and wide differences in views as to what should be spent and how.

There is however a second reason to tax, which is more recent (it has arisen only in the last century to any significant degree). This second reason is the consequence of political democratization, which has led to demands by the citizenry on the states to provide them with three major benefits, which have come to be seen as entitlements: education, health, and guarantees of lifetime income. When these benefits were first provided in the nineteenth century, state expenditures were quite small and only existed in a few countries. Throughout the twentieth century, the definition of what the states were expected to provide and the number of states which provided something steadily grew in each of these domains. It seems virtually impossible today to push the level of expenditures back in the other direction.

As a result of the increasing cost (not merely in absolute terms but as a proportion of world surplus) of providing security, building infrastructure, and offering the citizenry benefits in education, health, and lifetime guarantees of income, taxation as a share of total costs has been steadily rising for productive enterprises everywhere, and will continue to rise.

Thus it is that the three costs of production—remuneration, inputs, and taxation—have all been rising steadily over the past five hundred years and particularly over the past fifty years. On the other hand, the sales prices have not been able to keep pace, despite increased effective demand, because of a steady expansion in the number of producers and hence of their recurring inability to maintain oligopolistic conditions. This is what one means by a squeeze on profits. To be sure, producers seek to reverse these conditions constantly, and are doing so at present. To appreciate the limits of their ability to do so, we must return to the cultural shock of 1968.

The world-economy in the years after 1945 saw the largest expansion of productive structures in the history of the modern world-system. All the structural trends of which we have been speaking—costs of remuneration, costs of inputs, taxation—took a sharp upward turn as a result. At the same time, the antisystemic movements, which we previously discussed, made extraordinary progress in realizing their immediate objective—coming to power in the state structures. In all parts of the world, these movements seemed to be achieving step one of the two-step program. In a vast northern area from central Europe to East Asia (from the Elbe to the Yalu Rivers), Communist parties governed. In the pan-European world (western Europe, North America, and Australasia), social democratic parties (or their equivalents) were in power, or at least in alternating power. In the rest of Asia and most of Africa, national liberation movements had come to power. And in Latin America, nationalist/populist movements gained control.

The years after 1945 thus became a period of great optimism. The economic future seemed bright, and popular movements of all kinds seemed to be achieving their objectives. And in Vietnam, a little country struggling for its independence seemed to be holding the hegemonic power, the United

States, in check. The modern world-system had never looked so good to so many people, a sentiment that had an exhilarating effect, but in many ways also a very stabilizing effect.

Nonetheless, there was an underlying and growing disillusion with precisely the popular movements in power. The second step of the two-step formula—change the world—seemed in practice much further from realization than most people had anticipated. Despite the overall economic growth of the world-system, the gap between core and periphery had become greater than ever. And despite the coming to power of the antisystemic movements, the great participatory élan of the period of mobilization seemed to die out once the antisystemic movements came to power in any given state. New privileged strata emerged. Ordinary people were now being asked not to make militant demands on what was asserted to be a government that represented them. When the future became the present, many previously ardent militants of the movements began to have second thoughts, and eventually began to dissent.

It was the combination of long-existing anger about the workings of the world-system and disappointment with the capacity of the antisystemic movements to transform the world that led to the world revolution of 1968. The explosions of 1968 contained two themes repeated virtually everywhere, whatever the local context. One was the rejection of U.S. hegemonic power, simultaneously with a complaint that the Soviet Union, the presumed antagonist of the United States, was actually colluding in the world order that the United States had established. And the second was that the traditional antisystemic movements had not fulfilled their promises once in power. The combination of these complaints, so widely repeated, constituted a cultural earthquake. The many uprisings were like a phoenix and did not put the multiple revolutionaries of 1968 in power, or not for very long. But they legitimated and strengthened the sense of disillusionment not only with the old antisystemic movements but also with the state structures these movements had been fortifying. The long-term certainties of evolutionary hope had become transformed into fears that the world-system might be unchanging.

This shift in worldwide sentiment, far from reinforcing the status quo, actually pulled the political and cultural supports from under the capitalist world-economy. No longer would oppressed people be sure that history was on their side. No longer could they therefore be satisfied with creeping improvements, in the belief that these would see fruition in the lives of their children and grandchildren. No longer could they be persuaded to postpone present complaints in the name of a beneficent future. In short, the multiple producers of the capitalist world-economy had lost the main hidden stabilizer of the system, the optimism of the oppressed. And this of course came at the very worst moment, when the squeeze on profits was beginning to be felt in a serious way.

The cultural shock of 1968 unhinged the automatic dominance of the liberal center, which had prevailed in the world-system since the prior world revolution of 1848. The right and the left were liberated from their role as avatars of centrist liberalism and were able to assert, or rather reassert, their more radical values. The world-system had entered into the period of transition, and both right and left were determined to take advantage of the increasing chaos to ensure that their values would prevail in the new system (or systems) that would eventually emerge from the crisis.

The immediate effect of the world revolution of 1968 seemed to be a legitimation of left values, most notably in the domains of race and sex. Racism has been a pervasive feature of the modern world-system for all of its existence. To be sure, its legitimacy has been called into question for two centuries. But it was only after the world revolution of 1968 that a widespread campaign against racism—one led by the oppressed groups themselves, as distinguished from those previously led primarily by liberals among the dominant strata—became a central phenomenon on the world political scene, taking the form both of actively militant "minority" identity movements everywhere and of attempts to reconstruct the world of knowledge, to make the issues deriving from chronic racism central to intellectual discourse.

Along with the debates about racism, it would have been hard to miss the centrality of sexuality to the world revolution of 1968. Whether we are speaking of policies related to gender or to sexual preferences, and eventually to transgender identity, the impact of 1968 was to bring to the forefront what had been a slow transformation of sexual mores in the preceding half-century and allow it to explode onto the world social scene, with enormous consequences for the law, for customary practice, for religions, and for intellectual discourse.

The traditional antisystemic movements had emphasized primarily the issues of state power and of economic structures. Both issues receded somewhat in the militant rhetoric of 1968 because of the space given the issues of race and sexuality. This posed a real problem for the world right. Geopolitical and economic issues were easier for the world right to deal with than the sociocultural issues. This was because of the position of the centrist liberals, who were hostile to any undermining of the basic political and economic institutions of the capitalist world-economy, but were latent, if less militant, supporters of the sociocultural shifts advocated by the militants in the revolutions of 1968 (and afterward). As a result, the post-1968 reaction was actually split, between on the one hand an Establishment attempt to restore order and solve some of the immediate difficulties of the emerging profit squeeze and on the other a more narrowly based but much more ferocious cultural counterrevolution. It is important to distinguish the two sets of issues and therefore the two sets of strategic alignments.

As the world-economy entered at this time into a long Kondratieff B-phase, the coalition of centrist and rightist forces attempted to roll back rising costs of production in all three components of costs. They sought to reduce remuneration levels. They sought to re-externalize the costs of inputs. They sought to reduce taxation for the benefit of the welfare state (education, health, and lifetime guarantees of income). This offensive took many forms. The center abandoned the theme of developmentalism (as a mode of overcoming global polarization) and replaced it with the theme of globalization, which called essentially for the opening of all frontiers to the free flow of goods and capital (but not of labor). The Thatcher regime in the United Kingdom and the Reagan regime in the United States took the lead in promoting these policies, which were called "neoliberalism" as theory and "the Washington consensus" as policy. The World Economic Forum at Davos was the locus for promoting the theory, and the International Monetary Fund (IMF) and the newly established World Trade Organization (WTO) became the chief enforcers of the Washington consensus.

The economic difficulties faced by governments everywhere from the 1970s onward (particularly in the South and in the former communist zone) made it extremely difficult for these states, governed by old antisystemic movements, to resist the pressures for "structural adjustment" and opening frontiers. As a result, a limited amount of success in rolling back costs of production worldwide was achieved, but a success far below what the promoters of such policies had hoped for, and far below what was necessary to end the squeeze on profits. More and more, capitalists sought profits in the arena of financial speculation rather than in the arena of production. Such financial manipulations can result in great profits for some players, but it renders the world-economy very volatile and subject to swings of currencies and of employment. It is in fact one of the signs of increasing chaos.

In the world political arena, the world political left would increasingly make electoral objectives secondary, and began the organization rather of a "movement of movements"—what has come to be identified with the World Social Forum (WSF), which met initially in Porto Alegre and is often referred to by that symbol. The WSF is not an organization, but a meeting-ground of militants of many stripes and persuasions, engaging in a variety of actions from collective demonstrations that are worldwide or regional to local organizing across the globe. Their slogan, "another world is possible," is expressive of their sense that the world-system is in a structural crisis, and that political options are real. The world is facing increasingly a struggle on many fronts between the spirit of Davos and the spirit of Porto Alegre.

The dramatic attack by Osama bin Laden on the Twin Towers on September 11, 2001, marked a further indication of world political chaos and a turning-point in political alignments. It allowed those on the right who wished to cut their links with the center to pursue a program centered around unilateral assertions by the United States of military strength combined with an attempt to undo the cultural evolution of the world-system that occurred after the world revolution of 1968 (particularly in the fields of race and sexuality). In the process, they have sought to liquidate many of the geopolitical structures set in place after 1945, which they have seen as constraining their politics. But these efforts threatened to worsen the already-increasing instability in the world-system.

This is the empirical description of a chaotic situation in the world-system. What can we expect in such a situation? The first thing to emphasize is that we can expect, we are already seeing, wild fluctuations in all the institutional arenas of the world-system. The world-economy is subject to acute speculative pressures, which are escaping the control of major financial institutions and control bodies, such as central banks. A high degree of violence is erupting everywhere in smaller and larger doses, and over relatively long periods. No one has any longer the power to shut down such eruptions effectively. The moral constraints traditionally enforced both by states and by religious institutions are finding their efficacity considerably diminished.

On the other hand, just because a system is in crisis does not mean that it does not continue to try to function in its accustomed ways. It does. Insofar as the accustomed ways have resulted in secular trends that are approaching asymptotes, continuing in customary ways simply aggravates the crisis. Yet continuing to act in customary ways will probably be the mode of behavior of most people. It makes sense in the very short run. The customary ways are the familiar ways, and they promise short-run benefits, or they would not be the customary ways. Precisely because the fluctuations are wilder, most people will seek their security by persisting in their behavior.

To be sure, all sorts of people will seek middle-run adjustments to the system, which they will argue will mitigate the existing problems. This too is a customary pattern, and in the memory of most people one that has worked in the past and should therefore be tried again. The problem is that in a systemic crisis, such middle-run adjustments have little effect. This is after all what we said defined a systemic crisis.

And others will seek to pursue more transformative paths, often in the guise of middle-run adjustments. They are hoping to take advantage of the wild swings of the period of transition to encrust major changes in operating modes, which will push the process toward one side of the bifurcation. It is this last form of behavior which will be the most consequential. In the present situation, it is the one to which we referred as the struggle between the spirit of Davos and the spirit of Porto Alegre. This struggle is perhaps not yet at the center of most people's attention. And of course, many most active in the struggle may find it useful to divert attention from the intensity of the struggle and its real stakes, in the hope of achieving some of their objectives without arousing the opposition which the open proclamation of these objectives might arouse.

There is only so much that can be said about a struggle that is just beginning to unfold, one of whose central characteristics is the total uncertainty of its outcome, and another of whose characteristics is the opacity of the struggle. We might think of it as a clash of fundamental values, even of "civilizations," just as long as we don't identify the two sides with existing peoples, races, religious groups, or other historic groupings. The key element of the debate is the degree to which any social system, but in this case the future one we are constructing, will lean in one direction or the other on two long-standing central issues of social organization—liberty and equality—issues that are more closely intertwined than social thought in the modern world-system has been willing to assert.

The issue of liberty (or "democracy") is surrounded by so much hyperbole in our modern world that it is sometimes hard to appreciate what the underlying issues are. We might find it useful to distinguish between the liberty of the majority and the liberty of the minority. The liberty of the majority is located in the degree to which collective political decisions reflect in fact the preferences of the majority, as opposed to those of smaller groups who may in practice control the decision-making processes. This is not merely a question of so-called free elections, although no doubt regular, honest, open elections are a necessary if far from sufficient part of a democratic structure. Liberty of the majority requires the active participation of the majority. It requires access to information on the part of the majority. It requires a mode of translating majority views of the populace into majority views in legislative bodies. It is doubtful that any existing state within the modern world-system is fully democratic in these senses.

The liberty of the minority is a quite different matter. It represents the rights of all individuals and groups to pursue their preferences in all those realms in which there is no justification for the majority to impose its preferences on others. In principle, most states in the modern world-system have given lip service to these rights to exemption from majority preferences. Some have even lauded the concept not merely as a negative protection but as a positive contribution to the construction of a historical system of many different strands. The traditional antisystemic movements placed priority on what we are calling the liberty of the majority. The world revolutionaries of 1968 placed great emphasis rather on expanding the liberty of the minorities.

Even if we assume that everyone is in fact in favor of liberty, which is a rash assumption, there is the enormous and never-ending difficulty of deciding what is the line between the liberty of the majority and the liberty of the minorities—that is, in what spheres and issues one or the other takes precedence. In the struggle over the system (or systems) that will succeed our existing world-system, the fundamental cleavage will be between those who wish to expand both liberties—that of the majority and that of the minorities—and those who will seek to create a non-libertarian system under the guise of preferring either the liberty of the majority or the liberty of the minorities. In such a struggle, it becomes clear what the role of opacity is in the struggle. Opacity leads to confusion, and this favors the cause of those who wish to limit liberty.

Equality is often posed as a concept in conflict with that of liberty, especially if we mean relative equality of access to material goods. In fact, it is the reverse side of the same coin. To the degree that meaningful inequalities exist, it is inconceivable that equal weight be given to all persons in assessing the preferences of the majority. And it is inconceivable that the liberty of the minorities will be fully respected if these minorities are not equal in the eyes of everyone—equal socially and economically in order to be equal politically. What the emphasis on equality as a concept does is point to the necessary positions of the majority to realize its own liberty and to encourage the liberty of the minorities.

In constructing the successor system (or systems) to our existing one, we shall be opting either for a hierarchical system bestowing or permitting privileges according to rank in the system, however this rank is determined (including meritocratic criteria), or for a relatively democratic, relatively egalitarian system. One of the great virtues of the existing world-system is that although it has not resolved any of these debates—far from it!—it has increasingly brought the debate to the fore. There is little question that across the world, people are more fully aware of these issues today than a century ago, not to speak of five centuries ago. They are more aware, more willing to struggle for their rights, more skeptical about the rhetoric of the powerful. However polarized the existing system, this at least is a positive legacy.

The period of transition from one system to another is a period of great struggle, of great uncertainty, and of great questioning about the structures of knowledge. We need first of all to try to understand clearly what is going on. We need then to make our choices about the directions in which we want the world to go. And we must finally figure out how we can act in the present so that it is likely to go in the direction we prefer. We can think of these three tasks as the intellectual, the moral, and the political tasks. They are different, but they are closely interlinked. None of us can opt out of any of these tasks. If we claim we do, we are merely making a hidden choice. The tasks before us are exceptionally difficult. But they offer us, individually and collectively, the possibility of creation, or at least of contributing to the creation of something that might fulfill better our collective possibilities.

GLOSSARY

This is a glossary of terms used in this book. A glossary of concepts is not a dictionary. There exists no definitive meaning for most of these terms. They are quite regularly defined and used differently by different scholars. The particular usage is often based on different underlying assumptions or theorizings. What we have here are terms I use and the ways in which I use them. Some of my usages are standard. But in some cases, my usage may be significantly different from that of other authors. In several cases, I have indicated my usage of a term in relation to that of another term because I consider the two terms to be a relational pair. All these terms are for the most part already defined, explicitly or implicitly, in the text. But it may be useful to the reader to be able to refer to them quickly and precisely. Cross-references from one entry to another are indicated by SMALL CAPITALS.

antisystemic movements. I invented this term to cover together two concepts that had been used since the nineteenth century: social movements and national movements. I did this because I believed that both kinds of movements shared some crucial features, and that both represented parallel modes of asserting strong resistance to the existing historical system in which we live, up to and including wishing to overthrow the system.

Asiatic mode of production. This term was invented by Karl Marx to refer to what others think of as centralized imperial systems organized around the need to supply and control irrigation for agriculture. The key point for Marx was that these systems lay outside what he otherwise thought was a universal progressive sequence of successive "modes of production," that is, different ways in which systems of production were organized.

asymptote. A concept in mathematics, referring to a line which a particular curve cannot reach in a finite space. The most frequent usage is in referring to curves whose ordinal is measured in percentages, and for which 100 percent represents the asymptote.

axial division of labor. A term used in articulating the argument that what holds the capitalist world-economy intact is an invisible axis binding together core-like and peripheral processes (*see* CORE-PERIPHERY).

cadres. This term is used in this text to refer to all those persons who are neither in the top command positions of the social system nor among the vast majority who fulfill the bottom tasks. Cadres perform managerial functions and usually receive remuneration somewhere between that for the top and that for the bottom. In my view, worldwide today we are talking of 15 to 20 percent of the world's population.

capital. Capital is an extremely contentious term. The mainstream usage refers to assets (wealth) that are or can be used to invest in productive activities. Such assets have existed in all known social systems. Marx used "capital" not as an essential but as a relational term, which existed only in a capitalist system, and which manifested itself in the control of the means of production confronting those who supplied the labor-power.

capitalism. This is an unpopular term in academia because it is associated with Marxism, though in terms of the history of ideas the association is at best only partially true. Fernand Braudel said that one can throw capitalism out the front door but it comes back in by the window. I define capitalism in a particular way: as a historical system defined by the priority of the *endless* accumulation of capital.

capitalist world-economy. It is the argument of this book that a WORLD-ECONOMY must necessarily be capitalist, and that capitalism can only exist within the framework of a world-economy. Hence, the modern world-system is a capitalist world-economy.

circulationist-productionist. These terms only make sense within an orthodox Marxist critique of world-systems analysis. Some Marxists argue that for Marx, the crucial defining feature of a mode of production was the system of production. Hence, anyone who wishes also to emphasize the crucial importance of trade is a "circulationist" and not a "productionist." Whether these were the views of Marx himself is a matter of considerable debate. And that world-systems analysis can be labeled "circulationist" is something that world-systems analysts deny.

civil society. This term, invented in the early nineteenth century, became very popular in the last decades of the twentieth century. Originally, it was used as the antinomy of "state." In France at that time one contrasted *le pays légal* (the legal country, or the state) with *le pays réel* (the real country, or the civil society). Making this kind of distinction implied that to the degree to which the state institutions did not reflect the society (all of us), the state was somehow illegitimate. In recent years, the term has been used more narrowly to mean the panoply of "non-governmental organizations" and has carried with it the suggestion that a state cannot be truly democratic unless there is a strong "civil society." The term is also used, especially in this book, to refer to all those institutions that are not narrowly economic or political.

class conflict. The persistent cleavage within the modern world-system between those who control capital and those who are employed by them.

comparative advantage. The nineteenth-century English economist David Ricardo argued that even if a country produced two items at a lower cost than another country, it would still be to the first country's advantage to concentrate its production on only one of them, the one of the two for which it was the lowest cost producer, and trade that item with the second country for the second product. This is called the theory of comparative advantage. Ricardo illustrated this with the example that Portugal should concentrate on producing wine and trade it with England for textiles, even though it produced textiles at a lower cost than England. This theory underlies much of the case today for globalization.

conservatism. One of the three basic ideologies of the modern world-system since the French Revolution. Conservatism has many versions. The dominant themes have always included acute skepticism about legislated change and an emphasis on the wisdom of traditional sources of authority.

core-periphery. This is a relational pair, which first came into widespread use when taken up by Raúl Prebisch and the UN Economic Commission for Latin America in the 1950s as a description of the AXIAL DIVISION OF LABOR of the world-economy. It refers to products but is often used as shorthand for the countries in which such products are dominant. The argument of this book is that the key element distinguishing core-like from peripheral processes is the degree to which they are monopolized and therefore profitable.

economism. This is a term of criticism, suggesting that someone insists on giving exclusive priority to economic factors in explaining social reality.

elasticity of demand. A term used by economists to refer to the degree of priority that the collectivity of individuals give to purchasing a certain good over alternative goods, regardless of price.

endogenous-exogenous. This pair is used to refer to the source of key variables in explaining social action, whether they are internal or external to whatever is defined as the unit of social action.

epistemology. The branch of philosophical thought that discusses how we know what we know and how we can validate the truth of our knowledge.

Eurocentrism. This is a negative term, referring to any assumption that the patterns discerned by analyzing pan-European history and social structure are universal patterns, and therefore implicitly a model for persons in other parts of the world.

exogenous. See ENDOGENOUS.

externalization of costs. A term used by economists to refer to practices that allow certain costs of production not to be paid by the producer but "externalized" to others or to society as a whole.

feudalism. The name normally given to the historical system that prevailed in medieval Europe. It was a system of parcelized power, in which there was a ladder of lords and vassals who exchanged social obligations (for example, use of land in return for some kind of payments plus social protection). How long this system existed in Europe and whether similar systems existed in other parts of the world are matters of considerable scholarly debate.

free market. According to the classical definition, a market in which there are multiple sellers, multiple buyers, perfect information (all sellers and buyers know everything about price variations), and no political constraints on the operation of the market. Few markets, real or virtual, have ever met this definition.

geoculture. A term coined by analogy with geopolitics. It refers to norms and modes of discourse that are widely accepted as legitimate within the world-system. We argue here that a geoculture does not come into existence automatically with the onset of a world-system but rather has to be created.

geopolitics. A nineteenth-century term referring to the constellations and manipulations of power within the interstate system.

globalization. This term was invented in the 1980s. It is usually thought to refer to a reconfiguration of the world-economy that has only recently come into existence, in which the pressures on all governments to open their frontiers to the free movement of goods and capital is unusually strong. This is the result, it is argued, of technological advances, especially in the field of informatics. The term is as much prescription as description. For world-systems analysts, what is described as something new (relatively open frontiers) has in fact been a cyclical occurrence throughout the history of the modern world-system.

grand narrative. A term of criticism used by postmodernists to refer to all those modes of analysis which offer overarching explanations for historical social systems.

hegemony. This term is often used loosely merely to mean leadership or dominance in a political situation. Antonio Gramsci, the Italian communist theorist, following Machiavelli, insisted on an ideological and cultural component, in which leadership was legitimated in some way by the population, a process which he saw as crucial in enabling élites to maintain power. The term has a narrower use in world-systems analysis. It refers to those situations in which one state combines economic, political, and financial superiority over other strong states, and therefore has both military and cultural leadership as well. Hegemonic powers define the rules of the game. Defined in this way, hegemony does not last very long, and is self-destructive.

hermeneutics. Originally, scholarly interpretation of Biblical texts. The term now more generally refers to an epistemology that allows the analyst to empathize with and interpret the meaning of social action, as opposed to analysis through some set of "objective" modes of knowing, say statistical analysis.

heuristics. Exploratory problem-solving that aids in knowing, without necessarily being definitive.

historical social sciences. See UNIDISCIPLINARITY.

historical (social) system. This combination of "historical" and "system" into one phrase is used by world-systems analysts to stress that all social systems are simultaneously systemic (they have continuing characteristics that can be described) and historical (they have a continuing evolving life and are never the same from one moment to the next). This paradoxical reality makes social analysis difficult, but if the contradiction is kept in the center of the analysis the results are more fruitful and more realistic.

household. In the special usage of world-systems analysis, a group of persons (usually between three and ten) who "pool" multiple varieties of income over a long period (say thirty years). New members enter and old ones die. The household is not necessarily a kin group and not necessarily co-resident, though frequently it is both.

identities. See STATUS-GROUPS.

ideology. Usually, a coherent set of ideas that inform a particular point of view. The term can be used either neutrally (everyone has an ideology) or negatively (the others have an ideology, as opposed to our scientific or scholarly analysis). The term is used more narrowly in world-systems analysis to mean a coherent strategy in the social arena from which one can draw political conclusions. In this sense, there have been ideologies only since the French Revolution, after which it was necessary to have a coherent strategy about the continuing demand for political change, and there have been only three: CONSERVATISM, LIBERALISM, and RADICALISM.

idiographic-nomothetic. This pair of terms was invented in Germany in the late nineteenth century to describe what was called the *Methodenstreit* (battle of methods) among social scientists, one that reflected the division of scholarship into the TWO CULTURES. Nomothetic scholars insisted on replicable, "objective" (preferably quantitative) methods and saw their task as one of arriving at general laws explaining social realities. Idiographic scholars used largely qualitative, narrative data, considering themselves humanists, and preferred HERMENEUTIC methods. Their principal concern was interpretation, not laws, about which they were at the very least skeptical. (Note that idiographic is different from ideographic. "Idio-" is a prefix derived from Greek and means specific, individual, one's own; hence idiographic means of or relating to particular descriptions. "Ideo-" is a prefix derived from Latin and means picture, form, idea; hence ideographic means of or relating to a non-alphabetic writing system, such as Chinese characters.)

infrastructure. Roads, bridges, and other community structures which are seen as the basic underpinnings of a system of production and trade.

knowledge activity. A neutral term to refer to any kind of scholarly or scientific activity, one that avoids taking a position on the TWO CULTURES.

Kondratieff cycles. These are the basic cycles of expansion and stagnation in the capitalist world-economy. A cycle, consisting of a so-called A-phase and B-phase, generally lasts fifty to sixty years. The very existence of Kondratieff cycles is contested by many economists. Among those who utilize the concept, there is much debate about what explains them and particularly what explains the upturn from a B-phase to an A-phase. The cycles are named after Nikolai Kondratieff, a Russian economist who wrote about them in the 1920s (although he was far from the first to describe them). Kondratieff himself called them long waves.

leading products. A recent concept among economists who argue that leading products exist at any given time, and that they are leading because they are highly profitable, are relatively monopolized, and have significant impact on the economy (so-called backward and forward linkages). Because leading products are loci of great profits, producers constantly try to enter the market as competitors, and at some point a given leading industry ceases to be leading.

liberalism. Liberalism emerged as a term and as a reality in the early nineteenth century as the antagonist to conservatism. In the phraseology of the time, liberals were the Party of Movement, conservatives the Party of Order. The term "liberalism" has the most diverse usage conceivable. For some today, especially in the United States, liberal means leftist (or at least New Deal Democrat). In Great Britain, the Liberal Party claims to occupy the center between the Conservatives and Labour. In much of continental Europe, Liberal parties are those that are economically conservative but non-clerical. For some, the essence of liberalism is opposition to state involvement in the economy. But since the late nineteenth century, many "liberals" have proclaimed themselves reformers in favor of the welfare state. For others, liberalism reflects a concern for individual liberties, and therefore a willingness to limit the state's power to constrain these rights. Adding to the confusion is the emergence in the late twentieth century of the term neoliberalism, which tends to mean a conservative ideology that emphasizes the importance of free trade. As one of the three ideologies (*see* IDEOLOGY) referred to in world-systems analysis, liberalism is primarily centrist, favoring the steady (but relatively) slow evolution of the social system, the extension of education as the foundation of citizenship, MERITOCRACY, and giving priority to the role of skilled specialists in the formation of public policy.

longue durée. See SOCIAL TIMES.

manu militari. Latin phrase, meaning "by force."

meritocracy. A recent phrase, meaning the assignment of people to positions according to merit, as opposed to family connections, social position, or political affiliation.

modern world-system. The world-system in which we are now living, which had its origins in the long sixteenth century in Europe and the Americas. The modern world-system is a CAPITALIST WORLD-ECONOMY. *See also* WORLD-SYSTEM.

monopoly-oligopoly. A monopoly is a situation in which there is only one seller in the market. True monopolies are very rare. What is more common are oligopolies, in which there are only a few, usually quite large, sellers in the market. Often these large sellers collude to set prices, which makes the situation approximate that of a monopoly. Because monopolies and even oligopolies are very profitable, they tend to self-destruct when their prices are undercut by the entry of new competitors into the market.

nation-state. The de facto ideal toward which all, or almost all, modern states aspire. In a nation-state all persons can be said to be of one nation and therefore share certain basic values and allegiances. Being a nation is defined differently in different countries. It almost always means speaking the same language. It often means having the same religion. Nations are said to have historical ties which, it is usually claimed, predate the existence of a state structure. Much of this, not all, is mythology. And almost no state comes really close to being a genuine nation-state, though few admit this.

national movements. Also called nationalist movements and national liberation movements. They are movements whose objective is to defend a "nation" which its adherents argue is being oppressed by another nation, either because the other nation has colonized them, or because their "national" (often meaning linguistic) rights are being ignored within the state, or because persons of the particular ethnic group that is asserting "nationhood" have been assigned to inferior social and economic positions within the state. National movements often seek formal independence of the oppressed nation, that is, separation from the state said to be the oppressor.

nomothetic. See IDIOGRAPHIC-NOMOTHETIC.

oligopoly. See MONOPOLY.

particularism. See UNIVERSALISM-PARTICULARISM.

periphery. See CORE-PERIPHERY.

positivism. This term was invented by the French nineteenth-century thinker Auguste Comte, who also invented the term "sociology" to describe what he was doing. For Comte, positivism meant non-theological, non-philosophical scientific thought (including social analysis) and was the quintessence of modernity. Positivism took on a broader usage to mean adherence to a scientific agenda using methods represented best by physics (at least the Newtonian physics largely uncontested among natural scientists until the latter part of the twentieth century). In this usage, positivism and nomothetic (*see* IDIOGRAPHIC-NOMOTHETIC) methodology are largely synonymous. However, empirical historians are often called positivists because they insist on sticking close to the data, even if they reject nomothetic aspirations.

proletarians-bourgeoisie. The term "proletarians" came into use in late-eighteenth-century France to refer to the common people, by analogy with ancient Rome. In the nineteenth century, the term came to be used more specifically for (urban) wage-laborers who no longer had access to land and therefore depended on their employment for income. Proletarians, for the SOCIAL MOVEMENT and for radical IDEOLOGY, were seen as the social antagonists of the bourgeoisie in the modern CLASS STRUGGLE. The term "bourgeoisie" has been in use since the eleventh century. It referred originally to city-dwellers, specifically those of an intermediate social rank (less than an aristocrat but more than a serf or common worker). The term was associated primarily with the professions of merchant and banker. From the nineteenth century on, bourgeoisie as a term moved slowly from middle rank to top rank, as the importance of aristocracies declined. The term "middle class(es)" is often substituted for bourgeoisie, except that it tends to encompass a larger group of persons.

radicalism. With liberalism and conservatism, this is the third of the great ideologies of the nineteenth and twentieth centuries. Radicals believe that progressive social change is not only inevitable but highly desirable, and the faster the better. They also tend to believe that social change does not come by itself but needs to be promoted by those who would benefit by it. Marxism (in its many varieties) is a radical ideology, but it has been by no means the only one. Anarchism is another. And in the late twentieth century, there emerged many new claimants for the title of radical ideology.

semiperipheral. There are no semiperipheral products, as there are core-like and peripheral products. However, if one calculates what proportion of a country's production is core-like and what peripheral, one finds that some countries have a fairly even distribution, that is, they trade core-like products to peripheral zones and peripheral products to core zones. Hence we can talk of semiperipheral countries, and we find they have a special kind of politics and play a particular role in the functioning of the world-system.

social movement. This phrase originated in the nineteenth century and was used originally to refer to movements that promoted the interests of industrial workers, such as trade-unions and socialist parties. Later, the term got wider usage, referring to all sorts of movements that were based on membership activity and engaged in educational and political action. Today, in addition to workers' movements, women's movements, environmentalist movements, anti-globalization movements, and gay and lesbian rights movements are all called social movements.

social time. This concept, particularly favored by Fernand Braudel, suggests that the analyst should look at different temporalities that reflect different social realities. Braudel distinguished between the two widely used social times: the short time of "events" used by idiographic scholars and the "eternal" time of nomothetic social scientists (*see* IDIOGRAPHIC-NOMOTHETIC). He much preferred two other social times which he considered more fundamental: the structural time that was long-lasting and reflected continuing (but not eternal) structural realities, which he called the *longue durée*; and the cyclical time of ups and downs that occurred within the framework of a given structural time.

sovereignty. A concept in international law that first received wide usage in the sixteenth century. It refers to the right of a state to control all activities within its borders. That is, sovereignty is a denial of both the right of subregions to defy the central state and the right of any other state to interfere in the internal workings of the sovereign state. Originally, the sovereign was the monarch or chief of state acting by himself. After the French Revolution, it became more and more the "people."

state. In the modern world-system, a state is a bounded territory claiming SOVEREIGNTY and domain over its subjects, now called citizens. Today, all land areas of the world (except the Antarctic) fall within the boundaries of some state, and no land area falls within the bounds of more than one state (although boundaries are sometimes disputed). A state claims the legal monopoly over the use of weapons within its territory, subject to the laws of the state.

status-groups. This term is the standard English translation of Max Weber's term *Stände*. Weber's term is derived from the feudal system, in which one distinguished between different *Stände* or "orders" (aristocracy, clergy, commoners). Weber extended the term to mean social groupings in the modern world that were not class-based (ethnic groups, religious groups, and so on) and showed certain kinds of solidarity and identification. In the late twentieth century the term "identities" came into use, meaning more or less the same thing, but with perhaps more emphasis on its subjective character.

surplus-value. This term has a heavy legacy of controversy and sometimes occult debate. All that is meant in this book is the amount of real profit obtained by a producer, which he may in fact lose as a result of UNEQUAL EXCHANGE.

syndical action. A general term for any kind of action in which people group together to defend their common interests. A trade-union is a notable example. But there are many other forms of workers' syndical action. And persons other than workers can engage in syndical action.

system. Literally, some kind of connected whole, with internal rules of operation and some kind of continuity. In social science, the use of "system" as a descriptive term is contested, particularly by two groups of scholars: idiographic (*see* IDIOGRAPHIC-NOMOTHETIC) historians who tend to doubt the existence of social systems, or at least feel that social systems are not the primary explanations of historical reality; and those who believe that social action is the result of individual actions (often called methodological individualists) and that the "system" is nothing but the sum of these individual activities. The use of the term "system" in social science implies a belief in the existence of so-called emergent characteristics. *See also* HISTORICAL (SOCIAL) SYSTEM.

TimeSpace. A recently invented concept. The capitalization and running-together of the two terms reflects the view that for every kind of SOCIAL TIME, there exists a particular kind of social space. Thus, time and space in social science should not be thought of as separate, measured separately, but as irrevocably linked into a limited number of combinations.

tribe. This is the term invented by nineteenth-century anthropologists to describe the unit within which most preliterate peoples located themselves. The term came under extensive criticism in the second half of the twentieth century, the critics arguing that it masked an enormous and important variety of systemic arrangements.

two cultures. A term invented by C. P. Snow in the 1950s. It refers to the quite distinctive "cultures"—really, epistemologies—of people in the humanities and the natural sciences. The split, sometimes called "divorce," of science and philosophy was consummated only in the late eighteenth century, and has again come into question in the late twentieth century.

unidisciplinarity. This term should be clearly distinguished from multi- or trans-disciplinarity. The latter terms refer to the now-popular ideas that much research would be better done if the researcher(s) combined the skills of two or more disciplines. Unidisciplinarity refers to the belief that in the social sciences at least, there exists today no sufficient *intellectual* reason to distinguish the separate disciplines at all, and that instead all work should be considered part of a single discipline, sometimes called the historical social sciences.

unequal exchange. This term was invented by Arghiri Emmanuel in the 1950s to refute the concept of COMPARATIVE ADVANTAGE of David Ricardo. Emmanuel argued that when products that had low labor costs (peripheral products) were exchanged with products that had high labor costs (core-like products), there was an *unequal* exchange going from periphery to core, involving the transfer of SURPLUS-VALUE. Emmanuel's book stirred considerable controversy. Many accepted the concept of unequal exchange without accepting Emmanuel's explanation of what defines or accounts for it.

universalism-particularism. This pair reflects the difference in emphasis of nomothetic and idiographic scholars (*see* NOMOTHETIC-IDIOGRAPHIC). Universalism is the assertion that there exist generalizations about human behavior that are universal, that is, that are true across space and time. Particularism is the assertion that no such universals exist, or at least that none are relevant concerning a specific phenomenon, and that therefore the role of the social scientist is to explicate how particular phenomena or structures operate.

world-economy, world-empire, world-system. These terms are related. A world-system is not the system of *the* world, but a system *that is a* world and that can be, most often has been, located in an area less than the entire globe. World-systems analysis argues that the unities of social reality within which we operate, whose rules constrain us, are for the most part such world-systems (other than the now-extinct small minisystems that once existed on the earth). World-systems analysis argues that there have been thus far only two varieties of world-systems: world-economies and world-empires. A world-empire (such as the Roman Empire, Han China) is a large bureaucratic structure with a single political center and an AXIAL DIVISION OF LABOR, but multiple cultures. A world-economy is a large axial division of labor with multiple political centers and multiple cultures. In English, the hyphen is essential to indicate these concepts. "World system" without a hyphen suggests that there has been only one world-system in the history of the world. "World economy" without a hyphen is a concept used by most economists to describe the trade relations among states, not an integrated system of production.

world religion. This concept came into use in the nineteenth century to describe the limited number of religions that exist in wide areas, as opposed to the religious structures of tribes (*see* TRIBE). The standard list of world religions includes at least Christianity, Judaism, Islam, Hinduism, Buddhism, and Taoism.

BIBLIOGRAPHICAL GUIDE

For the reader who wishes to pursue the subject further, I have constructed a bibliographical guide in four parts: (1) other writings of mine, which elaborate the arguments in this book; (2) writings by other world-systems analysts, which present some of these issues somewhat differently; (3) writings that specifically critique world-systems analysis; (4) writings of predecessors that are most relevant, especially those to whom we have referred in this text. There is no pretense that this is a complete guide, merely a start.

I. Writings by Immanuel Wallerstein

There exists a collection of twenty-eight articles, published originally between 1960 and 1998, which puts together my essays on the whole range of themes that are caught up in the rubric of world-systems analysis. The book is entitled *The Essential Wallerstein* (New Press, 2000). The themes discussed in chapter 1 are elaborated in the report of an international commission that I chaired, *Open the Social Sciences* (Stanford University Press, 1996) as well as in my own *Unthinking Social Science* (2d ed., Temple University Press, 2001) and *The Uncertainties of Knowledge* (Temple University Press, 2004).

The themes of chapters 2–4 are addressed in my *The Modern World-System* (3 vols. to date, Academic Press, 1974, 1980, 1989) and in *Historical Capitalism, with Capitalist Civilization* (Verso, 1995). There are also three collections of essays published by Cambridge University Press: *The Capitalist World-Economy* (1979), *The Politics of the World-Economy* (1984), and *Geopolitics and Geoculture* (1991). A more recent collection, *The End of the World as We Know It* (University of Minnesota Press, 1999), provides a juncture between the epistemological and substantive issues in world-systems analysis.

Two books speak to specific themes. One is *Antisystemic Movements* (with Giovanni Arrighi and Terence K. Hopkins, Verso, 1989). The second is *Race, Nation, Class* (with Etienne Balibar, Verso, 1991).

Finally, the analysis of the present and the future, discussed in chapter 5, is elaborated in three books published by New Press: *After Liberalism* (1995), *Utopistics* (1998), and *The Decline of American Power* (2003). There is also the collection of essays coordinated by Terence K. Hopkins and me, entitled *Trajectory of the World-System, 1945–2025* (Zed, 1996). A full bibliography is available on the web at http://fbc.binghamton.edu/cv-iw.pdf

II. Writings by world-systems analysts.

I include here only persons who identify themselves as using world-systems analysis. And I am including only works which are wide in scope (as opposed to being empirical studies of particular situations). In order not to make invidious distinctions, I list the authors in alphabetical order.

Janet Abu-Lughod, *Before European Hegemony: The World-System, A.D. 1250–1350* (Oxford University Press, 1989). This book seeks to trace the story of the modern world-system back to earlier times than did *The Modern World-System*.

Samir Amin, *Accumulation on a World Scale: A Critique of the Theory of Underdevelopment* (Monthly Review Press, 1974). Published in French in 1971, this was perhaps the earliest full-scale presentation of a world-systems account of modern capitalism. A recent work on the future of the world-system is *Obsolescent Capitalism: Contemporary Politics and Global Disorder* (Zed, 2003).

Giovanni Arrighi, *The Long Twentieth Century: Money, Power, and the Origins of Our Times* (Verso, 1994). Despite the title, this book is about the development of the modern world-system through long cycles of accumulation from the thirteenth century to today. Also, a book written by Arrighi and Beverly Silver (plus others), *Chaos and Governance in the Modern World System* (University of Minnesota Press, 1999), is a comparative study of successive hegemonic transitions.

Chris Chase-Dunn, *Global Formation: Structures of the World-Economy* (Basil Blackwell, 1989). A theorization of the structures of the capitalist world-economy. Also, a book by Chase-Dunn and Thomas D. Hall, *Rise and Demise: Comparing World Systems* (Westview, 1997), is the best example of efforts to compare multiple kinds of world-systems.

Arghiri Emmanuel, *Unequal Exchange: A Study of the Imperialism of Trade* (Monthly Review, 1972). A refutation of Ricardo's theory of mutual benefit in international trade, this book launched the term and concept of "unequal exchange."

Andre Gunder Frank, *World Accumulation, 1492–1789* (Monthly Review, 1978). The clearest and fullest presentation of his views from the earlier period of his work. His later work, *ReOrient: Global Economy in the Asian Age* (University of California Press, 1998), involved a radical revisionism, in which he argued that there had been a single world system over five thousand years, that it had been largely China-centered, and that capitalism was not a meaningful concept. See the critique of *ReOrient* in three essays by Samir Amin, Giovanni Arrighi, and Immanuel Wallerstein in *Review* 22, no. 3 (1999).

Terence K. Hopkins and Immanuel Wallerstein, *World-Systems Analysis: Theory and Methodology* (Sage, 1982). The essays by Hopkins are the major methodological essays in the world-systems tradition.

Peter J. Taylor, *Modernities: A Geohistorical Interpretation* (Polity, 1999). An interpretation of some geocultural patterns in the modern world-system.

In addition, there are the annual conferences of the Political Economy of the World-System (PEWS) Section of the American Sociological Association. These result in one or more volumes per year. They were published as the Political Economy of the World-System Annuals by Sage from 1978 to 1987, then as Studies in the Political Economy of the World-System by Greenwood from 1987 to 2003. As of 2004, they are being published by Paradigm Press. There are two quarterly journals that publish materials in the world-systems tradition. One is *Review* (Journal of the Fernand Braudel Center for the Study of Economies, Historical Systems, and Civilizations), the other an electronic journal, *Journal of World-System Research*, http://jwsr.ucr.edu.

Finally, there is a collection of sixteen essays, edited by Thomas D. Hall, under the title *A World-Systems Reader* (Rowman and Littlefield, 2000), which includes a range of viewpoints on various topics.

III. Critiques of World-Systems Analysis

This section includes only those authors who have specifically criticized world-systems analysis for its various shortcomings. Most of these critiques appeared as journal articles rather than books.

The earliest critique, and one of the most famous, was by Robert Brenner: "The Origins of Capitalist Development: A Critique of Neo-Smithian Marxism, "*New Left Review* I/104 (July–August 1977): 25–92. It was aimed at Paul Sweezy, Andre Gunder Frank, and me and renewed the orthodox productionist, England-centered Marxism of Maurice Dobb.

Soon thereafter, there were two major critical reviews of *The Modern World-System* (vol. 1) from the "state-autonomist" school: Theda Skocpol, "Wallerstein's World Capitalist System: A Theoretical and Historical Critique," *American Journal of Sociology* 82, no. 5 (March 1977): 1075–90; and Aristide Zolberg, "Origins of the Modern World System: A Missing Link," *World Politics* 33, no. 2 (January 1981): 253–81. Both Skocpol and Zolberg acknowledge their indebtedness to the views of Otto Hintze.

The culturalist critiques have been continuous. The earliest and most complete is that by Stanley Aronowitz, "A Metatheoretical Critique of Immanuel Wallerstein's *The Modern World-System*," *Theory and Society* 10 (1981): 503–20.

Not quite the same is the critique from some Third World scholars that world-systems analysis has not shed Eurocentrism. See Enrique Dussel, "Beyond Eurocentrism: The World System and the Limits of Modernity," in F. Jameson and M. Miyoshi, eds., *The Cultures of Globalization* (Duke University Press, 1998), 3–37.

While the critique from staunch positivists has been severe, they have seldom deemed it worthwhile to make a systematic critique of world-systems analysis.

IV. Relevant Works: Forerunners or Influential Writings of Other Large-Scale Analysts

Here again, we shall list the authors alphabetically, and indicate only one or two principal works.

Perry Anderson, *Lineages of the Absolutist State* (New Left Books, 1974). An account of the history of early modern Europe which argues that absolutism was still a form of feudalism.

Anne Bailey and Josep Llobera, eds., *The Asiatic Mode of Production: Science and Politics* (Routledge and Kegan Paul, 1981), is a good introduction to the debate.

Fernand Braudel, *Civilization and Capitalism, 15th to 18th Century*, 3 vols. (Harper and Row, 1981–84). The classic methodological article, "History and the Social Sciences: The *longue durée*," which appeared in *Annales* ESC in 1958, has three English translations, of unequal validity. The best is in Peter Burke, ed., *Economy and Society in Early Modern Europe* (Routledge and Kegan Paul, 1972).

Ludwig Dehio, *The Precarious Balance: Four Centuries of European Power Struggle* (Alfred A. Knopf, 1962). A succinct and major overview of the geopolitics of the modern world-system.

Frantz Fanon, *The Wretched of the Earth* (Grove, 1968), is the major theoretical work justifying the use of violence by national liberation movements.

Otto Hintze, *The Historical Essays of Otto Hintze*, edited by Robert M. Berdahl (Oxford University Press, 1975). Major influence on the state-autonomist school of historical interpretation.

R. J. Holton, ed., *The Transition from Feudalism to Capitalism* (Macmillan, 1985). This contains the Dobb-Sweezy debate, with the contributions of many others.

Nikolai Kondratieff, *The Long Wave Cycle* (Richardson and Snyder, 1984). A recent translation of the classic essay of the 1920s.

Karl Marx, *Capital* (1859), and *The Communist Manifesto* (1848) are probably the most relevant works.

William McNeill. Generally considered the foremost practitioner of "world history," which emphasizes both the continuity of human history and the worldwide links going back a very long time. The best introduction is the work he wrote with his son, J. R. McNeill, *Human Web: A Bird's-Eye View of World History* (W. W. Norton, 2003).

Karl Polanyi, *The Great Transformation* (Rinehart, 1944). His classic and most influential work is a critique of the view that the market society is in any way a natural phenomenon.

Raúl Prebisch. The first executive secretary of the United Nations Economic Commission for Latin America, he is generally considered the initiator of the core-periphery analysis of the world-economy. Very little exists in English. The best overview is in *Towards a Dynamic Development Policy for Latin America* (UN Economic Commission for Latin America, 1963). A three-volume collection in Spanish is entitled *Obras, 1919–1948* (Fund. Raúl Prebisch, 1991).

Ilya Prigogine, *The End of Certainty: Time, Chaos, and the Laws of Nature* (Free Press, 1997), is the last and clearest overall presentation of his views. The title tells the essential.

Joseph Schumpeter, *Business Cycles*, 2 vols. (McGraw Hill, 1939), the most relevant of his books, argues that long cycles did not begin in the nineteenth century but rather in the sixteenth.

Adam Smith. *The Wealth of Nations*, written in 1776, is oft quoted but less often read, which is a pity. Marx said he was not a Marxist, and Smith was surely not a Smithian.

Max Weber, *General Economic History* (Collier, 1966), the best source for Weber's analysis of the historical development of the modern world.

Eric Wolf, *Europe and the People without History* (University of California Press, 1982), emphasizes the history and fate of non-European peoples in the modern world-system.

INDEX

working classes, 12, 21, 32, 34–35, 62, 67, 70–71, 97

workplace rules, 47

world-economy (capitalist), x, 1, 9, 12, 15–17, 20, 23–41, 46, 52, 57–59, 67, 83–87, 92–94, 99–100, 103, 105

world-empire, 8, 16–17, 24, 57–58, 99–100

world history, 105

world revolution of 1848, 63–65

world revolution of 1968, x, 16, 75, 77, 84–85, 87, 89

World Social Forum, 86–87

world-system (modern), 1–2, 9, 16–18, 23–25, 28, 32–33, 36–44, 48, 51–52, 54–58, 60, 65–66, 74–75, 77–78, 82–85, 87–89, 93–94, 96, 98–100, 103–5

World War, First, 65

Yalu River, 83

Yugoslavia, 45

Zolberg, Aristide, 20, 104

Immanuel Wallerstein is Senior Research Scholar
at Yale University and director of the Fernand Braudel Center at
Binghamton University.

Library of Congress Cataloging-in-Publication Data
Wallerstein, Immanuel Maurice, 1930–
World-systems analysis : an introduction / Immanuel Wallerstein.
"A John Hope Franklin Center Book."
Includes bibliographical references and index.
ISBN 0-8223-3431-3 (cloth : alk. paper)
ISBN 0-8223-3442-9 (pbk. : alk. paper)
1. Social history. 2. Social change. 3. Social systems.
4. Globalization—Social aspects. I. Title.
HN13.W35 2004   303.4—dc22   2004003291